George Galloway, [barcode obscures text]
Hillshead, is a foreig[...] [barcode] [...]
of Yasser Arafat a[...] [...]sonal
friends. His travels r[...] [...] revolutionary
upheavals: from the [...]ut ruins of Beirut, the
firestorms of Gaza, Soweto, Kashmir and Nicaragua to the
rebel-held fiefdoms of the Philippines and Central
America.

A frequent broadcaster and orator, Galloway writes for
the *Sunday Times*, the *Evening Standard*, the *Guardian*,
Spectator, *Glasgow Herald* and *The Scotsman*.

Bob Wylie is a freelance journalist whose work in recent
years has made him an eye-witness to the drama of events
in South Africa, the Middle East and Eastern Europe. He
worked for nearly two years in Cape Town and Johannes-
burg during P.W. Botha's State of Emergency to chart the
youth revolt and the rise of the black unions, then went to
Israel and the Occupied Territories to follow the Palestinian
intifada, and most recently he has marched in the
footsteps of the unfolding anti-communist revolutions in
Poland, Yugoslavia, and Romania.

Wylie, formerly a prominent Marxist, prides himself on
getting both sides of the story, and his writings in the
British and European press demonstrate a sharp eye for
detail, and a keen ear for quote. He is an Honours gradu-
ate of Glasgow University and was a teacher and then
social worker before becoming a journalist. He says his
working maxim now is 'Things are never what they seem'.

DOWNFALL

The Ceausescus and the Romanian Revolution

George Galloway and Bob Wylie

Futura

A Futura Book

First published in Great Britain in 1991 by
Futura Publications, a division of Macdonald & Co
(Publishers) Ltd, London & Sydney

Typeset by Leaper & Gard Ltd, Bristol, England
Printed in Great Britain by
BPCC Hazell Books
Aylesbury, Bucks, England
Member of BPCC Ltd.

ISBN 0 7088 5003 0

Futura Publications
A division of
Macdonald & Co (Publishers) Ltd
Orbit House
1 New Fetter Lane
London EC4A 1AR
A member of Maxwell Macmillan Pergamon Publishing Corporation

To the people of Romania, our parents and our children

——————— ACKNOWLEDGEMENTS ———————

There are many people we have to express our gratitude to for their help in the writing of this book. But there is one man without peer where these debts are concerned. He is our faithful, honest, indefatigable translator, Constantin Sfeatcu. Without him this book would never have been written. He kept telling us that in Romania anything is possible and he proved it. Constantin, you are 'some man'. Thank you.

We owe great thanks also to our Romanian friends Ioan Pascu, Augustin Buzura and Nicu Bujor. Their assistance, advice and encouragement were invaluable. The list of other Romanians who need to be thanked is as long as the welcome they have given us everywhere we have gone. However, Dinu Giurescu, Adrian Manole, Paula Jacob, Isabela Prina, Petru Clej, Rodica Matusa, Sorin Rugina, Marian Popescu, Radu Grigoriu, George Doros, Florian Cnejevici, Virgiliu Ancar, Nicolae Beldescu, Sergiu Celac, Adrian Sirbu, Vasile Secares, Radu Dop, Florian Nicodim and Ion Faida all deserve separate mention.

We have interviewed too many people in the writing of this book to thank them all individually, but wish now to record our debt to them. However, we want to mention our thanks to those who gave us more than one interview. They are: Radu Campeanu, Valentin Ceausescu, Nicolae Croitoru, Dinu Giurescu, Claudiu Iordache, Ion Iliescu, Paula Jacob, Valerica Matei, Iftene Pop, Ion Ratiu, Petre Roman, Moses Rosen, Adrian Severin, Gelu Voican, and Gheorghe Voinea. We want to thank Susan Laffey, at the

British Embassy in Bucharest also.

We do not consider this book to be a scholarly work but separate from our general sources we want to pay our dues to Mary Ellen Fischer. Her magnificent volume *Nicolae Ceausescu: a study in Political Leadership*, published in 1989 by Lynne Rienner, Colorado, has to be read by anyone seeking penetrating insight into the Ceausescu era.

At home, the support and companionship of June and Lilian was vital. We know we could not have done it without them.

Carole Hughes and Alan Hughes gave us extraordinary dedication in helping to create the first manuscript.

Billy Barnes, David Churchley, Christopher Silvester, Bill Speirs, Jeanette Wylie, Ian Bell then of *Observer Scotland*, and Andrew Neil of the *Sunday Times* have all contributed to our effort in different ways.

Special thanks is due to Belinda Harley, our agent. Pen would never have been put to paper without her. We hope her faith in us has been repaid. Thanks also to Alan Samson and Krystyna Zukowska at Futura, and Camilla Raab, who tackled the task of tidying-up the original typescript with gusto.

In autumn 1957 I had not yet experienced the Japanese film *Rashomon*, the dramatisation of the classic enigma of truth, the inescapable, ordained contradictions, life distorted to infinity in its own mirror.

I knew in Warsaw as I walked through the October events that I was walking in a hall of facets ... 30 years later I cannot be certain what was real and what was imagined ... which has caused me to return to *Rashomon* ... to study this metaphor of life and remind myself that there is no truth. There are many truths, some valid for one, some for another. Things are not what they seem ... It is a lesson we must learn and relearn because always we keep searching for certainty, and certainty does not exist.

Harrison Salisbury, *Disturber of the Peace*,
Unwin Hyman (1989).

——— CONTENTS ———

PART I
The Red Royal Family

1	The End, the Beginning	3
2	Ceausescu at the Summit	16
3	Czechoslovakia	23
4	Idolatry	28
5	Romania — A State of Morality	53
6	The Romanian Jews	65
7	Boulevard	88

PART II
The Revolution from Timisoara to Bucharest

8	Timisoara	97
9	17th December — the Day of Reckoning	113
10	Towards the Revolution — 18th, 19th and 20th December	122
11	21st December	131
12	22nd December	140
13	The Flight of the Ceausescus	166
14	The Days before Christmas	173
15	The Trial	181
16	The Execution	196

Contents

PART III
The June Days

17	From January to June	207
18	The Days Leading to 13th June	220
19	14th June and the Aftermath	242
20	Guilty or Not Guilty?	257
21	Miron Cozma and the Miners of the Jiu Valley	273
22	The Last and the First Chapter	283

Appendix 1 Romania — 20th May Election Results	292
Appendix 2 Eastern Europe: the Economic Facts	294
Sources	295
Index	296

PART I

The Red Royal Family

------ CHAPTER 1 ------

The End, the Beginning

In the early evening of Boxing Day, 1989 – the Year of Revolutions – television audiences, many of them still consuming the leftovers of their Christmas dinners, watched an old man and his wife pulled from the bowels of an armoured car. They saw the old couple, who clung together throughout, berated and harangued by a revolutionary drumhead court, and heard them sentenced to die by firing squad.

The old man was Nicolae Ceausescu: 'the Genius of the Carpathians', 'the Danube of the Thought', 'the Creator of the Golden Era'. The biggest 'Big Brother' of them all.

The old woman was his wife, 'Comrade academician, doctor, engineer' Elena Ceausescu.

Minutes later, in an anonymous barrack square, amid a hail of foul curses echoing from both victims and executioners, the Ceausescus were torn apart by uncontrolled automatic rifle fire.

The normal rites – of last words, and orderly soldierly commands to take aim, fire – went unobserved, and so premature was the first volley that the 'official' cameraman who had filmed the trial and sentencing was not in place, and missed the video-scoop of the decade. Few of the executioners missed their targets, and the bullets ripped through the expensive Astrakhan coats, the faces and heads of the head of state and his deputy. It was the final humiliation.

In Bucharest three days before, on 22nd December, 'the Genius' and his wife had clattered from the roof of the Communist Party Central Committee headquarters, squeezed into a helicopter with the most servile of their acolytes. A few seconds' delay would have seen them lynched and, as it was, the vengeful crowd almost caught hold of the helicopter's undercarriage as it took off.

Down in the square below, the people, whose lives the Ceausescus had bestrode like a Colossus, sang and danced with delight as they watched the unsteady flight of the escaping helicopter. 'Ole, Ole, Ole, Ole ... Ceausescu nu mai e!' With that chorus, redolent of football terraces across the world, Romanians hailed the dawn of their democracy. 'Ceausescu nu mai e!' 'Ceausescu is no more!' And now, literally, this statement was true. It had all ended in the blood and gore of the barrack square, and in the oversized coffins stuffed full of cheap yellow polystyrene pellets to stop the corpses rattling around.

It was the most extraordinary end, through the most extraordinary revolution, of the most extraordinary dictatorship in all of Eastern Europe. And yet the old man and woman who had walked as heroes through the corridors of the chancelleries of the free world, and who had been decorated by the Queen of England, had once seemed rather grand.

This is the story of the rise and fall of communism in Romania, and of the life and death of the communist world's only red royal family.

Nicolae Ceausescu was born on 26th January 1918 in a small village, Scornicesti, which nestles in the low hills of the county of Olt midway between the provincial capitals of Pitesti and Slatina, 100 miles west of Bucharest. He was the third of ten children, six boys and four girls. Like Stalin, with whom he was to share many characteristics, he was born into deep grinding poverty. His family were peasants not long freed from serfdom. His mother Alexandra was small and weatherbeaten, her back bent with hard work. His father Andruta was the village drunk, and may also have been the local police informer. Indeed there is evidence that this was the family's ancestral role in the village; the prefix 'ceaus' in the surname comes from the Turkish and means, among other things, 'informer'.

Like Stalin, Ceausescu received only the most elementary schooling and at weekends and during school holidays he and his brothers and sisters were hired out as agricultural labourers. At the age of eleven, as most of his brothers were to do, he left hearth and home for the lights of Bucharest. He arrived in the city in 1929, and eventually found a position as a cobbler's apprentice – as Stalin had been a cobbler's son. Life was hard even then on the bleak streets of the capital, and Ceausescu was quickly drawn by his own long hours, desperate wages and the squalor he saw around him towards the left and the clandestine revolutionaries of the Romanian Communist Party, at first through their myriad of front organisations.

At the tender age of fifteen, the apprentice cobbler took the public stage in Romania for the first time at an anti-fascist conference. In what was later described as a 'turbulent Carpathian torrent', he talked himself on to the National Committee of the organisation. Just five months later, on 23rd November 1933, he was arrested for the first time for 'inciting a strike' and 'seeking to undermine the security of the state'.

'The state' was far from secure in 1933, though the Romanian communists and the young Ceausescu were among the least of its worries. King Carol, an international playboy from the German house of Hohenzollern, had earlier renounced his rights to the throne to elope with an actress and society whore, Magda Lupescu (it was widely believed in Romania that Carol, an ageing Lothario, was remarkably physically endowed, and that the redoubtable Magda was one of the few women in Romania who could satisfy him), leaving his wife Princess Helen.

On his grandfather's departure in 1927, Carol and Helen's five-year-old son Michael became king. But in 1930, with Romania in deep turbulence and crisis, Carol, with Magda still in tow, brusquely returned to the country and reclaimed his throne. Like the rest of Europe, Romania was sliding into the great depression, and political troubles were endemic. Here, as in Germany, the street gangs of the far right, feeding on the anti-semitic hatred against the nearly one million Jews and the poisonous chauvinistic ire against the gypsies and other national minorities, had very much the upper hand. The Romanian right were fascists with a peculiarly religious, mystical and obscurantist feel. Their founder, Corneliu Zelea Codreanu, claimed to have seen a vision of the Archangel Michael who had appointed him the saviour of the nation. His organisation, the League of the Archangel Michael, became better known as the Iron Guard.

Though its electoral support never exceeded 16 per cent (still eight times the best prewar score of the young Ceausescu's 'Workers' and Peasants' bloc' – the legal front of the communists) their discipline and their jackbooted violent tactics gave them much greater political influence. In 1937, following a stalemated general election and with the Iron Guard sniffing power, King Carol dissolved the political parties and established a royal dictatorship. During its brief period, he grew fantastically rich by the granting of armament concessions, fuelling the Nazi preparations for war. The Iron Guard leader Codreanu was arrested, then killed, supposedly while trying to escape. A year later the Iron Guard assassinated the King's Prime Minister. Carol in turn carried out mass reprisals, killing and incarcerating hundreds of Iron Guardsmen. Although eventually, albeit briefly, he stilled the internal strife, the King proved powerless to prevent the dismemberment of the country.

In 1940 Stalin took Bessarabia, now Soviet Moldavia. Then Hitler's 'Vienna Diktat' gave northern Transylvania to his ally Hungary, creating such anguish that the King abdicated again, putting young Prince Michael on the throne for the second time. Carol left the country with his fortune and Magda Lupescu and, unusually for such a mistress, she was to outlive him and inherit all his ill-gotten gains.

The power behind the young King Michael's throne, however, lay with the army and General (later Marshal) Ion Antonescu, a Nazi collaborator, who first resurrected the Guard, then crushed them with the help of the Germans, who were worried about their strong Romanian nationalist credo. Under King Michael and Marshal Antonescu, Romania remained a Nazi satellite fighting alongside the German army virtually until the Soviet Red Army's tanks rolled in on 23rd August 1944. Through this brutal topsy-turvy time the young Ceausescu threw himself ever more wholeheartedly into what then must have seemed an Everest of a struggle. In June 1934 he was again arrested, this time for collecting signatures against the trial of striking railway workers in Craiova, one of whom was the man he would later succeed and attempt to obliterate from Romanian history – Gheorghe Gheorghiu-Dej.

In August of that year he was jailed for the third time, and again in September for the fourth, when the epithet 'dangerous communist agitator' was appended to his file in the Bucharest police headquarters. After this term he was exiled from Bucharest, confined by order to live with his parents in his home village of Scornicesti. Within months, he had clandestinely returned to the city and gone underground. Throughout that following year, Ceausescu's parents were regularly grilled by the royal police about the whereabouts of their wayward son, but this time his father Andruta, the village informer, was saying nothing. In his infrequent contact with his family during this period, through his sister Nicolina, he claimed that he was spending his underground hours 'studying Marxism'. A measure of the cultural impoverishment of the Ceausescu family was their lack of imagination in choosing names for their children. Ceausescu's younger brother was also christened Nicolae.

In early 1936 he was arrested again, described in the police report as an 'active distributor' of communist propaganda 'long known' to the police and the courts. He was eighteen years old. Acting under Party instructions, Ceausescu and his fellow defendants decided to turn their trial, which began in May, into a political demonstration to protest against 'fascist influence' in Romania. One of the accused, V. Tarnovski, grew so heated in the dock that he was dragged to the cells. The official court report then describes how another defendant, 'N. Ceausescu declared his support for Tarnovski, and incited the other defendants to follow his example, gesturing and offending the judges by his irreverent ... attitudes'. Ceausescu, who was then excluded from the trial, was given a six-month sentence for the interruption alone. The trouble in the court attracted wide publicity, with one contemporary report saying of Ceausescu that he 'spoke clearly, a bit too fast, as if he wanted to get all his words out at once'. The reporter, Eugen Jebeleanu, described the teenage rebel as 'small and dark with sparkling eyes ... like two peppercorns' and repeatedly stressed his youth, enthusiasm and courage. Jebeleanu concluded with the hope that the 'child with a young and generous heart' would receive a light sentence.

On 6th June Nicolae Ceausescu was sentenced to a further two years of imprisonment, a huge fine and a year's exile in his home village. However, like generations of revolutionaries before and since, for Ceausescu a prison sentence from his enemies was not so much a punishment as a badge of honour and, as a bonus, was a ticket to the 'Marxist University' of Doftana Prison where almost every leftist convict in the country was incarcerated. During those two years he studied under older and better communists than he, and indeed the graduates of Doftana Prison from this period provided both of Romania's communist leaders and many of their lieutenants over the next half-century. While behind bars, he studied not only Marxism but literature, economics and philosophy. One of his fellow prisoners, Vasile Dumitrescu, who later became Romanian Ambassador to Switzerland, said the prisoners studied 'Kant and Schopenhauer and read the poetry of Rimbaud out loud'.

When Ceausescu was released just before Christmas 1938, his file was now labelled 'Person dangerous to public order'. Unbowed, he threw himself back into politics and seems not to have even pretended to leave Bucharest. The following summer he attended a meeting which would eventually change his and many other lives.

The Bucharest police reports say that in August 1939 'the well-known communist Nicolae Ceausescu' was spreading communist slogans at a meeting of the Bucharest Guild of Leather and Footwear Workers. The reports continue that 'the communist Lenuta Petrescu, a worker at the "Jaquard" factory, spoke to the meeting, demanding "bread and justice" for the workers'. She lived near her fellow communist Ceausescu in an industrial, heavily working-class, district called, with prescient Orwellian irony, 'Park of Joy'. One day Lenuta Petrescu the young machinist would be known to the world as Elena Ceausescu, possibly the most loathed woman in the world. In September the fugitive Ceausescu was sentenced in his absence to three years and 200 days in prison. He remained underground and on the run from the authorities until July 1940, when he was finally captured.

This time he was incarcerated in a grim prison eight miles from Bucharest. Most of it, including the section housing the political prisoners, was deep below ground, making it the dampest and gloomiest jail in the country. A few months later, on 24th and 25th November, a 100-strong armed gang of the fascist Iron Guard forced their way into the prison and began a murderous pogrom, fighting from cell to cell, killing sixty-four political prisoners, mainly leftists. The communists, by now led in this jail by Ceausescu, were saved by a rearguard action fought by the soldiers guarding the block. The Ceausescu mythology was later to claim that the communists were saved by his intellectual dominance of the prison, which had spellbound the soldiers. The prison's name was Jilava, and the Ceausescu family would later have much cause to remember it.

By the time the Red Army came to his and his comrades' rescue in August 1944, Ceausescu, just twenty-six, had impeccable revolutionary and communist credentials by the score. Though he would later embellish those credentials as he airbrushed his way through the country's history-books, the genuine raw material of his life was sufficient to see him enter the postwar period, when the communists, who ended the war with fewer than a thousand members, gradually squeezed the life out of the other political forces under the cover of the Soviet tanks, in a pole political position. His 'time' in prison, his life in the underground, the courage and audacity noticed and reported by the journalist Jebeleanu, his friendship, forged in prison, with the older leaders of the Party, especially Gheorghiu-Dej, and above all his youth, saw him face the new red future with confidence – and considerable ambition.

This ambition was fired no doubt when he again met Lenuta (now Elena) Petrescu soon after the country's and his liberation. It is not clear exactly how long after his release they came together again, how intimate they were

when they did or to what extent Elena had waited faith-
fully for her hero. The later propaganda said that he was
reunited with Elena, 'the young militant who had waited
for him since those days so long ago ... The prisons had
separated them, but not divided them. They were married
as soon as Nicolae Ceausescu was free'. There is, however,
no record of when they married. Later still there is
mention of a wedding in the 'unceremonial tradition of
left-wing political activists'. It is more likely that the most
infamous married couple in the whole of communist
Europe in fact never legally tied the knot.

The official revolutionary love story turns sour when
one hears the testimony of Ceausescu's younger brother
Nicolae (sic), once the head of a Securitate Training
School near Bucharest and now languishing in prison.
According to him, not only was Elena unfaithful to her
companion but it was with a German soldier, and he
caught them *in flagrante*!

> I called round to her apartment to deliver a message
> from my brother from prison. I knew she hadn't gone to
> work and I thought she might have been sick. When
> there was no reply to my knock, I used my latchkey. As
> I entered the single room, the first astonishing sight was
> a German soldier's uniform folded neatly over the
> chair, his tall boots standing to attention in the middle
> of the floor. The second was even more astonishing: it
> was her large bare bottom staring me in the face. She
> was bent over, sucking the penis of a member of
> Hitler's army! Some communist; some partisan! She
> never forgave me for what I had seen. She hated and
> feared me ever after.

It is clear, however, from a study of the early postwar
editions of the Communist Party newspaper *Scinteia*
(*Spark*), that Ceausescu was already an important figure
in the ranks. His articles, reports of his activities and

photographs of the spindly awkward-looking young man – now leader of the Communist Youth Union – clearly chart his rise in the hierarchy.

A study of his writings and speeches from this period show that the narrow, almost primitive, Marxism he learned in prison and on the run with the mainly proletarian communists (most of the Party's best intellectuals lived out the war in Moscow) served as his guiding star from then till the end of his life – potted Marxism spiced with the often virulent Romanian nationalism which became increasingly *de rigueur* in the Romanian Communist Party.

Consequently, Romanian communism developed a fetish for centralisation and, despite the economic costs, diversification into all industrial fields. Thus huge projects of infrastructure and heavy industrialisation, emulating the Stalin school of economics, were promoted, even when this model was going out of fashion in Stalin's Moscow, and these economics of central command were combined with an attempt to diversify. Diversification was an expression of economic nationalism, to resist any attempts to subjugate Romania through economic dependency into the Comecon system. Neither Ceausescu, nor the more senior party leaders, ever did learn the central lesson of the failure of Stalinism, that socialism in one country was doomed.

In the immediate aftermath of the war, intense intra-party fighting broke out between the returning 'Moscow communists' and the internal or 'prison communists', a struggle which also pitted the more sophisticated and cultured intellectuals against the proletarians. Ceausescu's bruising experience of this seminal struggle would leave its fingerprints on the rest of his political career.

It was a complicated struggle inside the now renamed Romanian Workers' Party (following the compulsory merger with the much larger and more moderate Socialist Party), pitting Ceausescu's group, led by Gheorghiu-Dej, against a group led by an ultra-formidable Jewish woman,

Ana Pauker, whose husband Marcel had been murdered by Stalin. Stalin's enmity does not seem to have extended to the wife, however, because Ana returned with the Soviet tanks to become Foreign Minister and to struggle – unsuccessfully – for the leadership itself. In the power struggle, the young Ceausescu did not play a central role, but none the less clung closely to his mentor, mouthing the prevailing slogans of the Party's dominant 'workerist' wing. The struggle, which lasted for years, ended in the depressingly familiar Eastern bloc routine of denunciation: removal from state office, removal from Party office, criminal charges ranging from 'right deviationism' through 'Titoism' to 'advocating co-operation with the bourgeoisie and the entire peasantry', 'spying' and 'terrorism'.

Ceausescu, though he later claimed to have been too junior to have had any influence, watched and parroted the line as one by one his erstwhile comrades were incarcerated, reduced to 'non-personhood' or simply murdered. Gheorghiu-Dej's brutal dexterity in emerging victorious from the Party struggle was another lesson Ceausescu never forgot. In 1953 the lights went out all over Eastern Europe when the titanic leader Stalin died in Moscow. In Romania there was apparently genuine numbness and grief, and fear of what would become of the people now that the 'beloved leader and teacher' was gone. Even anti-communists remember the day sombrely: 'People were crying in the streets, the radio played funeral music, Beethoven, Tchaikovsky, Schubert and Schumann reverberated for three days and nights from loudspeakers erected in the centre of the city. Black flags were everywhere,' said one Romanian witness.

For the leaders of the Romanian Workers' Party, the death was more than a tragedy, it was a disaster. Gheorghiu-Dej had been a man after Stalin's own heart. It became clear at his funeral, however (at which Ceausescu was senior enough to be one of the eight RWP mourners), that Stalin's successors would be a different breed, favouring collective, more modern and moderate leadership. The winds of change would soon be blowing throughout the bloc. Gheorghiu-Dej returned to Bucharest determined to resist, and the parting of the ways with Moscow, for which Ceausescu was to receive much western credit (not to mention a weekend at Buckingham Palace and the Order of the Bath more than fifteen years later), began in earnest. Romania was better placed than the others in the bloc to make such a break. For a start, in recognition of their closeness, Stalin had agreed to Gheorghiu-Dej's request for the withdrawal of all Soviet forces from the country. Thus the traditional transmission channel of last resort of the Kremlin's orders, the Red Army, had gone.

Furthermore, Romania's tremendously fertile agriculture made the country both potentially self-sufficient in food and an attractive trading partner for points west. Romania's petroleum deposits, with the potential for downstream development in petrochemicals, and with a seaboard on the Black Sea (unlike landlocked Hungary and Czechoslovakia) all contributed to the self-confidence of the inveterate Romanian Stalinists. The RCP leaders refused Moscow's orders to 'de-Stalinise' their system, refused to begin to separate party and state power, refused the Comecon modernisations ordered by Khrushchev, the turning away from heavy industry, the attempts to woo the peasantry by small-scale private enterprise initiatives, the limiting of new investments in order to put more consumer goods on the shelves of the all but barren shops, and – of supreme importance to later western policy towards the regime – Gheorghiu-Dej made clear that, while he would give military support to the Soviet Union where he shared the goal of the Kremlin (for example the crushing of reform in Hungary in 1956), he would keep Romania effectively outside the Warsaw Pact's command structures. In effect, it was a unilateral declaration of military independence. Thus the 'anti-Sovietism' for which Ceausescu was later to be hailed, decorated and cosseted by the west on that most cynical of principles, 'my enemy's enemy is my friend', in fact predated Ceausescu's leadership by more than a decade, was a *sine qua non* of the Communist Party's uneasy contract with the Romanian people, and was in any case based not on a liberal moderate break with the authoritarian USSR, but a rejection of even the timid 'de-Stalinisation' of the Khrushchev years. It was also a retreat behind the barricades to consolidate the 'Park of Joy' that had become Romania.

—— CHAPTER 2 ——

Ceausescu at the Summit

On 20th March 1965 *Scinteia*, the daily '*Spark*' of the Romanian Workers' Party, arrived on the streets with the black-edged announcement that the leader, Gheorghe Gheorghiu-Dej, was no more.

The people were told that a rapidly advancing cancer of the liver had taken him, and that at his obviously crowded bedside when he passed away were no fewer than all fourteen ranking members of the Politburo, two Vice-Presidents of the Council of State and, no doubt as some kind of accidental domesticity, the dead man's son-in-law. But apart from the news of the death, the most important thing about the report was that the Party leaders at the bedside were captioned, frozen in equality, listed only in alphabetical order. Although the leader's demise had been expected for several days, it was thus obvious that the succession – that perennial problem of the communist system – had still to be resolved.

On the face of it, Nicolae Ceausescu was a far from obvious candidate to succeed his mentor. For a start, he was considerably younger than most of his rivals, with less seniority in the Party and the Government, having served the latter only as Deputy Minister of Defence and Deputy Minister of Agriculture. But he had learned, better than most, the art of the intra-party struggle, and at the feet of the masterful teacher Gheorghiu-Dej.

At the funeral, which was attended by such as Mikoyan, one of the Soviet leaders, and Zhou Enlai, the Chinese Prime Minister – this at the height of the Sino-Soviet split – the last of the four eulogies was given by Ceausescu. Threaded through the emotional and senti-mental tributes delivered by the previous three celebrants were scarcely veiled pitches for the leadership, empha-sising the speakers' own special qualities and constituency, rather than the deceased's. One orator alluded to his dedi-cation to collective leadership, the other to the centrality of the trade unions – his own constituency; a third talked of the need to place greater emphasis on consumer demands. Ceausescu, however, seized the occasion. Drawing on his experience as the Party Central Committee secretary for cadres and organisations, he spoke, not really to the audience or to the distin-guished fraternal mourners, still less to the Romanian people as a whole, but to the Party ranks and the apparatchiks.

Correctly assessing the feelings of insecurity that they felt at the prospect of a new era, Ceausescu stressed above all the power and prestige of the Party and the over-riding importance of preserving its role and its privileges. It was exactly the tack Stalin had successfully taken after the death of Lenin, and it worked equally well for Ceausescu.

By the time of the subsequent Party congress four months later, it was clear that by a mixture of guile, ambi-guity and peerless manoeuvring Ceausescu had emerged on top of the heap. The Ninth Party Congress, which opened on 19th July 1965, marked a successful start to the Ceausescu era. It was attended by no lesser personages than Leonid Brezhnev and Deng Xiaoping, Romania again bridging the by then monumental chasm in the world communist movement. Foreign observers, even from the United States, reported that, polite and efficient, communism in the colours of Romania looked to be well and securely in the saddle.

During the congress, unlike in the old days, although Bucharest was draped in flags and communist bunting, there were no pictures of the Party leaders on public view. It would never be so again. Ceausescu made only minor changes at the congress, through even they were significant in retrospect. He changed the Party's name back to the Romanian Communist Party, putting it on a par with the Kremlin – against the trend of most other Eastern European Parties – and he reintroduced Stalin's old title of 'General Secretary' of the Party instead of merely 'First Secretary' (thereafter no other organisation or institution in Romania would have any position entitled 'General Secretary' ever again). Leonid Brezhnev must have taken note, as he himself did the same in Moscow the very next year.

Ceausescu's main speech to the congress made clear that the twin planks of the Party credo remained: heavy industrial development and absolute national autonomy. It was not evident then that the first was beggaring the once abundant agricultural sector and would subsequently require massive foreign loans to sustain it, neither was it clear that the obsession with the second would eventually lead to Romania's total isolation.

Ceausescu in his speech, quoting from the nineteenth-century Romanian historian A.D. Xenopol, used words which revealed the mentality which would later bring about his downfall: 'To remain only agricultural would be to make ourselves for all times the slaves of foreigners.' Though this line would later be used to justify the disastrous hardships involved in clearing Romania's foreign debt, the first foreigners to feel the Romanian lash were not the 'imperialists' but the Soviets, who had installed the Romanian communists in power and without whose underwriting the Party would have been smashed. But, intoxicated with his new position, Ceausescu set out to bait the Russian bear.

He first commissioned an official history of the Romanian Communist Party. Though it was never published, a large number of monographs based upon its conclusions were. They amounted to a trenchant attack on the Soviet communists, denouncing the old prewar Comintern policies as they had affected Romania and the communist movement in general. Then a series of three state visits to Romania occurred, the treatment of which by the Romanian media is illustrative of the Ceausescu strategy.

First to arrive, in the spring of 1966, was the leader of neighbouring Yugoslavia, the first 'anti-Soviet' communist leader, Marshal Tito. Tito had used his enormous charisma and his internationally recognised credentials as possibly the finest partisan fighter of the Second World War to defy the Kremlin for more than a decade. His deviationism – 'Titoism' – was the 'crime' for which communists all over the Eastern bloc had paid with their lives – including in Gheorghiu-Dej's Romania, with Ceausescu's support.

On 17th April, the day before Tito's arrival, the front page of *Scinteia* carried a huge picture and glowing biography of the formerly reviled renegade. For a whole week, while in Romania, Tito completely dominated the front page, and all other parts of the Romanian media. On the day he arrived, he was driven in triumph through a cheering city bedecked in bunting, flowers, bilingual signs and slogans, and huge portraits of himself and Ceausescu.

At the airport to greet him when he touched down were the entire Government and the whole Party leadership. Zhou Enlai's state visit in June was a repeat performance. After several days of talks, Ceausescu took Zhou to the seaside for a break, before resuming formal talks. Zhou travelled the country, being feted at gala evenings and mass meetings, and again *Scinteia* was plastered with happy photographs. In blatant and unmistakable contrast one month before, on 14th May, *Scinteia* announced, *after* he had left, that Leonid Brezhnev had been in Romania from 10th to 13th May for 'friendly' talks! Ceausescu and Brezhnev were reported to have 'exchanged opinions on problems of continued development of co-operation'. This was the total extent of the coverage given to the all but secret state visit paid by the most powerful leader of the bloc, less than a year after Ceausescu took power, and more than two years before that seminal event, the Soviet invasion of Czechoslovakia.

The Romanian people loved it. In June the following year another critical step was taken on the path of 'national autonomy'. In a blitzkrieg attack lasting just six days, Israel pulverised the great Nasser and his Soviet supplied and trained Egyptian army, smashed nationalist Syria and seized the remaining Palestinian lands still outside their grasp. Hundreds of thousands of new Palestinian refugees streamed north to Lebanon, south to Egypt or east across the River Jordan.

For the Arabs it was an abject humiliation, and for Ceausescu's Eastern bloc allies it was only slightly less so, given the commitment of Warsaw Pact arms to the defeated Arab armies. Their response was swift, unequivocal and monolithic. Despite the fact that the USSR had been the first country in the world to grant recognition to the state of Israel in 1948, Moscow severed all links, and her allies followed suit. All that is except Romania, which refused to break diplomatic or any other links with Tel Aviv. Behind that decision lay the complex story of the love-hate relationship between Ceausescu, the Romanian communists, Romania's massive and historically reviled Jewish community and the state of Israel. But that story deserves a chapter of its own.

*

On the domestic level, Ceausescu intensified the drive for industrialisation and made a turn to tighter and more draconian Communist Party discipline. At the time when the Czechoslovak Party were limbering up for the 'Prague Spring' – the crushing of which by Moscow Ceausescu would sensationally oppose – he was writing at home such anti-reformist lines as these: 'Can a Party member be allowed to consider himself freed from the obligations to respect Party discipline on the ground that he has a different opinion? No. Nobody can be allowed this! No Party member has [this] right!' Simultaneously he began to shake up the Party apparatus by abolishing structures, creating new ones, enlarging some committees and shrinking others, finding ways of promoting new cadres loyal to him (including the rehabilitation of former comrades whose purging by Gheorghiu-Dej he had loyally supported).

By early 1968, Gheorghiu-Dej had been denounced. He had 'undeniable virtues', Ceausescu told a Bucharest Party rally in April, 'but no merits can excuse his abuses' of socialist legality. He was never to be referred to favourably again. By May 1968, Nicolae Ceausescu was in absolute command of the Romanian Communist Party, his only possible rivals retired or were discredited and purged. Though he would have some triumphs to come, he embarked then on a road that led him to become one of the world's best examples of the truism: absolute power corrupts absolutely.

But at this point for the Romanians, this road – which would eventually lead him to the blood and gore of the barrack square and them all the way to hell – seemed paved with good intentions. Ceausescu was talking tough to the Russians, he was plucking every heartstring of Romanian cultural pride, even snobbery, he was denouncing his previous mentor and cleaning the Augean

stables of the Party apparatus. And the warm days of
August 1968 were still to come. They were to bring his
greatest-ever triumph.

─── CHAPTER 3 ───

Czechoslovakia

Throughout 1968 the Warsaw Pact allies, utterly dominated by the sclerotic leadership of Leonid Brezhnev, had
been like sharks dangerously circling around Czechoslovakia and its reform-minded leader Alexander
Dubceck.

The so-called 'Prague Spring' does not look so very
radical now in these Gorbachev days, but in 1968 the
Czech attempt at 'glasnost' and 'perestroika' held out
hope for liberals in the west and incurred fear and loathing
among the regimes of the east in roughly equal measure.
During long weeks of crisis, Brezhnev turned up the heat
on the Government in Prague, calling several informal
Warsaw Pact meetings to which, illegally under the treaty,
he did not invite Romania.

Not that Ceausescu favoured the Czech reforms, but
his adamant insistence on the absolute autonomy of the
Warsaw Pact states made him an unreliable invitee. On
16th August, just five days before the invasion, Ceausescu
travelled to Prague to sign a Treaty of Friendship, Co-
operation and Mutual Assistance with the Czech Government. He publicly expressed his confidence in the Dubceck

leadership, and repeatedly urged caution on everyone else, insisting that differences of opinion in the bloc should be solved by 'comradely discussion'.

The day before the invasion, at a meeting in the Pitesti automobile factory, he stated his 'complete satisfaction' with the Czech communists, saying he was 'profoundly impressed' during his visit that the Czechoslovak people were 'in safe hands' under Dubceck and, again, that 'comradely discussion' was the way to solve disputes between ruling communist parties. The next day, 21st August, the world watched in horror as Brezhnev made his contribution to the 'comradely discussion'. The Warsaw Pact armies of the Soviet Union, Bulgaria, East Germany, Hungary and Poland steamrollered over the Czech borders, snuffing out any and all opposition, their tanks enforcing the Kremlin's writ at the point of a gun-barrel. They overthrew the Czech Party leadership, exiled Dubceck to a clerk's position in a Slovakian forest, installed a puppet Party leadership, and in the process softly, at first barely perceptibly, sounded the death-knell of the whole communist system.

On invasion day, Ceausescu held a rally in Palace Square in Bucharest – the same square from which he later fled to his death. To ecstatic acclaim from a gigantic crowd, he appeared on the balcony of the Central Committee building. It was, he said, 'a shameful moment in the history of the revolutionary movement'. The penetration of Warsaw Pact troops into Czechoslovakia was 'a grave threat to peace in Europe and to the fate of socialism in the world'. He announced to the rally the immediate formation of 'armed patriotic detachments of workers, peasants and intellectuals, defenders of the independence of our socialist homeland'. It is unlikely that these detachments kept Leonid Brezhnev awake at night, but their formation and Ceausescu's inflammatory rhetoric had a dramatic effect on the Romanian leader's standing at home and in the west.

At home, he became no less than a national hero; the most popular communist leader at any time in the whole communist bloc. Even years later, when his stock had plummeted and his domestic policies were crashing in failure, his compatriots would cite his stand during those August days as a reason why he was able to survive, and confessed a lingering affection for the good old days when Ceausescu successfully baited the Russian bear. The popularity, however, dazzled Ceausescu, convinced him that he was indispensable to both Party and nation and sealed the fate of any pretence at collective communist leadership. Henceforth, for Ceausescu in Romania, '*L'état, c'est moi*'.

The next summer, the American President Richard Nixon made a near-royal visit to Romania, the Stars and Stripes bordering the avenues of Bucharest. Three days after he left town, the Tenth Congress of the RCP took place. In contrast to the previous congress, this time the Chinese communists refused to come and the Soviets sent a minor functionary. Western interest in the congress, however, was intense.

Ceausescu spoke for five and a half hours – 'in a brisk monotone', reported one observer, 'his speech being punctuated every half-hour on the dot by a waiter in a white jacket bringing a glass of water'. In years to come, men in longer white coats would be hoped for during such congress marathons, but at this congress Ceausescu carried all before him, riding the crest of his brave 'Czechoslovak' wave. A free and fair election held then would have produced a landslide victory for Ceausescu, but he had no such nonsense in mind. His domestic policy announced at the congress remained unchanged: still more rapid industrialisation, a growth-rate of nearly 10 per cent was laid down, together with a staggering rate of what he called 'accumulation', which was in fact the share of the national income being reinvested (and therefore unavailable for consumer goods), of 30 per cent. It is clear from congress reports that the cult of the Ceausescu personality moved up a gear. Speakers from the rostrum apparently felt obliged to begin and end their speeches by hailing the leader by name. Some speakers, especially full-time apparatchiks, referred to him in almost every paragraph of their speeches.

The pre-Ceausescu era was almost never mentioned. It was as though the pre-Ceausescu history of communist Romania had never existed. To make sure, Ceausescu eliminated the two remaining leaders with whom he had inherited power just four years before. One was booted off the Central Committee but given a sinecure to allow him to retire with honour, the other was removed from his post as the head of the trade unions for 'inappropriate activity, for grave violations of communist ethics and the ethical principles of our socialist society'. During the next five years, and before the next time the Party assembled in congress, Nicolae Ceausescu would complete the journey from barefoot cobbler's apprentice to a position of omnipotence and a leadership cult surpassing even that of the cobbler's son Stalin himself.

The cult had an element of religious obscurantism, born of and appealing to the peasants from the deep cultural woods of Transylvania, Wallachia and Moldavia. It plucked at the heartstrings of Romanian nationalism, drawing on the siege mentality of a Latin island in a sea of hostile Slavs, reliving the legend of the lost Roman legion of Septimius Severus who fathered them. Above all, it was regal, with mace, sash and cloak, and under its shadow would be committed some of the most grotesque, even ridiculous, crimes committed in the name of communism. It would see the destruction of much of the old, the beautiful and the rural in Romania. It would beggar the country and pauperise its people, leaving them hungry and cold in an ill-lit gloom. For all its puritanism, it would see Romania become the septic abortion and child Aids capital of Europe. It was a cult which would reduce Romania not to a 'Park of Joy' but to a living hell.

CHAPTER 4

Idolatry

Even by the standards of the communist world wherein the body of Lenin lies embalmed and on public view, wherein Stalin's colossal image transfixed tens of millions of souls in worship, wherein Mao Tse Tung from within the walls of the Forbidden City ruled like the most majestic of emperors, inscrutable and infallible, the intensity of the cult of Ceausescu was astonishing to behold.

The cult started mildly enough. During his speeches, voices would rhythmically chant 'Ceausescu, PCR', 'Ceausescu si poporul' ('Ceausescu and the people'). It soon developed and would ultimately have an iconography of its own: the saturation of the country with touched-up, idealised portraits of the leader everywhere; scriptures, thirty volumes of his collected speeches on everything from agriculture, about which he knew little, to culture, about which he knew less; and rituals of worship, such that in years to come all artists, scientists, writers, poets and engineers would solemnly intone that the inspiration and guidance for their work had been the cobbler's apprentice with only primary school education.

It led to his merging the head offices of Party and state, to his determination to ensure hands-on control over every policy matter and virtually every appointment of every functionary for more than twenty years. It led, as we shall see, to his appointment of his family members to positions of power and influence: cousins, brothers, sisters, in-laws, his sons and, most especially, his wife Elena. Almost fifty members of the Ceausescu and Petrescu families were appointed to high government posts.

It was an attempt to touch all the bases; a new, red, 'royal family' for the backward peasantry with a touch of semi-religious mysticism thrown in. A rags-to-riches story to encourage the masses, to show that in the new Romania anything was possible. A blameless family life, pretended austerity, puritanical morals, marriage for procreation only and for ever.

If there was one thing on which every Romanian, except probably two, were agreed upon by the end, it was that, of their communist king and queen, the female was the deadlier of the species. This most extraordinary aspect of the cult – the attempt to transform their 'Marxist–Leninist' leadership into a dynasty – marks Romania out from all the other European communist countries. Until Raisa Gorbachev, few in the Eastern bloc ever knew whether their austere party leaders even had wives. When the geriatric Chernenko finally fell over after only a few months in the top position but a lifetime in the senior leadership of the USSR, it was only at his funeral, when she threw herself upon his open coffin, that the Soviet public knew Chernenko had a wife, and even then the media did not mention her name. Stalin's wife was never seen, neither was Khrushchev's, Brezhnev's nor Andropov's.

The wives and families of the leaderships of all Romania's Eastern European neighbours, with a very few exceptions, lived out their lives in comfortable anonymity. However comfortable, anonymity would never have been enough for Lenuta Petrescu.

When Nicolae Ceausescu first met his wife, she was the 'communist factory girl' of the Bucharest police report, demanding 'bread and justice' at the Guild of Leather Workers' meeting before the war. Before poverty and lack of opportunity drew her to Bucharest, she had been a farm-girl, principally remembered for her green eyes and her large 'Roman' nose. She was extremely short as a girl and during her elementary schooling – like her husband, she left school at eleven – she was regarded as backward. She was the daughter of poor peasants, her father a ploughman, from a village in the south-east of Oltenia. Her house was made of mud, her accent, never lost, aroused the particular contempt of the sophisticated Bucharestis in years to come. She failed her fifth-grade examinations, and failed also the school's alternative course of sewing and embroidery. At the age of fourteen she went off to the capital to join the factory workers in the 'Park of Joy'.

Vasile Dumitrescu, who recruited both Ceausescus to the Communist Party and eventually shared a cell with Ceausescu Nicolae, as he describes him, knew Elena as she was gravitating towards the Party agitators in the Bucharest slums. 'You could tell she came from the country; she was very much a farm-girl,' he says with the intellectual snobbery of which many Bucharestis, left and right, are guilty. 'She clumped across a room, head forward, backside out. Anything you put on her looked terrible. In Romania there is a saying that when clothes look like that on you, it's as if you put a saddle on a cow,' he says. Dumitrescu describes the small working-class alehouse, where the young revolutionaries did much of their courting, as 'rather sordid'. 'The local boys decided to elect a queen one night,' he says. 'To do this, you bought tickets, and the girl who inspired the purchase of the most tickets won. The more tickets you bought, the more you loved the girl,' explains the former Ambassador. Now, fifty years later, Dumitrescu is still wondering 'how

Ceausescu Nicolae managed to raise the funds to have plain Lenuta Petrescu elected queen of that tavern!'

This story is more significant than merely an indication of Nicolae Ceausescu's resourcefulness. It comes back in Technicolor in the Cecil B. de Mille-scale legend of the cult manufactured by the RCP's Department of Propaganda thus: the 'sordid' little pub becomes transformed to 'the local stadium'; the Saturday night dance becomes a 'May Day Ball' held by 'local workers'; the 'election' of Lenuta comes not through the purchase of lottery tickets but by a 'free vote of all the workers'. And her title, no longer 'queen' of the sordid little pub, but 'Miss Working Class 1939'. Thus the great revolutionary love story is manufactured.

After the war, Lenuta, now Elena Ceausescu, was wangled a job that taxed her elementary education, in the basement of the Ministry of Foreign Relations. There she was to sort and clip the foreign newspapers. 'She had great difficulties, because she couldn't tell the difference between the different nationalities of the newspapers. She constantly mixed up the French with the English for example,' said Pavel Campeanu, another former cellmate of Nicolae Ceausescu, and Elena's colleague at the Foreign Ministry. 'When she just upped and left one day, she was not missed. She was good for nothing, I'm afraid,' he went on. The next year she went to night school at the Politechnic Institute. During one of her examinations – ironically a test on Marxism – one of the invigilators found her copying answers out of a textbook. 'Comrade, that's not allowed,' he told her. After warning her again, he was forced to expel her from the exam room. Elena's lack of success with exams never again held her back, however.

Her elementary schooling, her failure at sewing and embroidery, her inability to tell French from English were no barrier to her next academic ambition. Having apparently decided after night school that the social sciences were not her forte, she turned to chemistry, the most difficult of the physical sciences, apropos, on the face of it, nothing at all.

Soon after taking over the top Party spot, Ceausescu created a National Council of Scientific Research. It had ninety members, and one of them was Elena Ceausescu. Two years later, without apparently completing any course of study anywhere at any time, Elena received her Ph.D. in industrial chemistry. No one knows who wrote her dissertation, but everyone knows that *she* did not. Some say that it was the work of a group of scientists at the Central Chemical Institute, of which she became a director. Others name a particular scientist who helpfully wrote not only her thesis, but the two books, ten patents and thirteen articles on the synthesis and characterisation of macromolecular compounds which bear her name. Certainly the said professor was, unusually, later allowed to emigrate with consummate ease. The thesis was due to be presented to an audience at the University of Iasi in Moldavia. The audience had been told to turn up to hear the great chemist make her presentation at 1 p.m. The amphitheatre was full and abuzz with expectation. At the appointed hour, a professor took the stage and announced bluntly, 'Thank you for coming to this ceremony today. I have to apologise. Comrade Elena Ceausescu has had to return on urgent business to Bucharest, and she therefore presented her thesis at 12 o'clock.' The professor then left the stage, and the amphitheatre emptied.

In Elena's defence, it must be said that uneducated she certainly was (the least of her sins), but stupid she was unlikely to have been. She did produce three children, all of whom went on to become mathematicians and scientists more or less genuinely (gaining overseas university degrees, with two of them still employed in their profession despite some hostility after the revolution). A look at her bookshelves, immediately after the revolution, that bore volumes from Charles Dickens to Romain Rolland, show that she had attempted to develop intellectually.

Nevertheless the notion that she could have come from nowhere to a Ph.D. in industrial chemistry is absurd beyond belief, and shows just how early in the tyranny the Ceausescus believed they could get away with any fraud. But what is one to say of the clutch of universities who awarded her honorary degrees in science because their Governments temporarily approved of her husband's policies towards the USSR? And what of the British Royal College of Chemistry, which awarded her membership when they must have known that she was a scientific quack, and that the regime ruthlessly exploited these honours for the aggrandisement of the dictatorship?

The question remains, however: why, of all the subjects in which to pretend expertise, did Elena choose one as specific and extremely demanding as chemistry? Was it an untutored love of the natural elements around her, an amateur's quest to unlock the scientific secrets of the universe? One man at least thinks he knows the answer, and it is a good deal more banal. Silviu Brucan, Ceausescu's neighbour in the 1950s, later a leading member of the Communist Party, one of the first anti-Ceausescu dissidents and one of the leaders of the December revolution, says simply: 'When Elena first emerged into the world of the nomenklatura, the two most important women in Romanian life were both chemists. One of them was her neighbour, my wife, and the other was Raluca Ripan, the rector of the historic University of Cluj. In my opinion, it really was as simple as that.'

For a leading communist in Romania, and indeed throughout the bloc, life was good. Not as good as for the elite in the west, but then they had chosen a different path. The nomenklatura could not bequeath their wealth, which passed with them or with their loss of political power, which differentiated them from the class-based elites of the west, but while the going was good, the position came, in Romania at least, with a Party gardener, a cook, a maid and a chauffeur. It furnished your house, though little inventory numbers on the back of the chairs reminded you that what the Party could give the Party could take away. A Party van would deliver the best quality food, which was unavailable to the mere masses, of whom you were the advance guard. The food would be cooked in a communal Party kitchen and given to you at the lowest prices. Your maid lived in, the Party gave you a car for your spouse, too. Your wife could frequent a special boutique (virtually all the nomenklatura were men) where she could order clothes not found in the people's shops.

Yet none of this grace and favour was enough for the Ceausescus, with Elena forcing the pace of the family's rise in the social stakes. By the end, the family had over forty homes, one in each province, all fully staffed, furnished and heated, even when the rest of the country was shivering. In addition, Nicolae Ceausescu maintained several hunting-lodges. Only he was allowed to hunt bear, anyone else would be jailed. Though enthusiastic, he was a poor shot, and the bears virtually had to be corralled into his gunsight. Some say the quarry was often drugged, so that the 'genius hunter' (as he was actually frequently described in the Romanian media) could pose triumphantly, his foot on the fallen Carpathian brown bear, one of the few remaining bears in Europe.

But the houses were very much Elena's province. She worked the staff's fingers to the bone. Two of her obsessions were the polished floors – everyone in the house had to wear ungainly foot mitts at all times, even though only the family, positively no aparatchiks, ever set foot there – and the combing of the fringes of the beautiful rugs which were scattered liberally through all forty villas. 'The floors, of course, had to be polished underneath the rugs, and she stood over you while you did it. But every time you replaced the rugs, and at all times of the day and evening, we had to use a special comb to separate the carpet fringes carefully,' said the maid in the seaside palace of Neptune. The furnishings, though occasionally kitsch, were on the whole of the highest quality, and many beautiful things were collected. Contrary to the flood of post-revolutionary propaganda from some western reporters, the interiors were neither universally tacky nor expensive imports. Ceausescu's chauvinism dictated that virtually everything was produced by the highly skilled and artistic Romanian craftsmen and women.

Clothes were another of Elena's weak points. Inevitably, because of her lifestyle, she was a heavy woman by the end, with large hips and a low-slung bottom. Nevertheless she coveted the latest fashions copied from her regularly airmailed *Vogue* or *Elle*. By the time of the revolution she had over two thousand gowns, and it is said that none of the other Party wives was allowed to own an identical dress. Her imminent arrival at the Party boutique, preceded by the news that 'The comrade is coming!', was a warning that the other women had to leave. She was hard to please as a shopper, especially if the dresses she had ordered proved unflattering when she later tried them on. 'She was always mutton trying to dress as lamb,' one of the boutique's couturiers said. 'Those employed to dress her were always a bundle of nerves.'

Though Nicolae Ceausescu ate frugally, perhaps due to his variety of medical conditions and his constant fear of being poisoned, Elena Ceausescu and the rest of the household had no such inhibitions. On her last birthday (Elena consistently lied about her age so that it was either her seventy-second or her seventy-third), the menu included three varieties of large grain caviar, *pâté de foie gras*, fifteen kinds of meat, fowl and fish: *filet mignon*, roast beef, baby pork, pork chops, pork loin, venison, roast turkey, Cornish game hens, pheasant, lobster, frogs' legs, smoked salmon and three kinds of trout.

In that year, the Romanian people were starving. Food was being exported by the wagon-load to pay off the foreign debt; foods such as oranges and bananas had not been seen on the market at any price for several years; babies were short of milk; large queues formed daily for such delicacies as sheep's head and pigs' knuckles. There was rarely any sign of the animals' intermediate parts. Pigs' trotters were known as 'patriots', since they had stayed in the country while the rest of the animal had gone abroad! Shoppers queuing for pigs' trotters – known laughingly in Romania as 'Adidas' – joked about their envy of the rest of the pig, which was being permitted to travel to Paris, Bonn or other European destinations long denied to them.

To head off the festering public discontent over food shortages, Ceausescu tried a variant of Bertolt Brecht's satirical solution to the popularity problems of the German communists: that the Party should abolish the people and elect a new one! In 1982, Ceausescu inaugurated a 'Rational Nourishment Commission', which devised a 'programme of scientific nourishment'. This solved the problem, Ceausescu-style. A number of segments of the population, it found, were over-eating for their types of jobs and lifestyles, and so the commission ordained the number of calories each type of person required, with most occupations henceforth being told to require less. George Orwell would no doubt have rejected this storyline as being too far-fetched.

If Elena Ceausescu had remained merely an expensive clothes-horse 'dressed as lamb', a glutton and a spendthrift, a bullier of servants, a fellator of German soldiers, an industrial chemist and a world authority on the synthesis and characterisation of macromolecular compounds, the cult, though grotesque enough, would have been merely different in quantity from some of the other Eastern bloc regimes. The qualitative leap, however, was achieved when Elena grew bored with mere sybaritic corruption and decided she wanted to go into politics.

'To the first woman of the country, the homage of the entire country; as star stands beside star in the eternal arch of heaven, beside the Great Man she watches over Romania's path to glory.' This, a gushing birthday tribute in the Party paper *Scinteia*, came to typify the worship paid her by the Romanian press which, by the end, easily equalled that paid to her husband.

The move began in 1971. Until then, if any wives of Party leaders did accompany them anywhere, they were referred to without names, as simply: wives. On 23rd August, Romanian National Day, Elena Ceausescu became the first wife to appear on the reviewing stand. The next year she was elected to the Communist Party Central Committee, and the year after that to the political executive committee – the all-powerful 'Politburo'. In 1979 she was appointed to the Council of Ministers as President of the National Council for Science and Technology. In 1980, most astonishingly of all, she was appointed First Vice-President of Romania's Council of Ministers, placing her as the third or fourth most important figure in the country.

Cynics said that of her importance there had never been any doubt, but its vivid confirmation in this way was unprecedented in Eastern Europe. Just as with the Ph.D., Elena Ceausescu ascended these political heights with no evidence of any work that could have justified it. She became the dominant figure in the country's chemical and petrochemical industries, on which untold billions were spent and wasted. She interposed herself between her husband and his advisers, interfering in both domestic and diplomatic appointments. She presided with him at Party and state ceremonies. She demonstrated her power by calling Romanian ministers by their first names (they, of course, were not allowed to reciprocate) and by speaking to them in the familiar, singular, form of the verb she should have reserved for children and animals.

Eventually she effectively took charge of the Ministry of Finance as it performed the Herculean struggle to pay off the foreign debt. She supervised the breakneck repayment of more than £8 billion well ahead of schedule, but at a price which broke the backs of the population and certainly proved the final straw for the regime. 'Life in the ministry was Kafkaesque,' says a young economist still working there and loath to give his name. 'Queries from either the International Monetary Fund or the Paris Club of bankers could not be dealt with by ministry officials, but had to be referred to Elena Ceausescu's advisers. Articles commissioned by Constantin Olteanu, the respected editor-in-chief of the magazine *Revista Economica*, were strictly censored by her men, and in any interviews given by Olteanu he was flanked by security men taking notes.' Olteanu eventually defected to the west, leaving the economy to the comrade academician, doctor, engineer.

Effective control of the magazine then passed to Barbu Petrescu, head of the Party and mayor of Bucharest – and Elena Ceausescu's cousin. On International Women's Day in 1982, *Scinteia*, reporting on the celebrations, rejoiced in the presence of 'comrade academician, doctor, engineer, Elena Ceausescu, outstanding activist of Party and state, eminent personage of Romanian and international science'. Even Elena's birthplace, which had been so disparagingly described by Vasile Dumitrescu – the village of Petresti – was, lo and behold, found to be of special scientific interest. Archaeological evidence found there showed that the village had been inhabited since Paleolithic times, and it was thereafter showered with privileges commensurate with its global archaeological significance. Not to be outdone, Nicolae Ceausescu's birthplace was also found to be scientifically important – indeed, one of the most significant sites in the world. The backward peasant area of Oltenia was found in 1976 to be 'the site of one of the earliest human presences on the continent of Europe'. As if such distinction were not enough, the area was found to yield 'one of the first decisive examples of anthropogenesis on the path to Homo Sapiens'. No wonder that, blinded by such science, Ceausescu could say in a raging argument in his office: 'A man like Me is born to a country only once in a thousand years.'

But it was a family affair, and not simply man and wife. In one of the earliest examples of the cult, a massive volume entitled *Homage* issued on Ceausescu's fifty-fifth birthday in 1973 gives a flavour of what was to come. Near the end of a biographical introduction, under a photograph of the family, the writer observes:

> We gaze with esteem, with respect, at the harmony of his family life. We attach special ethical significance to the fact that his life, together with that of his life comrade, the former textile worker and young communist militant in the days of illegality, today Heroine of Socialist Labour, scientist, member of the central committee of the RCP, comrade Elena Ceausescu, offers an exemplary image of the destinies of two communists. Their three children, Valentin a physicist, Zoia a mathematician, and Nicu a physics student, work, like any of us, following the example of their parents, to bring socialism to Romania. All this attests clearly to the truth: that work and personal example are obligations in the Ceausescu family.

In fact Elena and Nicolae Ceausescu ruined the lives of their children long before the revolution threw them into their current limbo, by interfering in their lives to the extent of proposing their marriage partners and disposing of the suitors who didn't suit them, choosing their subjects for study and then their jobs. The family grew up poor little rich kids, with everything and nothing. The result was depressingly predictable.

The original apple of the Ceausescus' eye was their younger son Nicu. Once the Dauphin of the Romanian Communist Party, Nicu now endures his revolutionary assizes in the eighteenth-century Bastille-like dungeon of

Jilava Prison, eight miles from Bucharest.

It will be remembered that in this prison, half a century before, Nicolae Ceausescu, the 'dangerous communist agitator', cheated death at the hands of the rampaging fascist death squad when his jailers made a last-ditch stand around cell blocks 22, 23, and 24 – the communist cells – on a wintry November night in 1940. Few in the prison today believe that his son will be lucky enough to outlive his imprisonment. The grounds are stark, with leafless trees and gaunt men in the grey striped pyjamas of the Eastern European convict. The convicts hew wood and draw water beneath the gaze of fierce German Shepherd dogs and bored, heavily armed guards.

In its soulless hospital block, the former crown prince Nicu lies in bed in considerable pain from a cirrhotic liver, the fruit of a legendary thirst for Scotland's 'water of life', and a varicose oesophagus. His sybaritic youth, when he partied, ate, drank and fornicated his way through Bucharest and beyond, seems far away. Yet he is only thirty-nine.

Summoning his dignity, he asks that we wait for him in the jailers' office, as he would prefer not to answer questions in his pyjamas. Inside the office, we have a long wait for the invalid. Finally the door opens, and slowly, almost theatrically slowly, the *enfant terrible* hobbles in, as though on fallen arches. Conspicuously thin and drawn, he looks ten years older than his true age.

It had not been easy to interview Nicu Ceausescu. Although the authorities had agreed quickly to our request, the prisoner, with little need now of sympathy after his twenty-year sentence, had played very hard to get.

The Ceausescu family lawyer, the redoubtable Jewish matron Paula Jacob, proved to be the key. Jacob is emerging as one of the personalities of post-revolutionary Romania, and her house in the centre of the city is one of the chicest salons in this most unchic of capitals. There of an evening will dine the ingathering Romanian intelligentsia, returning from exile to test the water of the new democracy. She seeks first to negotiate a price for access to the Ceausescu children to augment their now meagre incomes. 'They are like strays now, with not even enough money to clothe themselves for the winter,' she pleads. But she doesn't drive a hard bargain. At a musical dinner party in her home, with a blizzard blowing outside, and the giants of Romanian opera, Nicolae Herlea (once held in the 1950s and 60s in Pavarotti-like awe), Octavian Naghiu and Pompeiu Harasteanu warming her hearth, she relents on hearing our own duet of Tony Bennett's 'I Left my Heart in San Francisco'. Access to the jail is gained the very next morning. Gratis.

We travel to Jilava Prison via several spartan butcher's shops where Paula Jacob must purchase the beefsteaks and fruit juices that Nicu Ceausescu's poor health demands but which the prison regime cannot supply. A likely tale, we thought. But either Nicu Ceausescu is an actor in the Olivier class, or he is a very sick man indeed. He literally falls on to his hard prison chair, his right hand acting as cover for his half-closed eyes, his elbow resting on his knee, the thinning of his black hair evident. He is wearing an unflattering blue-patterned jumper, non-designer jeans and a green and red anorak jacket. All the colours of the rainbow, and definitely not dressed by Hugo Boss, he is not an inch the playboy.

We were joined at the entrance to the jail by his brother Valentin, another favour by Paula Jacob, and disconcertingly we list him as our translator for the visit. But it is a wise move, because although never close in years gone by, the uprooting of their family has drawn the brothers so close that only Valentin's presence persuades Nicu to talk.

The talking, mere drawling, is slow to start. Nicu asks – for the umpteenth time, we get the impression – for the brown-coloured Penal Codebook of Romanian justice, and scarcely intelligibly at first begins to quote from it chapter and verse to prove his point that his charges, trial and sentencing are a travesty. And that it all has nothing to do with justice and everything to do with the political needs of the hour.

It is not necessary to be an attorney to see that he is right. He stood trial for genocide, practised allegedly against the citizens of the important town of Sibiu. But when it became obvious that the state could find no one credible to say he'd given orders to shoot, and somewhat nonplussed by the steady stream of respectable citizens of the town, where he ruled as local Party boss, giving character references at his trial, the judge promptly found him guilty of 'economic sabotage'. It is a crime of which he may well have been guilty, but for which he had never been tried. No matter. He got the twenty years anyway. Soon he will be tried on further charges, namely, the pilfering of stock from the Communist Party shop in Sibiu.

He has lost hope of staying alive and, for what it's worth, his brother Valentin and his lawyer Paula Jacob have no doubt that he is dying. His doctor would not be drawn. As he sits hunched in his chair, wincing with pain and barely audible, we remember the description of him as the 'handsome and elegant young man' who had 'kicked the booze and straightened himself out here in Sibiu', in the imagination of Livia Birsan, the maid in the Sibiu Party villa. According to her, Nicu lived a modest life after his father exiled him from Bucharest, to dry him out, to break his profligate friendships, to get him away from the Olympic star Nadia Comaneci when their romance grew too public and too violent.

His maid says she saw him drink only the occasional beer, and that his bed, which she made every morning, was occupied by him alone. Ioan Preda, his *chef du cabinet*, said that Nicu took his job in Sibiu seriously and that his drinking was characterised by infrequent binges, which kept him from the office while they lasted. At all other times, he says, Nicu was the first one in to work and the last to leave.

But Nicu knows well that his early life in the bratpack has tipped the balance of public opinion heavily against him. Crazedly, and crazily, given the state of his health, he is drawing deeply on his third Kent cigarette in our first fifteen minutes.

He is reluctant to talk much about his parents. 'At this stage it's too early to evaluate his life – his political life, I mean. I never really knew him personally. You need decades, perhaps a century, to write history objectively. There were many mistakes, of course, but there were good things too.'

'What kinds of mistakes?'

He folds up in a fit of coughing which lasts many minutes. 'His biggest mistake was listening to my mother too much. Even a history written now would have to show that my mother was a very bad influence on him.'

Paula Jacob hands him some papers to sign, which he does without looking down, then checks himself, laughing. 'Sometimes I forget the old days are over ... I learned to sign then ... Now I'd better learn to read before I sign,' he says.

'I have appealed against my sentence, of course,' he goes on, 'but my appeal will surely fail. And even were it to succeed, you know that they are planning to charge me next ... With what? With pilfering goods from the Communist Party shop in Sibiu! Are these serious people?' He has now become animated, to the concern of his young woman doctor. He looks at her, and fires a winning wink in her direction. Some old habits die hard.

How would he explain the extraordinary collapse of his father's regime, especially in the light of its earlier popularity?

'Well, there is a simple reply to this question,' he says, lighting up again. 'It was all predictable, when the external structures, in the Soviet Union and the other Eastern bloc countries, began to collapse. Added to the internal problems of the regime, this made it impossible to survive for long. But I still think the change could have happened in a different way ... without the bloodshed ... I think the bloodshed was futile ... completely futile.' His voice dies away, and he lights up again.

Is he still a communist?

'Well, that's a big question. It depends on what you mean by communist. It is one thing to talk of communism or even socialism as ideas, centrally their advocacy of equality between people, their social goals, and so on. It is quite another thing to talk about how these ideas worked out in practice ... during the last forty-five years in Romania, for example. In practice, all the countries embracing communism have finished up as one-party states, which has led to totalitarianism. That is the big question ... There are many problems which need clarification,' he says.

Valentin is keen to change the subject, but Nicu, warming now to this rare audience, jokes, 'I have plenty of time. I won't be going anywhere for a very long time!'

What about today's Government, which keeps him here for fear of the Romanian people's wrath?

'We spoke of totalitarianism ... What is this new Government? ... No more than "*Jeanette autrement coiffée*" ("the same old Jeanette with another hairdo"). The people voted for them because they were afraid of a witch-hunt in the country. Now they are witch-hunting my family instead. We are the witch-hunt that might have been ...'

And his exile from Bucharest to Sibiu by his father: was it an exile, or a proving-ground?

He answers quickly, anticipating the question's real point. 'I never at any time had a discussion with my father about my succeeding him. I never believed that I would ever be President of this country, or the General Secretary of the Party.'

What were his relations with his father?

At this point he puts his head back and closes his eyes

for what seems a long time. His doctor grows anxious
again. He sits up straight, looks at Valentin, and answers
with a grin. 'Even worse than his!'

Well, his mother, then?

'Bad ... Not worse than with my father ... I was equi-
distant from them. My mother had a lot of influence, a
great deal of influence, and that was a bad influence, that's
obvious. But both my parents were to blame, although
others were to blame also. You can only take decisions
based on information. The quality of our information was
pathetic.... But I've told you ... I don't normally speak
about my parents.'

Had he known the end was coming?

'No one could have forecast the way the end came in
Romania; that what happened in the days from 16th
December to January would have happened. Anyone who
says they could have forecast it is a liar.'

His doctor is standing by him now, feeling his brow for
his temperature. 'All this talk; all these cigarettes,' she
sighs. As she mops his brow, it is obvious from his face
that he is missing the gentle company of women in the
coarseness of his prison life. The undeniable in his biography is the long string of suitors he loved and left, or was
forced by the interference of his mother to leave. A galaxy
of actresses, opera singers and professors of Marxist–
Leninism, the brightest star among them Olympic
gymnastics champion Nadia Comaneci, 'Heroine of
Socialist Labour of Romania'.

Does he? Miss women, that is?

'I was not a saint, but there were many with a vested
interest in lying about my loins,' he says, coughing. 'Take
Ion Pacepa, the defector, and his book *Red Horizons*, for
example. He had me pissing on oysters and God knows
what. Lies, lies, and not even good lies! I saw Pacepa
once in my whole life, in 1973, when I was twenty-three
years old.'

And Nadia Comaneci? Her mother had claimed, after

Nadia's defection to America with a father of four young children, that Nicu had raped her daughter.

'Rape ... Rape!' shrieks Paula Jacob, waking the dozing prison warder with a start. 'All Romania knows that Nadia Comaneci was grateful for everything she received from Nicu Ceausescu!' she bellows. The prison guard nods in agreement.

And, now, does Nicu believe in God?

He thinks deeply before answering this question, half asked in jest. 'This ... is a return ticket question ... Everyone has to have some hope ... some have religion. I have broken eggs at Easter, but that is a pagan custom, I suppose. I have nothing against God ... and I certainly hope He has got nothing against me!'

As we leave, Nicu takes the beefsteak with a grateful shrug. Paula Jacob is the last to bid him goodbye. She looks at him as only a mother can look at a son.

Leaving Jilava Prison with Valentin Ceausescu, at forty-two the Ceausescus' eldest child, the deference shown towards him by convicts and guards alike is surprising. Many prisoners doff their stripy pyjama caps as he goes past; every guard has a friendly word. Even the German Shepherd dogs have become his friends and he feeds two of them with biscuits as we leave.

Valentin modestly explains that the friendly response has nothing to do with politics, and indeed it is well known in Romania that he had very little interest in politics. 'No, it is because of my football,' he explains.

Valentin Ceausescu was chairman in all but name (strangely he had no formal title at all) of Steaua Bucharest, the European Cup winners in 1986. Steaua were the 'army' team while their rivals, Dynamo Bucharest, were patronised by the hated Securitate. As the son of the President of the country, Valentin's 'pull' in attracting and retaining players, in opening doors around Europe during the team's great overseas campaigns, during which he met all the greats – 'How is Graeme Souness doing now? – A brutal, but brilliant player' – was widely credited as being the driving force that made Steaua Romania's top team for the first time. This credit has stayed with him – except among Dynamo supporters – through the revolution and beyond.

Valentin Ceausescu is a scientist, but a real one, unlike his mother. He studied physics at Imperial College London in 1968, when European students, many inspired by the same Marx and Lenin whose theories titularly underlay the state run by his father, took to the streets looking for revolution.

'The student demands seemed very immature to me then. As to their leaders, I used to listen to the likes of Tariq Ali, and I could never imagine him coming to power in a country like Britain. I'm told he's an important member of the Labour Party now,' he says.

Valentin now works, as he did before his father's fall, in the Nuclear Physics Institute, where he is a capable and popular employee. He seems profoundly saddened by his life.

His former wife – the daughter of a former communist rival of his father, and a Jew – was hated by his mother, and many say the marriage was wrecked by Elena Ceausescu. She has now fled the country with Valentin's only child, and he is feeling the pain.

Valentin is so subdued that he can hardly be heard when he is speaking, and in any case he doesn't want to say much, especially about his dead parents. 'I warned my father ten years before that this was coming and that it would end like this. The night before he was overthrown I talked with him for about fifteen minutes. I begged him to make concessions, to receive a delegation from the people. He was listening, but he didn't hear. My mother told me, "Don't be stupid!" He was always listening far too much to my mother.'

He is more relaxed now in the salon of Paula Jacob. He

is a handsome man, with a 'feathered' hairstyle of the kind
fashionable nearly twenty years ago. Unusually in the land
where Kent cigarettes are king, he is a Marlboro man, and
his English has a distinct American twang. He is as slim as
a professional athlete, perhaps the footballer he would
have wanted to be. He is wearing a kingfisher blue sweat-
shirt, well-tailored grey needlecord trousers and black
suede 'brothel-creeper'-type shoes.

'I didn't really know my father,' he says. 'He was so
busy with politics, I never really got to know him. He was
a very dedicated man, my father. Whatever else anyone
says about him, he really believed in a communist
Romania. This was his faith. Maybe he was the only one
who believed it ... Yes, I suppose this did make me closer
to my mother, but of course eventually she became totally
involved in politics too.'

Was his mother a dominant person?

'Yes, I suppose she was.'

For the son of a dictator, Valentin is his dialectical
opposite. He is 'sure' about nothing. He 'supposes',
'thinks' or 'guesses' most of his opinions.

I think they overdid everything, my mother and father.
This personality-cult stuff, I was always against this.
When it came on the television I used to switch it off; it
offended me. Even when it started, around 1970, I
think, it had already gone too far, and although I used
to speak to them about it, mainly to my father, I guess
the decision had already been made to go in for that
stuff. I think the idea came from somebody else.

From 1980 I saw the end coming. It was definitely
all downhill from then on. I really was pinning my
hopes on my father retiring at the last Party congress,
just weeks before the end. He looked so old the last
year and a half ...

I learned by telephone that my parents had fled on
the revolution day. I was living with friends. They were

afraid that the revolutionaries would come looking for me, so I turned myself in. I was joined in my detention by my brother Nicu, and believe it or not I got to know him there. I didn't know him before. We are completely different, and he has problems which have resulted in his being witch-hunted more than me ... He's arrogant and sure of himself, and this makes him easy to hate. But he is my brother, and we are sticking closely now.

It was in prison that I learned that my parents were dead, and much later that I saw the kangaroo court which ordered their executions. I haven't watched the film of them being shot to death ... Would you, if it was your parents? In the film it is obvious that my father doesn't believe that it is the end. You might find this funny, but I think that my father went to his death believing that the working class in this country really supported him ... loved him, even.

That's what happens with this kind of personality cult, you see; it works both ways. You construct such a thing, and before long you have convinced yourself that it is true.

Valentin's first love, his child, is gone now, a casualty of who he is in every way. His second love, his football team, is gone too. Although he says there have been demonstrations at the stadium calling for his return, he knows it can never be. He faces his own criminal charges of 'economic sabotage' too. He now seems interested only in physics and his absorbing study of quantum mechanics.

Leaving, he fixes his eye on one of the authors, George Galloway, MP. 'You know, I have no time for politicians; I never have had. They have an innate duplicity in their characters. When I read your book, I will know if you are a politician or a writer of books.'

The most wretched of the Ceausescu offspring has none of her elder brother's bank of popularity to draw upon.

Zoia Ceausescu is forty-one and a mathematician. She currently works at the Institute of Mathematics, where before the revolution she held a senior position. Her professor, Nicolai Gusi, now in charge of the Institute, has placed her on a one-year probation as a junior member of the academic staff. She is a collector of antique books, and a believer that dogs, not diamonds and certainly not men, are a girl's best friend.

There is a deep well of misogyny in some of Romanian society, and from it is dredged much of the posthumous bile being thrown at Elena Ceausescu. The well is producing smears by the bucketful for Zoia, too. Foremost is the charge that hurts her most. Luridly expressed in tabloids, and other news-sheets around the world, is the allegation that the mathematician Zoia Ceausescu is a nymphomaniac. Not merely promiscuous, but a nymphomaniac. Lovers by the score are named or hinted at and paraded in European glossy magazines. Legends of the type inspired by Catherine the Great of Russia are attributed to her. The photographs used to illustrate these stories of scandal are out of date indeed. Zoia Ceausescu is an emaciated, alcoholic wreck.

Her former maid reports that Zoia used to lock herself in her room for days on end. 'She would run into the room, usually crying, with her dogs, her cigarettes and her booze. During these bouts, I was not allowed into the room to clean. When she eventually emerged, the stench was overwhelming. During one of these times, she was in such a stupor that she appeared not to realise that one of her dogs had given birth to several puppies at the bottom of her bed,' she says.

More than with any of the other children, Elena Ceausescu demanded total control over her daughter's life. She broke up several promising romances purely on the ground that they would not have been politically suitable for the regime. Either the boy was too high born, or too low. He was too political, and thus a threat, or he was politically ignorant and therefore a risk. Or he was the son of a Party functionary who was not trusted. Or, if his father was trusted, would marrying into the ruling family give his father too much power? Or he was a Jew.

Elena Ceausescu spied on her daughter, and ordered the Securitate to follow her and her beaux. Eventually, she even had her daughter's private quarters videotaped. Such lovemaking as was captured thereby has been said by some reporters to have been used by Elena for her vicarious sexual satisfaction. Much more likely is that the films were used systematically to eliminate successive lovers from Zoia's permanently disappointing life. Boyfriend after boyfriend would unexpectedly turn up in one far corner or another of the Romanian civil service – anywhere from obscure embassies in Central Africa to provincial universities miles from Bucharest. According to the defector Ion Pacepa, Elena even plotted to have one unusually persistent wooer killed.

Like her siblings, Zoia Ceausescu is fearful of letting her true feelings show. Her large dark glasses are not the only barrier to the woman behind them. She too is awaiting sentencing for her 'economic sabotage' of Romania, though she would certainly have a claim that Romania surely sabotaged her. But, weak though she is, some things make her very angry indeed.

It's true that I have a problem with alcohol, and it's true that I have had many troubles in my life – long before these latest ones. I have now lost both my mother and my father – in front of my eyes on the TV – my kid brother is serving what will turn out to be a life sentence, my other brother is awaiting sentence, and I too may soon be behind bars. What do they want, this regime? Do they want blood? They are welcome – but I warn them, I have not much blood left to give.

The world ... Do you understand what that means? ... The whole world has been told I am a nymphomaniac. What is a nymphomaniac? If I have slept with eight men in my whole life, does that make me a nymphomaniac, that is a freak, a medical case! How many of the men who have written these things have slept with eight women in their lives? Is such a man a nymphomaniac? What hypocrites men are!

She is shaking now, and crying. It is better to ask no more.

Nicolae and Elena Ceausescu brought about the ruin of their country, and were surely the architects of their own grisly and ignominious demise. But long hours in the company of their children convinced us that not the least of their victims were in their own 'red royal' household, among their own flesh and blood.

CHAPTER 5

Romania – A State of Morality

One of the many aspects of the Ceausescu dictatorship which marked it out from the other European communist states was its active pursuit of puritan ideals, as conservative in its approach to personal, social and family life as any clerical dictatorship. Characteristically, however, their puritanism backfired and their policies achieved the opposite of their intentions, leaving a train of ruined, corrupted and brutalised victims behind.

Sadly, Ceausescu's 'state of morality' was no more successful than any of his other grand designs, and it has left a most bitter legacy. Early in his rule – nearly two years before he stole the hearts of the west by opposing the Soviet invasion of Czechoslovakia – Ceausescu, and the Romanian Communist Party, climbed beneath the bedclothes of Romanian women and stole control of their fertility.

He acted out of a mixture of motives. On the one hand there was the puritanism of the Oltenian peasant. This had fathered successive fierce campaigns against long hair, smoking and, in the late 1960s, against the imminent invasion of the mini-skirt from swinging London.

On the other hand, there were more practical reasons. There is a constant fear among ethnic Romanians that their 'stock' is being subverted by the presence of large ethnic minorities in the country; in a total population of 23 millions, there are 1,500,000 Hungarians, 200,000 Germans and two million gypsies, as well as Serbian, Turkish and Russian minorities, and immediately after the war, at least, nearly half a million Jews. It became an article of faith in the dark Ceausescu years that the 'pure' Romanian birthrate was not keeping up with the others, and that the 'special' character of the Romanian genetic pool was under threat. The call went out: Boost the birthrate!

Thus Ceausescu began to legislate the moral tone of the nation. First, a decree was issued that, henceforth, all women under the age of forty with fewer than four children would be forbidden by law to practise any form of contraception. Second, in an accompanying decree, all abortions, except in life-threatening circumstances, were declared illegal. A breach of either of these decrees, which were supported by all religious denominations in Romania, was to be punishable by long periods of imprisonment, both for the woman concerned and anyone who assisted her in the commission of these 'crimes'.

A 'flying squad' of gynaecological policemen was assembled to enforce the dictator's writ at the point of a speculum, a branch of the hated Securitate. The inspectors of the squad raided every workplace – in Romania virtually all young women worked – randomly, but at least once every three months. All women of child-bearing age were compulsorily inspected, feet up in portable stirrups, for any signs of makeshift coils (imported rubber for condoms had long since been unavailable in Romania) or any evidence of abortions. Women with confirmed pregnancies were supervised weekly until their babies were born. The immediate result of this reign of obstetric terror was encouraging for the regime – a doubling in one year of the growth in the birthrate.

But it was quickly accompanied by an ever more desperate scramble by couples determined to avoid the new fertility trap. Soon there was the virtually universal practice of coitus interruptus. Worse, a dramatic growth in anal sex and, increasingly, loveless marriages. Then, inevitably, an ever more desperate scramble through the back streets of the big towns as the new moralistic Romania became the illegal abortion capital of Europe.

Cornelia Treveleanu, an attractive dark-haired factory worker from Bucharest, is thirty-eight years old. She bears the scars of an incredible thirty-six abortions, all but one of them during the days of illegality. The great majority were, in the cold words of the medical dictionary, carried out through physical dislodgement of the foetal embryo. In the back room of a house in Bucharest, this meant the rough insertion of a rubber tube carried out by an untrained crone with a bar of caustic soap. Some of Cornelia's abortions were of the type euphemistically described as 'manual massage'. In every single one of her abortions, she was subsequently hospitalised with heavy blood loss and septicaemia immediately afterwards.

'Every time, I was terrified. I thought to myself, this will be it, this time. God will surely make me die for this. A woman in Romania in those days had to be like a cat; she had to have nine lives,' she says.

Mrs Treveleanu lives in the Pantelimon district of Bucharest with her husband and the two children she wanted to bear. She is crystal clear about the number of terminations she has had in the back streets of the capital. She goes on, 'I know the number very well, because as a woman you can never forget. It is not thirty-seven abortions I have had, nor thirty-five. It is thirty-six, God forgive me. I didn't have any choice. It seems I become pregnant easily, and there was a law against using anything. It was abortion, or bringing a child into a world where there was no food, no money, no medicine, no room, and a cold, cold house.'

The Pantelimon district of the city is served by the 'August 23' Hospital, called after the day fascism in Romania was routed in 1944. Luckily for Cornelia Treveleanu, the doctors there found the fascistic fertility decrees just as abominable as she did. They helpfully hospitalised her after each of her abortions as having naturally miscarried.

When the regime, almost unbelievably, toughened up the decrees to include women up to forty-five years old with fewer than five children, many doctors were in a state of – secret – revolt. In the words of Professor Virgiliu Ancar, the consultant gynaecologist at the 'August 23' Hospital, 'Ceausescu's making abortions illegal didn't stop them happening – it just made sure they didn't happen in hospitals. The dictatorship made prostitutes out of our profession.'

But sympathetic or not, doctors like everyone else knew that the eye of the Securitate could see almost everywhere. In 1985, Professor Ancar's then superior, Henrietta Ciortoioman, a doctor of forty-five years' experience, said at a routine morning staff meeting in the hospital that, in her view, for women with heart problems the insertion of an intra-uterine coil was preferable to their risking their lives in back-street abortions. At lunch-time the same day, she was dismissed by the Ministry of Health.

Professor Ancar, for the crime of merely being her assistant, was banished to another hospital for two years. He believes that upwards of two million illegal abortions took place during the ban, and the consequences, he says, have been horrific. 'Probably 25,000 women have died from septic abortions, or abortion complications, during the period. Furthermore, perhaps half a million women have been permanently damaged, many now infertile. In the year 1989 alone, in just my own wards at the "August 23" we operated on nearly five thousand casualties of back-street abortions – mostly of the most basic type – women having had their waters burst early to puncture the membrane of the placenta. We did the mopping up,' he says.

The bitterest of ironies is that just like most of Nicolae Ceausescu's grand plans, this attempt at playing God was a dismal failure even in his own terms. Though the birthrate jumped from 14.3 live births per thousand inhabitants in 1966 to 27.4 the next year, by 1973 it had fallen again to 18.5. And by the time of Ceausescu's death, twenty-three years and a vale of women's tears later, the birthrate in Romania was lower than it had been when he started.

While anal sex and coitus interruptus are doubtless declining in the new Romania, the most serious legacy of the dictatorship's time between the sheets of the nation's marital bed will not go away so easily. This legacy lies in the grim iron cots of the country's Aids wards, where half of all the child Aids cases in Europe are incarcerated awaiting the merciful release of death.

As Romania's economy staggered through the 1980s and the country's families, trapped by the fertility decrees, plunged ever deeper into cold, damp poverty, tens of thousands of unwanted and abandoned children began to be offloaded into children's homes and orphanages. Those were the canyons of horror that were captured on unforgettable film by the first western TV crews arriving after the revolution.

With the collapse of the economy came a disproportionate crisis in the country's medical and ramshackle social work services. For example, by the 1980s, Ceausescu's refusal on economic grounds to allow the import of any rubber goods meant that even surgical gloves were unobtainable, and only doctors performing live deliveries were allowed to wear them. Thus, for example, the thousands of post-septic abortion 'mopping up' operations cited by Professor Virgiliu Ancar of the 'August 23' Hospital were carried out by men with bare hands, threadbare stirrups and crude-looking knives. Conditions in hospitals, orphanages and other institutions in the country were comparable with the worst British Victorian poorhouses and asylums of a century or more earlier.

The medical authorities buckled under the strain of ever-increasing caseloads. Food was becoming more scarce in what was one of the most fertile countries in Europe, because the wholesale export of food was fuelling the breakneck repayment of more than £8 billion in foreign loans.

Some genius – who knows, perhaps even 'the Genius of the Carpathians', Nicolae Ceausescu himself – hit upon the idea of giving micro-transfusions of blood to the grossly malnourished children in the institutions. Soon, this was the official policy of the Romanian Ministry of Health. Needles to transfuse the blood were in short supply, and were used again, and again and again.

Eventually, no one knows exactly when, the syringes were delivering not just blood, but the Aids virus as well. No one knows, either, or they aren't telling, where the infected blood came from. If it came from Romanian adult donors, clearly the country may be the unknowing epicentre of a European epidemic. Even now, virtually no testing of the adult population has been carried out, and most blood transfusions in the country still take place using unscreened blood. Some say Ceausescu made a bulk purchase of blood – unbelievably, from Africa! Others say it came from the private market in blood in the USA.

At first, Ceausescu declared that Aids was a capitalist world disease, which could not exist in his socialist paradise. He banned mention of it in the medical journals, and demoted those who dissented. Aids became the illness that dare not speak its name.

By all the normal parameters of epidemiology, the Black Sea town of Constanta would be an area at high risk of the Aids virus. It is a busy and bustling industrial port, with popular seaside holiday resorts to its north and south, and thus it combines a social cocktail of sailors, prostitution and the kind of transient population which is highly conducive to the spread of the infection. No one knows how many adults in Constanta are HIV infected. But what is known is that one in four of all the child Aids cases in Europe lie waiting to die there. It was into these killing-fields that the authors walked, quite unprepared, just weeks after the December revolution.

Nothing in any case could really prepare you for the authors' first visit to the Municipal Hospital in Constanta. It stands off the Boulevard Republica in the heart of the town not far from the railway station. A purple-blue plaque on the wall of a rear building announces 'Spitalul Municipal Sectia Contagioase', indicating the virulent diseases section where the Aids children lay. You climb with dread the sickly yellow marble staircase, up the three flights to the white-and-maroon-floored entrance hall, off which lies a ward entitled only 'Sector II'.

The day we walked through that door has never left us.

The ward comprised six rooms in which the children were kept in basic iron cots, one butting against the next. Many of the children had the faces of dying geriatrics, grey, sunken-eyed skeletons. That day there were sixty-three children sharing forty-three cots, so that the smallest were three to a bed, and two to a bed was common. They were, most of them, swaddled in old bed-sheets, and screaming. The stench of death and defecation was overwhelming. They lay on their backs, eyes wide in frozen watchfulness, hands outstretched as though begging to be lifted and hugged. This they never would be. Most were under two years old and nearly dead.

Children had been dying here since 1988, scythed by the grim reaper of Aids, but only the December revolution allowed the truth to be counted. In this hospital, nearly two hundred children have died since the counting began at the end of 1989.

To place this in perspective, in Scotland – with the terrible problem of Edinburgh at its heart – there have been three child Aids deaths since 1986. More than five hundred children in the town of Constanta have the Aids virus, three-quarters of them with full-blown Aids. In Scotland, there are currently ten such cases.

Sabin Borcea is one of the children in Constanta suffering from Aids, or Sida, as it is known in Romania. His mother Alina is a doctor, and so when in the summer of 1989, Ceausescu's last summer, she noticed that her baby son had developed an inflammation of the tonsils, she knew that it was potentially serious in a young child. She watched him carefully for two days, and when he developed a fever, she took him to hospital. After four days in hospital, the boy recovered and was allowed home.

Two months later Alina was asked to bring the baby back for tests because it was discovered that a baby with hepatitis B had been in the ward at the same time. She was told then, in August, that there was nothing to worry about, so she didn't ask too many questions. People didn't, in Ceausescu's Romania. Today the little boy is HIV positive and may die of Aids; he contracted the virus via an infected needle when being tested in hospital. He is terminally ill, and his mother the doctor seems terminally sad as she sits there on the wooden bench outside 'Sector II'.

Dr Rodica Matusa is the saintly, Florence Nightingale figure in charge of 'Sector II' in the Constanta Municipal Hospital and several smaller sanatoria. In between caring for one in four of all the child Aids victims in Europe, and dealing with the devastated mothers on the wooden bench, she tells her story.

In late 1988 I became worried about all the post-operative babies with hepatitis B whom I was seeing, and I feared, even then, that they might in fact be HIV infected. I sent the blood tests to the Ministry of Health in Bucharest. They confirmed that they were Aids cases, but they forbade me very sternly from telling anyone. Agents of the Securitate, two men in black leather jackets, came to my house and told me that I would be severely punished if I discussed the Aids babies with anyone. The 'chief' was on record, they said, as saying that there was no Aids in Romania. Later, these and other men began following me everywhere I went. They didn't even pretend to stay out of sight. They even, clumsily, bugged my telephone.

After the revolution I was shown a great thick file on me made by the Securitate, and reading it made it obvious that some of their informants were doctors with whom I had been working in the hospital. They had told them that within the hospital I had been constantly talking about the Aids babies. I refused to keep an illness a state secret.

As we toured the ward that day, Dr Matusa was at a low ebb. Somehow the agony of her colleague Dr Borcea, the doctor whose child caught Aids from a dirty needle in her own hospital, had destabilised her. As she discussed the ravages that the children face as their immune systems collapse – 'tuberculosis, diarrhoea, genital and facial herpes, bronchial pneumonia … Oh, and hepatitis, the toll of the bell …' She sheds a tear, and her gentle voice becomes hard with bitterness. 'These are Ceausescu's children,' she says, looking around the ward, 'and I hope that he is now burning in the hottest fires of hell!'

Despite Matusa's constant admonishments, the nursing staff in the hospital that day were, simply, frightened of the children. Terrified of catching 'the plague', as one said. They refused to approach the children without first donning such barrier clothing as made them look like cloth space-men on a moon walk. Other than Matusa's, no human skin had ever touched most of these children.

The authors' attempts to lift the children and cuddle them were met by loud shrieks of horror from the nurses, who beat a hasty retreat. There was not a toy, a scrap of decoration, a teddy bear in sight. These were the children doomed, it seemed, to live and die without ever having had a cuddle or a kiss.

Since those grey days, as the memories of the dictator's orders to wipe out not the disease but any mention of its name begin to fade, things have changed. 'Apart from anything else, the children are taking much longer to die than we expected,' says Dr Matusa.

In early 1990, the authors established the Romanian Child Aids Appeal. Press coverage in the *Observer* and *Independent on Sunday* newspapers in Britain, television coverage in New Zealand and Australia and some co-funding from a national appeal in the *Guardian* eventually enabled the Appeal to raise tens of thousands of pounds for the children and the staff of Constanta Hospital. This enabled the forging of a link between the City Hospital in Edinburgh, where the world-renowned child Aids specialist, Dr Jacqueline Mok, has her paediatric Aids clinic. The Appeal has now been taken over by the Romanian Angel Appeal, run chiefly by Olivia Harrison. This has guaranteed a continuation of the work, sending nursing teams to Constanta and the establishment of the first research project in Romania, to research the pathology of the disease there, headed by Dr Mok and Dr Matusa, and partly financed by the Angel Appeal and the

National Cancer Institute in the USA.

The key to the improvements in the hospital has been the change of attitude among Matusa's staff. Now the best-paid of the country's nurses, they have learned that Aids cannot be caught from a toilet seat (a lesson not learned yet among people who should know better in countries more advanced than Romania). The children are now bounced on the knees of staff who wouldn't touch them before. Neat romper suits are now the children's order of the day. Nappies have replaced the swaddling clothes, drugs are no longer in such short supply.

Two of the main reasons for this change are Dr Jacqueline Mok, the Malaysian-born child Aids expert and her assistant Sister Chris Rafferty. Through several visits, bearing drugs and up-to-the-minute techniques, giving moral support and confidence-building example, the two Edinburgh women have achieved near sainthood in the town. Dr Matusa speaks French, but little English; Dr Mok little French. Yet within minutes, the lingua franca of medicine is in play: Words like encephalopathy, lymphoid interstitial pneumonitis and cytomegalovirus pepper their exchanges, uninterrupted by the translator.

On the ward, Sister Rafferty bowls them over with her cheery confidence and skill as she dispenses soft toys and expertise in equal measure. Dr Matusa and her dedicated lieutenants Doctors Sorin and Claudia Rugina regard the women's arrival in this once hellish place as being 'a miracle'.

Yet still the haunting grey skeletons of that place confront you. The toys and the romper suits and the love allow the children to die in more dignity, but die still they must.

Out in the corridor, the doleful Dr Borcea, her son Sabin still hanging on in 'Sector II', asks Dr Mok, 'What would you do, Doctor, if he were your son?'

Dr Mok pauses for a long time before replying. 'I don't

know ... I would not know what to do. In fact, there is almost nothing you can do,' she says softly.

And you are reminded again: how hot are the fires of hell?

---------- CHAPTER 6 ----------

The Romanian Jews

One of the most brazen peculiarities of the Romanian communists was their attitude to the Jews, to the later creation of the state of Israel, and the development of the Israeli-Palestinian conflict which followed. Study of the twentieth-century history of the Jews in Romania provides a yardstick to measure against the events of the greater history.

As the three stars began to twinkle in the sky, marking the end of the Jewish Sabbath, high in the mountain resort of Poiana Brasov Romania's Chief Rabbi Dr Moses Rosen was in an agitated mood. Not merely because from around 8.40 p.m. his hotel room telephone had been ringing out – he would not profane the Sabbath by lifting the receiver – but more because he had just learned of another English language broadside heading in his direction from the pages of the *Spectator* magazine and the pen of the redoubtable Jessica Douglas-Home, widow of the former editor of *The Times*, Charles Douglas-Home, nephew of the former British Prime Minister, Sir Alec Douglas-Home.

The attack is part of a long season of abuse mounted by prominent figures on the British and American right, with Douglas-Home and other figures around the *Salisbury Review* intellectual Roger Scruton (with whom Ms Home was romantically linked), to the fore. The attack seems familiar to the Rabbi, though he has yet to read it.

'It is a blood libel,' he says as he sets out on his soliloquy. Blood and libel, it seems, have stained the history of the Romanians, their communists, and the Jews these fifty years past. When you listen to the Rabbi talking about his life facing the persecution of anti-semitism you can hear the echo of history.

Moses Rosen was born in Moinesti, in Moldavia, in 1912. His father, who was the local Rabbi, had been born in Galicia and his Rabbinical 'family tree' has deep roots. His father's grandfather was Rabbi Leibish Auerbach in Stanislawow, Galicia, and his ancestors include Rabbi Moshe Isserles of Cracow, the Noda Biyehuda of Prague, the Great Rabbi Loew in Prague and Rabbi Naftule Frankfurter whose son was the first Hacham-Basha of Moldavia in the eighteenth century. Moinesti was a typical Jewish Shtetl of the Eastern European type. Narrow cobbled streets, with dirt tracks running off them, small houses with flat roofs of the kind on which a fiddler played in the Hollywood film many years later. The little houses backed on to each other, even where there was no shortage of land, as if even the architecture of the Jews crouched in fear of the episodic bloody bouts of pogrom. Most of the Jews, then, lived in crushing poverty, with tradesmen trying to sell shabby clothing and trinkets to the equally poor peasants arriving in town with their animals and produce. Many went hungry.

Yet, as the Rabbi explained it, 'what made life bearable was the comradeship which the Shtetl created, the help they gave each other, and their love of traditional Judaism. Many of the simple artisans would spend hours at Torah, [the five books of Moses] after their often backbreaking work, and in the early morning, and the late evening they would sit there in the synagogues and continue to learn.'

Moses Rosen took his first stand against anti-semitism in 1926. Then, as the Austrian house painter Adolf Hitler barnstormed the great beer halls of Bavaria with his Nazi message, anti-semitic outrages conducted by Romanian fascists were becoming commonplace. In the town Cernauti, the Jewish student David Falik was shot dead by a fellow student Nicolae Totu. After a farcical trial, Totu was set free, sparking huge demonstrations of fascists and anti-semites who hailed Totu as a national hero. Moses Rosen, then fourteen, openly protested against the verdict and was promptly arrested for 'insulting King Ferdinand and Queen Maria of Romania by casting doubts on Romanian justice which is under their guardianship'. Next day, he was expelled not just from his own school, but from all state schools throughout the country. Sharing a cell with a man accused of cutting up another man after a drunken brawl, Rosen refused to be intimidated or to confess to guilt of any crime. He even went on hunger strike in protest at the absence of Kosher food. 'From that time I bore, in the minds of the Romanian right and the anti-semites, the stigma of being a Bolshevik'. It was a stigma which would resurface time and time again.

As the 1920s became the 1930s the Romanian Iron Guard grew to be a strong – and for a time – dominant force in Romanian life. Under the playboy King Carol, and then under the boy King Michael, his son, Marshal Ion Antonescu, the pro-Nazi military dictator, played the anti-semitic card well. Europe's depression and the rampage of Hitler's Brown Shirt National Socialists were the hammer and the anvil between which the Romanian Jews would face annihilation and genocide. Romania's prewar 800,000 Jews were affected by striking differences in appearance, culture and outlook. But whatever divided the

Jews of Romania, the fear of the pogrom was strong enough to bring them together.

By then another group was attracting the malignant gaze of the Romanian right – the numerically insignificant Romanian Communist Party. Marxist–Leninism has always existed in uneasy ambiguity with the Jews. Marx was himself a German Jew, and many of his early followers were European Jews from the teeming ghettos of London and Manchester, through Paris and Berlin to Moscow and Warsaw. These Jews, many of whom had been active in the creation of nascent trades unions, were drawn by the high intellectualism and humanism of Marx, and joined the Communist Parties and their allied fronts all over Europe. For the right, the 'Judeao-Communist' was born, and the 'Jewish communist conspiracy' was hatched.

For the communists, enemies of the Christian fundamentalism which underpinned much of European antisemitism, defenders of the poor and the workers, and drawn to the progressive culture of much of Jewish life at the time, the Jewish population of Europe were obvious allies. And as the continent drifted towards war and as the hordes of Nazism grew powerful enough to threaten not just Jews and communists but the Soviet Union itself, the alliance took on a note of urgent expediency.

On 10th May 1940 Moses Rosen, by then a candidate Rabbi, delivered his first sermon, and the army of the Third Reich entered Belgium and Holland. One month later they had occupied France. At the end of that month the Soviet army, as the result of the secret treaty between Hitler and Stalin, occupied the Romanian provinces of Bessarabia and northern Bucovina. The Romanian Government, in thrall to the Nazis, was powerless to resist. Popular anger among Romanian nationalists was intense, and the anti-semites knew just who to blame – the 'Judeao–Communists' in their midst. Pogroms broke out in various parts of the country, with mobs accusing the

Jews of having welcomed the arrival of the Red Army in the two provinces.

In Dorohoi in Moldavia, a Jewish army officer was killed by an anti-semite. There was a huge turnout for his funeral at the Jewish cemetery, where units of the Romanian army had turned out, ostensibly to honour the dead man. During the religious service, without warning, the soldiers opened fire on the Jewish mourners. Afterwards, eighty men and women lay dead on the ground. The Dorohoi massacre was accompanied by many others in towns and villages throughout the country. In the first flush of national humiliation over the loss of the two provinces, Jew equalled communist equalled Soviet equalled death and burning.

For Moses Rosen the equation was disastrous. On the night of 3rd July 1940 an army officer entered his parents' house and bellowed 'Hands up! You are the chief of the communists in the city!' He placed the cold steel of his revolver barrel at the Rabbi's temple. 'Give me the list of the communists in the town or I will kill you like a duck,' he said.

Rosen was dragged to the local police station where he was tortured for the non-existent list, then he was taken into the courtyard of his old school and placed against the wall. 'It was dark and cold,' he said, shivering as he relived the moment, 'and the officer told me "Say your last prayers because we are going to shoot you". Expecting that my moment had come I prayed silently and repeated the magnificent declaration that Jewish martyrs proclaim when they are facing death, "Shema Israel". But no shot came.' Rosen was dragged inside and tortured once more. One soldier took off his shoe and, in a frenzy, began beating the Rabbi. 'They tore at my hair and stamped on me; they tried to force me to cross myself and to polish their shoes, but I refused. I don't know how many people beat me ... ten? ... twenty? In a few minutes I was covered in blood and in great pain.' Two days later he was sent to a concentration camp for political offenders.

Miercurea Ciuc – the first concentration camp in Romania – had been opened a year earlier, ironically to house Iron Guardists who had fallen out with the dictator Marshal Antonescu, and who had murdered the Prime Minister Armand Calinescu. A large number of the Guard were, in turn, murdered by the authorities while held in the camp, and were laid to rest in a large grave in the centre of the camp compound. On the long list of fallen Iron Guardists, under two orthodox crosses, was the name of one Nicolae Totu, the young anti-semite who had killed the student, David Falik, back in 1926, the aftermath of which had seen Rabbi Rosen branded a Bolshevik for the first time.

'The words of the sage Hillel, from the Pirkei Avot, came to my mind. He once saw a skull floating on the water and he said: "Because you had drowned a man, you were drowned, and the end of him who drowned you will also be drowning",' said the Rabbi with a smile. But the quarrel with the Iron Guard had passed, and the camp was now full of their bitter enemies, the communists. And some Jews.

The next month the dismemberment of Romania continued, by the 'Vienna Diktat'; Romania bowed to Hitler's demand to hand over the northern half of Transylvania to the other fascist ally, Hungary. The month after that, in order to save his head as the flush of national humiliation became the burning shame of national betrayal, King Carol bowed to public demands and abdicated in favour of his young son Michael, who was then not even nineteen years old. But the real power in any case was Antonescu, who thereafter adopted the title which would return to haunt the Romanians: 'Conducator' (Leader).

Although an admirer of Hitler, Antonescu at first tried to stop the anti-semitic outrages being committed by the Iron Guard; however, later, he transported over 100,000 Jews from Bucovina to the camps of Transnistria in the

Ukraine. Nearly 80,000 of them perished there.

The ancient city of Iasi is where the world's first Yiddish Theatre and newspaper were founded. It has had a Jewish community for more than five hundred years. A tombstone in the Jewish cemetery there bears the date 1467. In late June and early July of 1941 it was where the very worst of the authentically Romanian pogroms took place.

In June 1941, when the Nazi army swept over the borders of the Soviet Union, Romanian troops under Antonescu's command were at their side. One week later the Iasi pogrom, one of the worst of the whole period, occurred, and again Antonescu was in charge. When the Soviet Air Force bombed German/Romanian positions at Iasi, which is close to the Soviet border, the 'Jewish-Communist' conspiracy was dragged out again. The Romanian troops alleged that the local Jews had signalled to the Soviet pilots. On Sunday 29th June 1941, the unsuspecting Jews of Iasi were ordered to go to the police station in the centre of the town, supposedly to have their identity cards changed. In order to enter the police station they had to pass through two lines of soldiers and policemen. When more than 6,000 of the Jews had gathered, men and women, many with small children in their arms, they were suddenly set upon in a way which was unique even for the holocaust. The soldiers and police began to beat the people to death with their rifle butts and clubs and rods of iron. The square courtyard began to fill with the bodies; their skulls smashed open, and the street became a river of blood. Every single one of the Jews who had gathered there to change their identity cards, in the morning in a European town, with the Christian population looking on, was beaten to death. The other Jews in the city who, for one reason or another, perhaps a prescient dread, had not turned up in the square, were then rounded up. They were packed into horse-wagons attached to trains. In wagons built for three horses, 150 people were crammed in the hot

July sunshine. The guards covered up the ventilation holes. The trains were driven to short distances outside of Iasi, and left there over the next few days.

In their agony the Jews clawed at their own flesh. By stabbings and shootings almost 12,000 Jews from Iasi were annihilated in just four days. Altogether nearly 300,000 Romanian Jews died under Antonescu's period as 'Conducator'. Later, when the tide of war began to change at Stalingrad where the German and Romanian armies were humiliated – and Romania began to change sides accordingly – Antonescu did offer asylum to a number of Jews escaping from the death camps of Hungarian-occupied Transylvania, but the stain of his enormous war crimes would follow him to his summary execution at the hands of the local communists in 1944.

After the war, communism came to Romania in the echo of the boots of the Red Army. What happens next in the story of the Romanian Jews cannot be separated from the importance of the Jews in the ranks of the RCP, and especially it cannot be separated from Romania's remarkable Chief Rabbi who walked every step of the way, suffered every blow, was blackguarded as a collaborator, yet even now is keen that history should tell the truth.

In the second half of 1948, the year in which the Soviet Union became the first country to vote in the United Nations for the establishment of the state of Israel, the year when the Soviet ally Czechoslovakia sent to the Jewish state arms which were crucial in routing the Arab armies fighting on the side of the Palestinians, two important events for Romania's Jews occurred.

First, the then Chief Rabbi disappeared. 'Notwithstanding his responsibilities as Chief Rabbi to 450,000 Jews, the largest community outside the Soviet Union, and without discussing it with anyone in Bucharest, Chief Rabbi Safran left his post and set up in Geneva, later becoming Chief Rabbi to the tiny Jewish community in

Switzerland,' says Rosen. Mr Safran and Geneva, his place of haven, are later to prove significant to this tale. Second, and, in the short term, more important, since the end of the war, unlike elsewhere in the Eastern bloc, Jews had been leaving Romania for Israel. One ship every week sailed from the Black Sea port of Constanta with a thousand Jews bound for Haifa.

In September 1948, the atmosphere was shattered by the publication of the notorious Ehrenburg letter in *Pravda* that was a full blown attack on 'Zionism' and which had the effect of re-opening hostilities against the Jews throughout the Eastern bloc. Henceforth, 'Zionists', that is those Jews who wanted to support the state of Israel which had just been ushered in with Soviet support, were to be regarded as spies and traitors. A wave of *Kristall-nachts* swept communist Europe, with Jewish property smashed and burned and Jews attacked. Yet from Romania, uniquely, throughout the dark nights, the Haifa boats kept on sailing.

Rosen played cleverly, even perhaps unscrupulously on the communist authorities, with their Jewish leaders prominently targeted. Appealing to their better instincts; calling upon the ghosts of their forefathers; withholding or granting international approbation for the religious 'toler-ance' of the RCP by contrast with their communist neigh-bours. The authorities in turn were stricken with a painful ambivalence. They wanted to show the Soviet Union their first signs of Romanian 'independence' of spirit, and anti-semitism in the country was such that the sight of the retreating black-coated backs of the Jews heading for Israel was potentially popular.

The Jewish communists in the ranks were demanding that the shutters come down, yet the Jews in the leadership were strangely open to Rosen's political manoeuvrings. And so, simultaneously, as Romania's jails were filling with 'Zionist agitators', as the Party press was filled with virulent denunciations of Israel, full boatloads of Jewish emigrants choked the harbour at Constanta and the will-o'-the-wisp Rabbi Rosen flitted the corridors of power keeping all the options open.

Over the four years 1948 to 1952, when the Jewish communist, 'the Empress of Romania', Ana Pauker was the power behind the throne of the new government and the young Chief Rabbi was spreading his wings, more than 100,000 Romanian Jews left for Israel, and this at a time when virtually no Jews were being allowed out of the communist bloc. Ana Pauker was overthrown in the next upheaval for Eastern European Jewry – the aftermath of the notorious Slansky trial in Czechoslovakia.

Then in early 1953 anti-semitic hysteria increased with the 'relevation' of the 'Doctors' Plot' in Moscow. In this plot, several leading doctors, all Jewish, were supposed to have collectively planned to poison the whole Soviet leadership. All of Eastern Europe's Jewry, gripped with panic, battened down the hatches fearing widespread pogroms and even a new round of extermination. Amazingly, in this case the Soviet authorities, just six weeks after Stalin's death, backtracked, declaring that their previous announcement was null and void and that the 'Doctors' Plot' was a fabrication.

The Romanian authorities, not wanting to believe it, refused to broadcast the news, demonstrating not for the first or last time that their 'independence' from Moscow was not always a good thing. Rosen meanwhile was keeping the candle burning despite intense repression, harassment and regular arrest. Through all of these troubled waters for Eastern European Jewry, some boats kept sailing from Constanta to Haifa, and despite great repression Jewish life continued, more freely than anywhere else in the bloc.

In 1957, when elsewhere in the Eastern bloc repression following the 1956 uprising in Hungary was redoubled and where, in the wake of the Suez crisis of the same year, the Party line against Zionism was more virulent than

ever, in Romania the gates of mass-emigration were
opened again. Rabbi Rosen's fancy footwork, his assid-
uous playing of the power of international Jewry, his logic
and his flattery, had succeeded once again in bucking the
trend and unlocking the gates.

Romanian Jews heard on Yom Kippur that they were
free to register to leave for Israel. Within days, literally
thousands of Jews lined up on the pavements of all the
cities and towns in Romania, seeking permission to leave.
'The queues stretched for miles ... it was an awesome
sight ... foreign newspapers reported it as a phenomenon
reminiscent of Messianic times,' says Rabbi Rosen.

The vast majority of Romania's remaining 300,000
Jews began to take places in the queue, but Rosen became
suspicious. Why were the authorities encouraging the Jews
to queue up so ostentatiously to leave in full view of
their no doubt envious Gentile compatriots? Why wasn't
the Government allowing those 60,000 Jews who had
long ago applied to leave, to go first?

Characteristically Rabbi Rosen took his questions to
the top. He sought an interview with the Romanian President of the Council of Ministers, Ion Maurer. 'Mr President, I hope you don't mind me telling you an old Jewish
joke,' said the bold Rabbi. 'After synagogue one Friday
evening, a Rabbi announced in a loud voice, "All those
who like fish should come to my house this evening".
Many people turned up expectantly at the Rabbi's house.
He was sitting at his table and eating fish, obviously
enjoying his meal. He asked the visitors to sit down. They
did so, obviously expecting fish to be served, but no fish
was forthcoming. The Rabbi continued to eat oblivious of
the looks of astonishment around the table. Eventually
one of them remonstrated with him about his rudeness.
He looked at the man steadily and said, "Did I say I was
going to give fish to anyone? Certainly not. What I said
was that I wanted to know who liked fish. Now I know ...
and I thank you!".'

After telling the joke, Rabbi Rosen asked President Maurer, 'Is it by chance possible that you are forming these queues in order to find out how many of our people want to go to Israel rather like the Rabbi wanting to find how many people liked fish? And that those queuing for visas will end up as disappointed as those who were queuing for the fish?' The President smiled, but he didn't reply.

However, thousands were given permission to go and began to leave for Israel. In 1958–1959, long before the coming to power of Nicolae Ceausescu, 130,000 applied to leave and over a quarter of a million left Romania over the next fifteen years. The Romanian communists discovered that a great number of people liked fish.

Rabbi Rosen's style of work was guaranteed to raise hackles around the world in those cold war days. For some Zionists, the shrill 'Let my people go' type of approach was the only way to deal with communist governments who refused Jewish emigration. By mounting virulent anti-Soviet propaganda; by campaigning against western 'normalisation' efforts towards the East; by organising noisy demonstrations to embarrass Soviet bloc diplomats and trade delegations; by the use of economic sabotage and even terrorism they believed they could eventually prise open the gates in Eastern Europe.

But for these, the critics of the Rosen approach, there was a fundamental problem; namely that their methods weren't working, while his were. During all the long years of anti-Soviet agitation by the 'Let my people go' brigade, hardly a single Jew left the Soviet Union, and those who did went straight to America. In Romania, on the other hand, under Rosen's leadership a steady flow of emigrants were permitted to leave for the Jewish state. Rabbi Rosen gave us some details. 'And, furthermore, our Jews went to Israel as observant religious Jews; able to speak Hebrew, having studied their faith and its teachings out in the open in the only "free" Jewish institutions in Eastern Europe.

Our Jews left for Lod and not for Vienna, and they ended up living in Israel not in Philadelphia,' says Rabbi Rosen.

However, the hawks could not bear his anti-cold war approach, nor his frequent criticisms of Israeli Government policies across a whole range of issues. There were few more ferocious hawks or more ferocious critics of the Rabbi than Golda Meir.

'The Romanian Government should award you a special decoration for the services you have rendered them and for the speeches you have been making on their behalf,' a red-faced and angry Golda Meir told Rosen in New York in 1961. 'I don't believe a word you say,' she said to him.

Rosen was to have his revenge upon her scepticism when in 1967 Romania, by then much influenced by him, would be the only communist country not to break off relations with Israel after it attacked and occupied its Arab neighbours in the Six-Day War. 'You – not we – were right ... and your way and not ours was right,' said the Israeli President Salman Shazar, to Rosen, in his office just after the Israeli victory.

The non-Jewish cold warriors hated Rosen too. As part of their unremitting crusade against communism, it was vital to show that all communist countries were the same, and that no kind of freedom, least of all freedom to worship or to emigrate, could exist behind the Iron Curtain. Rosen insisted that, notwithstanding a fierce ideological struggle which in the earlier years certainly qualified as repression, the Jews were worshipping happily in Romania, bringing up their children as Jews, and leaving for Israel in large numbers.

However this was certainly not the song the anti-communists wanted to hear, and there were few cold warriors as coldly determined as the Eastern European émigrés in their bitter exile. It was in these communities that Rosen made his most dangerous enemies, enemies who continue to dog his steps to this day. Rosen was an anti-communist, but equally, having seen what he had seen, he was an anti-fascist too.

Many of the war-time Romanian fascists had fled to the United States, and many indeed were encouraged by the US Government to make their new lives there. By the end of the war, the Americans were a good deal more worried about 'the reds' than about Europe's former black- and brown-shirted fascists.

During Rosen's visit to New York in 1961, on which occasion he had the angry clash with Golda Meir, he embarked upon a campaign which, while successful, incurred for him the enduring enmity of the Romanian émigrés and their right-wing allies in the USA and throughout the west. He describes the situation:

One of the leaders of the war-time anti-semitic pogroms perpetrated by the Romanian fascists was a young Romanian Orthodox priest called Valentin Trifa. By telling a series of lies Trifa had managed to get into America after the war and when I arrived in New York in 1961 I found he was now a Bishop serving the 100,000 Romanian Orthodox émigrés, mainly in Detroit, Michigan and Cleveland.

I had been in Bucharest during the pogrom there in January 1941 when the Iron Guard had killed every Jew they could find. They looted Jewish homes, burned Jewish shops and synagogues. Rabbis were taken to the nearby Jilava woods and shot, others were taken to the municipal slaughterhouse where they had their throats cut and their bodies hoisted on hooks, with placards hung around their necks saying 'Kosher Meat'.

The leader of this outrage was Father Valentin Trifa. I saw with my own eyes the manifesto signed by him calling for the killing of every Jew. I heard, with my own ears, Trifa's voice on the radio saying, 'We'll kill every Jew. The Jew will not escape us even if he hides himself like a snake in a hole'. Trifa was one of the leaders of the Iron Guard and one of the most venomous. He went to Nazi Germany in 1944 and at the war's end told the Americans he was a 'displaced person'. He denied he had ever been a fascist. I discovered however that like other major war criminals Trifa had powerful allies. I learned to my sorrow that he had obtained the protection of the CIA, who had recruited him and many others into the fight against communism.

When I arrived in America and confronted him with my own and other eye-witness evidence that he was a war criminal, he was deeply shocked. With the aid of the late Robert Kennedy [then US Attorney General] and Philip Klutznick [then US Ambassador to the UN] I was able to bring the matter before the highest circles in the USA. I persuaded Congressman Halpern to denounce Trifa's crimes and lies in Congress. I called press conferences and appealed directly to American public opinion. Trifa's lawyer asked me, at the US Justice Department, 'Did you see Bishop Trifa kill Jews?' 'No,' I replied, 'but I did not see Hitler kill Jews either.'

Eventually, despite his protectors, and after many years, Trifa lost his case. He was stripped of his American citizenship and deported to the then fascist Portugal, one of the few countries willing to accept him. He died there a few years later. It didn't make me popular in certain circles, and in those circles you can say I'm still not so popular.

The issue around which all Rosen's enemies were able to unite and which remains controversial today was his campaign to make the US Government grant Romania 'Most Favoured Nation' treaty status, by which Romania's goods could enter the USA at preferential rates. This was granted in 1975. The American administration is now widely criticised for extending such a favour to the Romanian dictatorship, though it is worth remembering that this concession was granted before the British Labour Government (on the recommendation of Dr David Owen, then Foreign Secretary) lodged Nicolae and Elena Ceausescu in Buckingham Palace and persuaded the Queen to award the dictator the Order of the Bath. It is worth remembering also, that by then 'Most Favoured Nation' status had been granted by the US to both Poland and Hungary.

None the less, the remarkable public campaign by Rabbi Rosen, by frequently travelling to Washington on Romanian Government expenses to lobby Congress, clashing violently with those seeking to block the treaty, ready at a moment's notice to go anywhere to testify to the religious tolerance of the Ceausescu regime, was bound to be a red rag to the right-wing bulls. Ceausescu was a monster, they said, and he was selling Romanian Jews to Israel in exchange for American taxpayers' dollars, aided and abetted by Rabbi Rosen, the 'Red Rabbi'. Even now, Rosen is unrepentant about his role.

It is a lie to say that I was close to Ceausescu. He received me perhaps seven or eight times only during his reign. In the last years of his life he consistently refused to see me though I sought audiences with him. By the time Ceausescu came to power I had been Chief Rabbi of Romania for seventeen years. Hundreds of thousands of Jews had left Romania for Israel before I began lobbying for 'Most Favoured Nation' status ... not for him but for Romania, the country of my birth and in which my compatriots and my Jewish brethren desperately needed the economic boost which MFN could bring. It was true, what I was saying about the relative religious freedoms enjoyed by the Jews in Romania. But it is not true that these privileges were bestowed by Ceausescu. Almost all of our gains were made during the period of Stalin's regime, and the subsequent era, long before Ceausescu came to power. It is true that increasingly, Ceausescu was becoming a monster, but he was not a monster when I lobbied for MFN. Of course he was a dictator, but he was better than the other communist dictators then.

Remember that I am a Jew, and my first responsibility as a Jewish leader was to the Jews. In addition to our freedom to be Jews under Ceausescu, and our freedom to emigrate to Israel – 97 per cent of all Romanian Jews were allowed to leave for Israel under communism – remember that Ceausescu was the only communist leader to maintain relations with Israel; the only one to vote in the UN against the resolution equating Zionism with racism; and the only one to oppose the Soviet invasion of Czechoslovakia. This was a different Ceausescu from the one we saw in his last years. And there is one last point I want to make to you; I was frequently asked during the communist period … is there anti-semitism in Romania? My answer always was, 'there are anti-semites, but not anti-semitism'. The difference between the situation under the communists and that which existed under the previous, so-called democratic Governments or the royal dictatorship period was that the communists suppressed displays of anti-semitism and punished them without eradicating the hatred which gave rise to them. In the earlier periods – the so-called democratic, Christian, monarchist times … so beloved of your readers of the *Spectator* of Miss Douglas-Home; and of those émigrés who hate me: these courtiers of the Pretender, King Michael in Geneva, or the devotees of the late Bishop Trifa in Detroit and in Cleveland – the situation in those times was very different. During those times, the rulers of Romania actively encouraged and organised anti-semitism. It was a so-called democratic Government in Romania that organised the pogroms against the Jews and killed us in large numbers.'

What is his answer to the latest broadside from the *Spectator*?

'I have told you my life,' he thundered, 'and I have told you the lives of our people. It has been a strange and wonderful life, full of dangers, tests and miracles. Tell King Michael, the *Spectator* and all the others: this story is my answer.'

Postscript: The Arabs

The other side of the coin to the communists' relations with the Jews and Israel was their equally bizarre connections with the Palestinians. As we have seen, the Romanian Communist Party under Ceausescu was the only Party in the communist bloc not to sever relations with Israel when it attacked and smashed the Arab armies in the Six-Day War. On the contrary, Ceausescu kept not only his Embassy open, but all other doors to the Jewish state.

New citizens for the expanded state of Israel continued to flow from Romania's remaining ghettos. The Israeli hawks Golda Meir and Menahem Begin both made state visits to Bucharest. Romania broke ranks with the bloc and much of the non-aligned movement in voting against the UN resolution equating Zionism with racism.

But none of that stopped Ceausescu from seeking and succeeding to establish a close working relationship with the Arabs, particularly later with the Egyptian President, Anwar Sadat, but also with the PLO. This notwithstanding the obvious fact that it was the Palestinians who were paying the price – in the further colonisation of their country by Jews who had been hounded from Europe either by 'Christian' anti-semitism, or in this case by Ceausescu's opportunism and his eye for the main chance.

'I personally was not involved in articulating the Palestinian response to Ceausescu's decision to break ranks with his allies in the aftermath of the 1967 war and the seizure by Israel of what remained of our country,' says the PLO leader, Yasser Arafat. (Arafat's 'Fatah' group did not assume control of the PLO until 1969.) 'Nevertheless, of course we were clear as to why he was doing what he did – it was about his distancing himself from the Soviet Union first and foremost. Of course, over the years we raised the issue with him many times, but at the end of the day, we took what I believe to be the principled stance of non-interference in Romania's internal affairs. They had the right to their own foreign policy.'

Most hurtful to the Palestinians was the huge reserve of new Israelis provided by Ceausescu's emigration policy. Here Arafat is unforgiving, both of Ceausescu and of the Zionist movement which, in his view, helped to stampede Romania's Jews into 'Aliyah'. He put the question:

Was it a real emigration or a forced stampede similar to other, now well charted, episodes? It is obvious that a great many people wanted to leave Romania – not just Jews – but the non-Jews weren't allowed to go; the Jews were permitted to go only to the occupied Palestinian lands, and nowhere else. Most of them, it is clear, wanted to go west, particularly to the United States, which refused to have them. Thus we paid the price of western anti-semitism twice – the fascism of the 1930s and 1940s and then the postwar denial of the rights of European Jews to travel and settle in the countries they really wanted to go to.

Believe me, we tried hard to convince Romania to change its position on this dangerous and sensitive problem – as we are trying today to convince the Soviet Union, now that they are allowing this problem to multiply. You must know that the vast majority of these emigrants – and incidentally many of them are simply pretending to be Jews – do not want to come to Palestine but merely want out of the Soviet Union, preferably to the United States, which is refusing them.

None the less, Ceausescu was careful to keep all lines of influence open to the Palestinians. 'During many years, the Romanians helped our needs, particularly in the medical field, and in the provision of academic scholarships, places for our long-suffering students scattered around the world away from their homeland, desperate to educate themselves in a largely indifferent world,' says Arafat.

Neither should Ceausescu's delusions of grandeur as a world-class statesman be underestimated in this strange love–hate affair. As a country, Romania was well placed to act as a bridge between the Arabs and the Jews, and this he tried to do.

Although the world well remembers the Camp David agreements between Sadat and the Israeli leader Menahem Begin, the ill-fated and ultimately counter-productive attempt to end the Arab–Israel dispute, few are aware that the talks came within an ace of being held not at Jimmy Carter's ranch, but in one of Nicolae Ceausescu's communist palaces!

The one chosen, ironically, was the former royal palace in the mountain town of Sinaia, and for more than a year Ceausescu secretly negotiated with Cairo and Jerusalem to bring the former foes face to face for the first time, in what would have been his greatest ever *coup de théâtre*, eclipsing even his sensational stand over Czechoslovakia.

Agreement in principle had been reached, and Ceausescu had even briefed an astonished Leonid Brezhnev, when the Americans informed the Romanians that Sadat had opted for Camp David, figuring that the doughty Menahem Begin would be under more pressure to compromise on the soil of his bankroller, the US taxpayer. Seeing his chance of the Nobel Peace Prize slipping from his grasp, Ceausescu was reportedly incandescent with rage, and according to his former Intelligence Chief, Ion Pacepa, furiously declared that 'the snake Sadat should be bumped off'.

Of Ceausescu's attempts, then and later, Arafat will only say, enigmatically: 'Occasionally Ceausescu carried our messages to others, and carried theirs to us.'

To Ceausescu's credit, it must be said that he never allowed his closeness with successive Israeli Governments to stop him from telling them of the need to solve the Palestinian problem with justice. From the beginning he argued that there should be two states in Palestine, side by side, with each being internationally guaranteed.

Rabbi Moses Rosen remembers the first meeting of the Romanian Parliament after the 1967 war when, due to Ceausescu's brazen defiance of the Moscow line, newsmen from all over the world turned up. 'Ceausescu made a courageous speech. He was not seeking the applause of one or the other of the protagonists to the conflict. He spoke about the necessity of a Palestinian Arab state – back in 1967 – and he was the first European leader to make this call.'

There are many lurid accounts of what purports to be the darker side of Ceausescu's links with Arab groups and states. Ion Pacepa, the Romanian Intelligence Services Chief who defected to the United States in 1978 and published his memoirs, *Red Horizons*, under CIA direction, makes a remarkable number of blood-curdling allegations about the sexual, financial and physical appetites of all America's least favourite Arabs, in particular of Yasser Arafat. But few outside the feverish circles of the US intelligence community will believe that top PLO leaders were paid spies, or that the ascetic Arafat would choose, of all places, one of Ceausescu's bugged and video-taped guesthouses to have two-day sex orgies. Arafat says, 'I tell you frankly, there is nothing in that book that deserves comments or answers ... So far as it deals with us, I can tell you that there is not one sentence which is true.'

More serious is the anger, frequently expressed in Romania, that Arafat was the only figure of any importance who attended what turned out to be Ceausescu's final Party conference. All the other regular attenders at such conferences had decided to send only minor functionaries in protest at what had become the Romanian nightmare.

More serious still is the charge, broadcast frequently in the tumultuous days of the December revolution, that Palestinian fighters closed ranks with the diehards of the Securitate, in the counterblast to restore Ceausescu which killed hundreds. Arafat says:

It is simply a lie, that there were any Palestinians fighting on any side in the Romanian revolution. You will find that the first rumours of this came from outside Romania. At one point they said that there was an air and sea landing of hundreds of Palestinian commandos coming to fight for Ceausescu! It is just rubbish. The Romanian Government – which consists of the people who overthrew Ceausescu – have consistently denied this calumny. We had three thousand students in Romanian universities at the time of the revolution, and not a single one of them took up so much as a stone against the Romanian people's revolt.

As for my attendance at the final conference of the then ruling Party, it was traditional for us to attend all the conferences of the ruling parties in Eastern Europe – as it was traditional for them to attend our conferences and meetings. We had good relations with these countries. Yes, of course I felt ridiculous making more than sixty standing ovations during Ceausescu's speech, but what could I do when I was in the hall and everyone else was standing – remain seated?

In any case, let us talk honestly. For many years you in the west feted Ceausescu. The world's great leaders accepted from him medals and gave him high-ranking awards in return. They gave him loans and favours worth billions of dollars and opened up the doors of their capitals for him. As for us, we didn't have any money or recognition to give him. We are a small people, struggling only for our freedom. We are forced to accept help wherever we can find it.

CHAPTER 7

Boulevard

Within the designs of the extraordinary personality cult of Ceausescu there was of course room for foreign influence. While most of the cult was authentically Romanian, there were for example straight emulations of Stalin. But most who were close enough at the time to observe, say that an important watershed occurred with the state visit to Asia in 1971, when Ceausescu was at the height of his powers.

The dictator and his wife travelled to China, then in the immediate aftermath of the great Cultural Revolution, to North Vietnam – then still locked in battle with Ceausescu's friend Richard Nixon and his US armed forces – to Mongolia and, perhaps most importantly, to the People's Democratic Republic of Korea, ruled by the red emperor Kim Il Sung.

With them on the North Korean trip was the then recently appointed Secretary for Ideology, now democratically elected President of free Romania, Ion Iliescu. He told us:

I recognised some important changes in the Ceausescus

during that visit. In China we met Madame Mao, who might have been invented as a role model for Elena. Her eyes shone as she watched Mao's wife in action. In particular I remember Mrs Mao setting up a session of 'self-criticism' by the university professors of Peking. Elena was very impressed by that.

But it was North Korea that fascinated the Ceausescus the most. You could see they were envious of the way that Kim Il Sung was treated with the reverence of a god.

I had been to Korea the year before. On the way there, I met the son of the President of Sierra Leone, Siaka Stevens. We met again on the aeroplane home, and he asked me what I had thought of the country.

I told him I was impressed by the industry of the people, which was colossal, and by what they had achieved following the destruction of the Korean War. In the countryside there was not a single patch of land that was not worked. Nobody wasted time; everybody worked.

But then I told him I could not live in such a society. I said that in a week I had not been able to speak to anyone, as soon as I spoke to anyone they quoted me Kim Il Sung. It drove me crazy. I wondered how Kim Il Sung had achieved such horrors.

I told Ceausescu this story, making the point that the African, from his poor under-developed country, had been well able to see the backwardness of the situation in Korea.

Ceausescu's reaction to this story amazed me. 'That stupid African!' he said. 'He was incapable of recognising the greatness of these people.'

On their return to Romania, Elena really moved into politics in a big way in her own right, and both began to elevate Ceausescu from the ranks of the great to a fully-fledged god-king.

Then they began to lay the foundation-stones of what they thought would be the ultimate legacy of their rule, a new socialist-realist capital city built on the rubble of what was old and beautiful from the past. This road led to the 'Boulevard for the Celebration of the Victory of Socialism', and the grandest palace of them all. Forty thousand buildings were demolished in the centre of Bucharest to make way for the Boulevard, many of them the very buildings which had earned prewar Bucharest the epithet 'The Paris of the East'.

International opinion was outraged. Ceausescu abusing his people was his own affair, but when it came to old buildings ...

The Israeli and United States Governments were mobilised to threaten dire economic consequences if Ceausescu carried out his threat to flatten the last remaining redoubts of Bucharest Jewry.

His Royal Highness Prince Charles, the heir to the British throne and an energetic conservationist, made a most undiplomatic attack on Ceausescu's bulldozing, for which he was chastised by the British Foreign Office, who were keen to avoid overt criticism of the man they had decorated with the Royal Order of the Bath.

'After the blitz against the centre of his own capital was over, we named Bucharest "Ceau-shima" after Hiroshima,' says Dinu Giurescu, the latest in a family line of distinguished Romanian historians, now again Professor of History at the University of Bucharest. Giurescu can list the historic buildings that were smashed, giving the dates of foundation and demolition as he does so.

'At least a dozen historic churches were pulled down. There was the Pantelimon monastery built in 1735, there was the church of Nicolae Sirbi erected in 1692, and many others, reduced to dust for this mad scheme to turn one of Europe's grand old capitals into downtown Pyongyang,' says the history professor bitterly.

The idea for such a celebration of socialism may have originated in the benighted North Korean wonderland, but Paris, as in much else, unwittingly dictated many of the co-ordinates. The Boulevard is, for example, five feet wider than the Champs Elysées and five yards longer, in a neat piece of one-upmanship for the francophile Bucharestis. Further, Hitler's unbuilt 'Grand Avenue', which he planned for Berlin to be the centrepiece of his thousand-year Reich, is surely another architectural inspiration.

Lining both sides of the Boulevard are mile upon mile of contiguous golden-brown eight-storey apartment blocks in which Ceausescu had intended to install the elite of the Party and state, the better to guarantee his ticker-tape progress down the Boulevard's three miles to the House of the People, which was to house his government.

The House of the People, which stands at the western end of the Boulevard, completes what is an architectural wonder of the world. It stands on the site of what was Bucharest's highest hill, which was levelled in June 1984 to create the 380,000-square-metre site that it would occupy. With its thousand rooms, many bigger than football pitches, many of whose ceilings are thirty feet high, it is now the largest white elephant in the world.

Only the Pentagon in Washington is larger than this Colossus. Romania's treasury was looted to provide the 65,000 tons of structural steel, 42,000 tons of rolled steel and 480,000 cubic metres of cast concrete needed to erect the structure. The interior of the building was never completed, partly because of the constant redesigning of everything from internal staircases to chandeliers that was personally ordered by the dictator.

Every Friday, 'The Chief' would wander through the belly of the monster, second-guessing the architect Anca Petrescu (allegedly yet another of Elena's relatives) and the scores of the country's best craftsmen. The central interior staircase alone underwent nineteen complete redesigns on the whim of 'The Chief'. No wonder Petrescu could reply, when asked what the dominant architectural influence would be, 'We can actually create a Ceausescu style.'

But the real show-stopper for the House of the People was the people's overthrow of its creator in the December revolution. But, by then, miles of beautiful marble had been laid in the interior and gallons of liquid gilt had been consumed to decorate its fine cornices with gold leaf. This was at a time when Romanians just a street away shivered with cold and went hungry and when, a block away, doctors performed operations without surgical gloves or sterilised instruments.

Dinu Giurescu paid a high price for his campaign to stop the Boulevard, a campaign involving public meetings and petitions to save specific buildings. In 1985 he publicly accused the Patriarch of the Romanian Orthodox Church of 'collaborating in the destruction of the religious heritage of Bucharest'. When the holy man replied that these were the words 'of a foreign defector', Giurescu knew his time was coming. He was sacked from his post, and it was no surprise when an order was made that his family home, too, must be demolished as part of the 'systemisation'. Eventually, in despair, after he had been banned from speaking in public Giurescu did indeed leave for the United States.

Giurescu takes strong issue with those, like the authors, who say they can see the grandeur, and yes the beauty, of the Boulevard and the House. 'You misunderstand this scheme. This whole enterprise was the development of the programme of "systemisation" to its highest level. At the very heart of that is the humiliation of the individual by the scale of the collective ... symbolised in concrete by the mass destruction of single family homes and their replacement by huge apartment complexes. Of course there is more to it than that. It represented the attempt to destroy all of Romanian history that existed before Ceausescu, as though to declare that all that had gone before in Romania was worth nothing.'

Yet it is impossible to stand in what is now re-named Unity Boulevard and not be affected by the scale of its vistas and the sight of its Versailles-like palace at the end. It is, frankly, breathtaking.

Of course the obscenity occurred in the destruction which preceded it, and its opportunity cost in cold hungry children. None the less, many see the Boulevard, as Ceausescu might have put it, as 'a thing of beauty and a joy forever'.

This view is certainly shared by the families now moving in to the sandstone apartment blocks. Doru Ursu's is one of them. 'Perhaps in the fullness of time, future generations who have no personal experience of the tyranny of the Ceausescus will look on this Boulevard with wonder,' he says.

The flats are being allocated first to those whose houses were destroyed in the revolution. So, though Doru Ursu is the new Minister of the Interior in the elected Government, his immediate neighbours include a waitress, a doctor, an engineer and a building worker.

'We like life here. My children lived with rats and dampness in our last flat,' says Victoria Petreanu, the waitress, mother of three young children. They pay £10 per month rent for the five-roomed flat, about 10 per cent of her earnings in a downtown restaurant. 'But rents are graded according to income under the new government, and so the doctor living above pays double my rent for the same-sized flat.'

In a proudly guided tour, Mrs Petreanu takes care to point out the double radiators. 'To have central heating is a dream for me. To describe for you how it was in my last flat, I shall tell you one of the bitter jokes of the Bucharestis. The woman of the house rushes through to the living-room and scolds her husband, "Quick, shut that window, you'll give a passer-by out there his death of cold!"'

She has only one complaint: that the lifts have never been finished. 'I'm going to see Madame Ursu, the wife of the Minister of the Interior. She lives just two floors above me!' laughs the waitress.

And what of Ceausescu?

'Well, he did one thing for us: he left the legacy of these buildings ... But don't forget, we would never have been able to live here without the revolution,' she says.

Postscript

On Boxing Day 1989, the day after the Christmas execution of the perpetrators of the architectural genocide of Bucharest, Prince Charles and his wife Princess Diana were taking lunch at the cottage of the celebrated English socialist, wit and raconteur Stephen Fry.

Just before 1 p.m., Prince Charles enquired if he might be so rude as to ask if he could turn the television on to catch the BBC News. 'I want to see what's happening in Romania,' he explained.

As the pictures of the executed tyrants came on the screen, the Prince raised his glass and toasted their demise, while explaining the reason for his apparent, and uncharacteristic, callousness.

'That pair destroyed the heart of one of the most beautiful cities in the world,' he said.

PART II

The Revolution from Timisoara to Bucharest

CHAPTER 8

Timisoara

Claudiu Iordache worked as a technician in the Institute of Construction Design in Timisoara. He was actually a writer, but had paid the price for not becoming one of Ceausescu's apostles of the personality cult. His plays and manuscripts had been blocked from performance for seventeen years. On 15th December 1989 one of the leading literary critics of the Ceausescu regime telephoned to seek his permission for one of his stories to be published in the prestigious *Theatre Almanac*.

Iordache is an honest and proud man, given to obduracy. He had been humiliated too long. He told the influential critic, 'I am a playwright ... and the regime does not see fit to allow my plays to appear, so if my plays are not good enough for performing, then my stories cannot be published either. So you're not getting my permission.'

The critic replied, 'My dear Claudiu, you are letting your heart rule your head. If we print this one story in the *Almanac*, it could change a lot of things for you. Don't be so obstinate!'

'There's only one change I'm waiting for in Romania,'

Iordache replied to Ceausescu's lackey, before slamming the phone down.

Five days later, on Wednesday 20th December, Iordache stood at the head of a huge general strike demonstration of tens of thousands in the Opera House Square of the town. The Opera House was originally built as a smaller-scale replica of the Vienna Opera House from the days of the Austro-Hungarian Empire, although its facade was altered by the Ceausescu regime to blot out this memory. Along with the cathedral started in 1936 by King Michael, three hundred yards opposite, it dominates the square.

On 20th December, that three hundred yards was a seething mass of humanity. Every factory in Timisoara was on strike, their banners held high in manifestation. There were Romanian flags, too, with the communist hammer and sickle cut from the middle, a harbinger, after Byron's 'Yet Freedom, yet, thy banner torn but flying, streams like a thunderstorm against the wind.' Protest was accumulating the reserves for revolution.

Iordache had not been elected to lead the crowd, neither had his counterpart, Lorin Fortuna, but the trials of history were inexorably throwing them both forward into the vacuum of leadership. They were brave men, but clever too, and this combination, in both, would make them the voices for the many.

They tell the story of the time in the same measure. At this point they were seized by the recognition of the necessity of getting to the balcony of the Opera House to stand between its four white marble portals to address the crowd. They wanted to affirm the protest and attempt to organise it into something more far-reaching than a demand for an inquiry into the killings of the last few days. Ranks of soldiers, bayonets fixed, stood in front of Fortuna and Iordache, barring the way to the Opera House. Behind them stood tens of thousands.

The sight of the square packed with the workers of

Timisoara had filled Iordache with emotion. The bell of history tolled. He stepped forward, and addressed the soldiers: 'You are the Romanian army, the army of the people!' he yelled. 'It is we, the people, who pay for you and for the bullets in your guns ... So shoot us now with the bullets we have paid for, our own bullets, or stand aside!' The soldiers' ranks stirred, and as Iordache marched forward, they divided and the crowd broke through massively. The bell was tolling for Nicolae and Elena Ceausescu and their communist regime.

It is necessary to look back to understand this moment. The seminal influences pushing the people towards revolt were want and poverty, and the soul-breaking police state. Thomas Carlyle, in *The French Revolution*, comments on the mood of the sans-culottes before the French Revolution as: 'Yes, here with us is famine; but yonder at Versailles is food enough and to spare.' If the palace were changed to Cotroceni, Ceausescu's palace in Bucharest, the same words could have been used to describe the feelings of Romania's poorest. But poverty alone does not beget revolution, otherwise the Third World would never be still.

There has to be a focal point to channel desperation in a political direction. But, because of the Securitate, there were no definable circles of organised opposition operating in Romania. There was no Gdansk shipyard. There were no Solidarity priests either. In fact the Orthodox Church was sickeningly collaborative, many of its priests suspected of being Securitate officers.

The miners' rising in 1977, and the strike struggle in Brasov some ten years later, had given notice that in the depths of Romanian society there was a burning desire for change, but on the surface things seemed to be forever accepted, in the way the mule accepts the whip. So much so that the poet Mircea Dinescu could write in apparent disillusion, practically on the eve of the revolution, 'There

would appear to be only one dissident for every two
million inhabitants here.'

It took the appearance of Gorbachev, the Berlin Wall to
tumble and the march of revolution throughout Eastern
Europe for the idea to permeate the consciousness of
Romania's poor, and particularly its youth, that it was
better to die standing up for liberty than to suffer tyranny
forever on your knees. Then Leipzig, Berlin, Budapest and
Prague all demonstrated that it was possible to win. Once
that realisation was welded to the willingness to struggle,
it was only a matter of time before all the factors necessary
to produce a social explosion, from the accumulation of
resistance to misery and oppression, would coincide somewhere. That happened in Timisoara on 16th December.

The history of the October Revolution in Russia is spat
upon by most Romanians because of its association with
communism, but there are some historical parallels worth
drawing on. Want and poverty had been recruiting
sergeants for revolution in Russia for decades. The Tsar,
Nicholas II, and his wife Alexandra had, by the early years
of the twentieth century, become objects of scorn and
hatred in the eyes of the ordinary people. There was politically combustible material accumulating year after year in
the impotent rage of the suburbs of St Petersburg. It only
needed a match thrown on it to begin a social conflagra-
tion. The original match came in the shape of an unwitting
priest, Father Gapon, who led a demonstration to the
gates of the Winter Palace, in January 1905, to demand
bread. The Cossacks opened fire, and the 1905 revolution,
which was a turning-point in the calendar for October,
had begun.

The Tsar and Tsarina of Romania had their priest, too,
in Laszlo Tokes of the Hungarian Reformed Church in
Timisoara. He would become the Father Gapon of the
Romanian revolution, his protest the dropped lighted
match that was to ignite a social inferno.

Father Laszlo Tokes went to Timisoara in June 1986 to

begin his probation as the pastor of the Hungarian
Reformed Church there. The Hungarian Protestant population in the city then was 10,000 out of a total of
400,000. Of these, only one quarter were still on the church
roll. Tokes described the situation on his arrival in
Timisoara thus: 'The congregation was in complete
disarray. We had only 2,500 on the church roll and very
few indeed actually worshipped in the church each
Sunday. There was no momentum; the church was slowly
grinding to a halt.'

But after his first two years, Tokes had doubled the
church roll, and the income of the church had risen from
250,000 lei per annum to 600,000 lei. By that time the
young Hungarian-born pastor was attracting such interest
in his sermons that people travelled from all over Transylvania to hear him, and the church had to institute two
services on a Sunday to cope with the numbers who
wanted to attend. But soon there were more than Sunday
church-goers interested in him.

Tokes was a rebel whose rich vein of analogy and
powerful oratory drew the attention of the quisling local
bishop and the Securitate, since criticism of the communist
regime was implicit in all his parables. 'He had a way of
talking about honesty and truth and decency so that you
knew he was criticising the regime ... without ever
mentioning any names,' a former parishioner said.

His first formal rebuke came from his local bishop,
Laszlo Papp, a shameless collaborator with the Ceausescu
regime. The bishop summoned Tokes to his offices in
Oradea and told him: 'Pastor Tokes, you are giving me
cause for concern ... cause for considerable concern.'
According to Tokes, the bishop then continued, 'You are
permitting the membership to grow too quickly. You are
drawing too much attention to the church.' Tokes says in
his autobiography, *Laszlo Tokes*, that the interview ended
with the bishop declaring: 'I do not speak only for myself.
I have contacts with the Ceausescu family, you know.' He

was on the road which would lead him from identification as a 'social nuisance' in the Securitate files to an 'enemy of the people'.

Early in 1988, the 'turbulent priest' became involved in discussion within the church on what stand it should take on the so-called 'systemisation' or 'modernisation' programme that the Ceausescu regime had devised for the Romanian countryside. Systemisation meant the destruction of at least 8,000 Romanian villages, and Tokes argued that the church could not stand aside from this. At the time he argued, 'Our church communities cannot be indifferent to these programmes ... There may be economic and political reasons for them, but we believe the moral consequences are so incalculable that the churches must fight to gain a compromise ...' Papp took a different line. He said in one debate with Tokes, 'If the state should even decide that the great church in Oradea should be demolished – if for the good of the people that were necessary – it would not matter. The first Christians worshipped under the sky and in the catacombs ...' A clash was guaranteed.

In due course Tokes found himself once again at a disciplinary hearing before the bishop. Along with two others, he was harangued about the stance he had taken on the issue. According to the recollections of his autobiography, the discussion finished with the inspector from the Department of Cults – the government body that supervised the agreed terms for religious worship – accusing Tokes of being a troublemaker and oppositionist who was following the pattern of his previous charge in Dej, where he had been disciplined twice and thrown out of the church. The threat was implicit.

On 31st October 1988 Tokes organised a joint ecumenical festival service with the Catholic Church in Timisoara. It brought a significant section of the students and intellectuals together in one gathering. During the service, Tokes allowed three students to recite poetry; this was prohibited by the state laws concerning religious worship. Fomenting a unity between students and intellectuals, which was spiced liberally with the Hungarian national question, was a provocation that the authorities could not ignore, especially in Transylvania. 'From that time on, the serious persecution of our parish began,' Tokes says. He was then watched day and night by the Securitate from behind the dirty net curtains of the windows in the sandstone building opposite his anonymous church in Timotei Cipariu Street.

Tokes was suspended from the ministry in March of 1989, by Bishop Papp. Tokes resisted further, and Papp tried to strike a compromise that Tokes could continue to preach but only if he was prepared to transfer to another church, out of harm's way in the remote countryside, at Mineu. But with the people of the parish fully behind him, Tokes dug his heels in. A signed petition was gathered by the parishioners and presented to Bishop Papp in Oradea.

Then the physical persecution of Tokes and his congregation was stepped up. His parishioners were harassed, eventually having to pass through a cordon of Securitate goons jingling their handcuffs each time they went to church on Sunday. And on 26th July 1989 the event that determined the final phase of the long-drawn-out battle between priest and bishop, church and state, came. Tokes appeared on the influential Hungarian TV programme *Panorama*, and launched a blistering attack on all those who were persecuting his church, the Hungarian minority in Romania and the horrible realities of life under Ceausescu. He said on *Panorama*:

... It is our duty to speak out when everybody, including the highest ranks of church leadership, is silent. There are questions torturing my brother pastors and members of my congregation, and they are too frightened to say anything. I feel an irresistible urge now to say openly all the things I have choked back so many times before. Why should we always build ourselves into this wall of silence? This wall is more solid than the Berlin Wall. And I feel that someone should start dismantling this wall ... Step by step our homes, our institutions, our human rights are being destroyed ... There is a deliberate attempt to eradicate our Hungarian culture.

This was unprecedented. A day after the broadcast went out on Hungarian television, the rebel pastor received a phone call at his manse. The caller shouted 'You're a man who no longer has a country!' before slamming the receiver down. One month later, Tokes was informed by Bishop Papp that he had been dismissed as a pastor of the Reformed Church and that if he did not leave the manse, he would be evicted. Tokes took legal action to defend his position.

In September, Ernö Ujvarossy, a leading figure in the Tokes church, was found dead in a forest near Timisoara in what could only be described as suspicious circumstances. Ujvarossy was the man who had delivered the signed petition to Bishop Papp in March that year, and he had been responsible for organising most of the restoration work earlier carried out on the church. Tokes completely rejects the assertions that Ujvarossy's death was suicide.

Then, in October, as though working hand in hand with Bishop Papp, the authorities withdrew Tokes' temporary residence permit for Timisoara, insisting that he return to Cluj, where his main residence visa was valid. Tokes challenged this ruling successfully in court on two occasions. In November, he was attacked and badly beaten by four thugs who entered his home. Then in early December, now virtually under house arrest, he lost a third court hearing on his appeal, and 15th December was set for his eviction from the church, since he had no right to reside in Timisoara. Another gang of thugs arrived some four weeks after the first mob, and smashed all the windows of his house.

By this time, all the tricks that the totalitarian regime knew for forcing submission – surveillance, intimidation, violence – had been used on Tokes and his wife Edit. Edit was pregnant with their second child, and now on the verge of a nervous breakdown. Tokes was also showing the strain, so much so that he now admits that in the early part of December he wrote a Christmas sermon in which Ceausescu was cast as the persecuting Herod and his own position compared with that of the infant Christ.

On Sunday 10th December, during what was to be his last sermon from the pulpit of the church in Timotei Cipariu Street, Tokes said to the packed congregation: 'Dear Brothers and Sisters in Christ, I have been issued with a summons of eviction. I will not accept it, so I will be taken from you by force next Friday ... It is an illegal act ... and they want to do it in secret because they have no right to do it ... Please come next Friday and be witnesses of what will happen. Come and be peaceful, but be witnesses ...'

As the congregation filed out, Tokes wondered how many of them would turn up on the following Friday, 15th December. He says that he expected few, on account of what people had already suffered. He was wrong, because 15th December would prove to be the beginning of ten days that would shake one of the world's most powerful dictatorships to the core. Ten days after that Friday, Tokes' 'Herod', Ceausescu, would be before a firing squad, and the Christmas sermon the pastor had prepared would have been changed. In distant Mineu, instead of a parable on Herod, Tokes would preach on Isaiah, chapter 16, verse 4: 'For the extortioner is at an end, the spoiler ceaseth, the oppressors are consumed out of the land.'

Early in the morning of 15th December Laszlo Tokes moved across his office in the Hungarian Reformed

Church. He looked at the oil-painted portrait of Istvan Debreczemi, one of the founder members of the church that had existed in Timisoara for almost a century. He could not help reflecting that perhaps the pioneers from the 1890s had had an easier road to walk than he. He opened the wooden shutters covering the shattered remains of the window, reminders of the last serious assault on the premises by the Securitate thugs. It was a beautiful crystal-clear winter's day.

In the street below were some thirty or forty people standing in knots of four or five, most of whom he recognised as members of his congregation. The protest had begun. No mean beginning, either, in a state where you had to have police permission for a birthday party if more than ten people were to attend! There were Securitate officers in their black Dacia cars at each end of the street, and three or four of them stood, as ever, by the street doorway at the stairs that led to the church buildings. One of the men in a knot near the window shouted up to Tokes, 'We are here now. What can we do for you?'

Incredibly, Tokes, fearing for their welfare, suggested they should leave. When they stoutly refused, he asked them to bring him bread and milk, since under the conditions of house arrest, he was rarely allowed to go out to purchase any. He then glanced at the old brown marble wood-burning stove in the corner of the room, thinking about his log supply, but enough had been smuggled to him that week already. 'Besides,' he thought, 'who knows if we shall be here tomorrow?'

By mid-morning, the crowd had grown to more than a hundred, and the Securitate officers made an attempt to move those immediately under his windows. The people stood their ground, and remarkably, around 11 a.m., all the policemen left. At first, no one could believe it. For the first time in months, people could move freely in and out of the Tokes' flat. It was a remarkable turn-round, filling all those involved with an optimism that perhaps something could be done. Clearly the authorities had not expected that people would support the outspoken cleric when the chips were down.

Twenty-nine-year-old Romeo Sofrone remembers driving down the Boulevard 6th Martie late in the afternoon of the 15th. 'There were hundreds if not more than a thousand people in the street where the Tokes church was. My works colleague, who was a Party member, went white when he saw it ... When I saw the look of him, I remember thinking, "My God, they are scared of what is happening!",' he said. Already, by the time Sofrone passed, a decisive change had taken place in Timotei Cipariu Street. The demonstration, which had started as essentially an ethnic Hungarian protest about the treatment meted out to one of theirs, was now overwhelmingly composed of Romanians who were there to use the persecution of Tokes to protest against the Government in general.

At just after 10 p.m., the mayor of Timisoara, Petru Mot, a small stout man in his early sixties, arrived with several of his leading Party comrades to push his way through the crowd of more than a thousand to negotiate with Tokes. When he demanded to know what was going on, he was told that the protest was against the eviction of Pastor Tokes. Surprisingly, Mot said that there was no such plan to evict Tokes, promising that the pastor would be issued with a new temporary residence permit. Tokes then demanded that the mayor guarantee the lifting of the Securitate restrictions on him and his wife, and the repair of the damage done in recent weeks to his house. The mayor agreed, provided that Tokes asked the crowd to disperse.

Lorin Fortuna, a lecturer in telecommunications at the local university, had gone to the Tokes' flat after work. He had heard about the demonstration by word of mouth: 'Everyone was talking about it that day.' He says he went 'out of curiosity, and a wish to participate', hoping that 'something might happen'. He heard Tokes come to the window that night after speaking with the mayor, explain the mayor's promises and plead with people to disperse. He listened, astonished, as people in the crowd yelled back 'Don't trust the mayor. He's a communist ... He's lying!' and, 'We are staying all night.'

But after the shutters were closed and the mayor had left with his entourage, the Securitate men arrived, clubs in hand. Fortuna decided it was time to go, to fight another day. He made his way home and told his family about the demonstration. His thirteen-year-old daughter asked, 'Are there still people on the streets?' 'Yes,' he replied, to which she said, 'Well, why are you not with them?' The anguished father then said, 'Well, darling, I have you and your mother to look after, don't you see?' The thirteen-year-old voice of the nascent Romanian revolution then countered, 'Are those now on the streets fighting for today or for tomorrow? ... Or are you telling me none of them have families and children to think about?'

The Fortuna family went to Timotei Cipariu Street on Saturday 16th December as did Claudiu Iordache, his wife Antoneta and their daughter, Alice, who was nineteen. So did thousands of others. By mid-morning, the authorities had made good several of their promises to Tokes – people had been allowed to bring food to him in quantity; all the broken windows had been repaired and the mayor, visiting their flat, was still promising that when the town hall offices were open on the following Monday, their residence permit would renewed.

Accordingly, at around 11 a.m., Mot asked Tokes to tell the crowd to disperse. Tokes went to his window for the first time that day, but not the last, to plead with those gathered to go away. He told them that the mayor had kept his promises, that the situation was much improved, and that it was dangerous for them to maintain an illegal gathering. 'We've gained what we wanted. Please go home now,' he said. The crowd would have none of it, for, unknown to Tokes and Mot, they had subconsciously raised the stakes of the game. Tokes was cheered, but the shouts told him that the people would not be moved off. These, the bravest of Timisoara, symbolised the idea that the Tokes protest had generated a mood among a certain section of the people that it was now or never. Besides, as one hour followed the next, the swelling of their ranks made them more and more bold. They did not know what they wanted precisely, only that they would not accept whatever Mot had to offer.

The mayor left in the early afternoon, then later sent a message that if the crowds would not disperse, force would be used. Clearly he and his comrades thought that if they raised their swords above this thousand-voiced tumult, it would scatter in fright. When Claudiu Iordache reached Timotei Cipariu Street at about 5 p.m. that night, the demonstration was overflowing into the Boulevard 6 Martie, blocking the tram-lines on the main avenue. He says he pushed his way through the crowds to get near the Tokes' window, and recalls:

> You have to bear in mind that I am a writer when I tell you this, but there in that street was a tension and a feeling of power that you could almost touch. There was a kind of joy in people's eyes, mixed with apprehension about where this would lead. But on top of that, a celebration that they were saying to the powers that be at last, 'Go to Hell! We have had enough!' It was as if they were drinking the wine of liberty, and never mind the consequences.

He stood among the turmoil around the Tokes' window for an hour or more. People were now clamouring for Tokes to lead them in a demonstration to the town centre. Iordache said: 'Tokes came to the window and told us the Securitate were coming, that we should go home. He advised us to leave the area so that it should not all be interpreted as an anti-communist demonstration. He said, "We are powerless against them ... I ask you to leave quietly".' Tokes says in his own writings that at this stage he chose to be a pastor, not a political crusader. From this point on, like a Father Gapon, history would really have little further use for him.

Then, somewhere between 6 and 7 p.m., it rose, hesitantly at first, then growing louder. A woman near Iordache started it. 'Li-ber-ta-te,' she chanted. Fears evaporated as it got louder and louder, echoing the growing resolution of the crowd. 'Li-ber-ta-te ... Li-ber-ta-te ... Li-ber-ta-te!' They had found a voice for their purpose. Freedom was its name. As though on cue, the strains of 'Desteaptate Romane' ('Romanians Awake'), an anthem long banned under communism, filled the air next, and, minutes later, the unimaginable ... 'Jos Ceausescu! ... Jos Ceausescu! ... Jos Ceausescu!' 'Down with Ceausescu!' There could be no turning back now, so when the first ranks of the police militia arrived, the people fought. 'The women were amazing, yelling at their men to fight, literally pushing them forward. People were throwing anything they could get their hands on ... bottles, stones ... breaking anything for missiles,' Iordache says.

Next, helmeted soldiers were repulsed and a fire truck followed, spraying jets of foam into the street. 'They were weak – we could see that ... They were impotent, and I thought for the first time, "This is the beginning of the end",' Iordache remembers. Then heavily reinforced ranks of militiamen came wielding their clubs mercilessly, and their superior arming and weight of numbers began to tell. The crowd started to give ground, and retreat became flight. The militiamen scrambled through the back courts after people. The whole Iordache family were clubbed as they ran, but Claudiu says, 'With all our hearts we had shouted "Jos Ceausescu!" It was the freeing of our souls. Once we had shouted like that, we believed that he was finished.'

Fresh forces came out on to the streets, the students and the poorest of the poor being the most clearly distinguishable groups. The town was dissolving into civil war with the poorest looting shops and burning as they went, in an orgy of revenge delivered out of their excoriating poverty. 'There was no tomorrow for us anyhow,' as one poor man put it later. Street fighting was developing everywhere, its ferocity astonishing the forces of law and order.

In the distant Calea Aradului area, Romeo Sofrone remembers opening his living-room window and listening to the far-off roars early that evening. 'At first,' he said, 'we thought it was a football match … then it dawned on us. A demonstration! We left for the town centre immediately.'

In the Circumvalatiunii area, people had gathered from all the surrounding houses, and chanted in the local square 'Jos Ceausescu!' in a frenzy. The Iordaches were now among their number. The crowd then moved off for the town centre, chanting, 'Romanians come with us!' As it left the square, the leading column was attacked by a phalanx of soldiers wielding billy-sticks. Heads were being broken, limbs bludgeoned, and one nameless hero had had his teeth smashed out by the time the Iordaches beat a hasty retreat to their seventh-floor flat. Claudiu says:

In the street below there were at least ten army trucks each carrying more than fifty or sixty soldiers. The soldiers were pouring on to the streets, armed with wooden clubs and pickaxe handles, and together with the police, they were beating and arresting anyone they could get their hands on. When they eventually retreated, I went back into the street. The shops had been broken into and looted in my area. I went home and talked with my wife through the early hours of the morning. She was worried that, since I was wearing a distinctive white raincoat, I would be identified.

It took the militiamen and the soldiers well into the following morning to bring things to order.

Nicolae Ceausescu had a sleepless night, constantly phoning the Minister of the Interior, Tudor Postelnicu, and the Minister of Defence, Vasile Milea, for progress reports. Ceausescu told them both repeatedly that live ammunition was to be used to quell the disturbances, but his orders were not obeyed. In the course of the late evening of the 16th and early morning of the 17th, he phoned Postelnicu, the man responsible for the Securitate, more than fifteen times.

CHAPTER 9

17th December – the Day of Reckoning

The vanguard of the most desperate returned in mid-morning to the smoking fields of the previous night's battle. Most of the leaders of those clashes had been badly beaten or arrested by the Securitate in punishing sweeps through the city in the early hours. But the abyss threw up fresh soldiers of Nemesis, and inexorably they made their way that morning to the head offices of the Communist Party in Timisoara County, in effect the county council offices of the Party, in Boulevard 23 August.

By late morning, a crowd of two or three hundred had assembled, chanting anti-Government slogans, and the rebellion reached a new stage when, at around noon, a group of the most adventurous stormed the building. The soldiers around the HQ seemed to be moving in slow motion as the horde poured up the stone stairs under the ubiquitous stone pillars that adorn the facade of Party offices everywhere in Romania. Inside, petrified Party apparatchiks clung to the walls as the demonstrators tore Ceausescu pictures from the walls, Ceausescu books from the bookcases and grabbed any other obvious communist totems and threw them out of the window into the street.

Romeo Sofrone was down in the street with the demonstration at that time. He says he watched in utter astonishment as books and portraits crashed from the balcony and upstairs windows. The shattering of each icon was met with a huge cheer. He says he was overjoyed at the sight, while thinking simultaneously, 'He's finished now', because such protest was unthinkable otherwise. He added, 'I wasn't afraid then ... I did not think they would shoot.'

At this stage the army held its fire, but it is likely that the first martyrs of the revolution fell here, for, as the Party offices were being ransacked, three columns of soldiers moved down Boulevard 23 August and began to use their bayonets on the people for the first time. Sofrone saw one man bayoneted in the stomach, another in the back, an old man with blood streaming from his head, his ear hanging by a thread of skin, and another falling under a rain of soldiers' rifle butts. Another spiral of vengeful rioting and brutal counter-offensive from the forces of state had begun. It would end in massacre.

'Do you know what I should do with you two? I should put you before a firing squad and have you shot. What you have done is treasonable!' Nicolae Ceausescu yelled, enraged at his Minister of Defence, Vasile Milea, and his Minister of the Interior, Tudor Postelnicu. They were arraigned before Ceausescu and his wife Elena at an emergency meeting of the political executive committee of the Romanian Communist Party at its Central Committee building in the centre of Bucharest. It was late in the afternoon of the 17th.

Ceausescu was enraged on two counts. First, that his orders for the soldiers and the Securitate to use live ammunition the previous night had not been implemented, and second, because law and order in Timisoara had deteriorated to the point where the sacking of the Communist Party headquarters there had become possible. Throughout the hour-long meeting, Ceausescu repeated the same question again and again. 'I ordered that the security forces be armed, that warning shots be fired first, and that then the demonstrators should be shot in the legs. Why was this not done?'

Postelnicu grovelled before the Ceausescus. 'I fully agree with the measures that will be taken against me ... As the Party activist in charge of this field of activity, I have no wish to absolve myself whatsoever ... I am an honest soldier, faithful to the Party, yet I have to confess that I did not know that the units were to come out with arms and war cartridges ... What I mean is that I took firm action based on the guidelines and directions given by you last night. I have done my best,' he said. Elena Ceausescu retorted, 'You have not done anything,' and her husband added, 'You went to suppress this riot with only truncheons, and so in effect you did nothing.'

General Milea offered his excuses. 'I am guilty. It did not strike me that it would reach such serious proportions.' Iulian Vlad, the Head of the Securitate, supported Milea by saying, 'We thought it was a minor disturbance that we could settle without war cartridges ... We made a fundamental error.'

Ceausescu then railed, 'I ordered you to fire warning shots, and then, if they don't withdraw, shoot them in the legs. I didn't think for a minute that you were using blank cartridges. This is eyewash! Those who broke into the Party County Committee headquarters should never have got out alive. They should have been shot dead.'

Then Ceausescu returned to the proposal he had made in the early part of the meeting that Milea and Postelnicu be sacked for their failure to contain the situation properly, saying, 'Look, comrades, I suggest that we take some severe steps ... If you are of a different viewpoint, I ask you to speak your mind now ... because we are confronted with actions concocted both by the East and the West, which have joined forces with a view to destroying socialism.' Not one of the twenty-nine members of the political executive committee attending the meeting expressed any difference of opinion with Ceausescu on the fundamental issue that the rebellion be put down using live ammunition, but there were some dissenting voices concerning the dismissals of Milea and Postelnicu.

A political pantomime then ensued. Ceausescu offered his resignation as General Secretary in a fury that his proposals were not received with immediate unanimity. He scattered his papers on the table and shouted as he made his way to the door, 'You can get yourselves another General Secretary!' As he went out, Curticeanu ran after him, beseeching him to stay, followed by Dinca. Dascalescu, the Prime Minister, who would try to hijack the first government after the revolution five days later, stood up and implored the 'Conducator', 'No, no, no, Comrade Ceausescu, you cannot do that … Don't leave us!' And then the two women on the committee apart from Elena Ceausescu, Ana Muresan and Lina Ciobanu, shouted, between sobs, 'Stay, stay, Comrade Nicolae! We shall always be on your side.'

Elena Ceausescu suggested to the committee that she have a word with 'the Comrade', to try to persuade Ceausescu not to resign. After she had a whispered conversation with him at the doorway, he returned and agreed to withdraw his resignation. The performance allowed Ceausescu to compromise in the short term on the sackings, having secured support, without one voice raised in opposition, for the demonstrators to be fired on. He concluded the meeting by putting the motion that all Romania's borders be closed, and that, during his absence on a state visit to Iran over the next two days, Elena Ceausescu be put in charge.

The dictator then left to prepare for his telephone conference with the army generals and Party leaders in

Timisoara, and thereafter his state visit to Tehran. In his telephone conference, he told those present in Timisoara, 'Some very serious events have been occurring in Timisoara in the last two days ... Mistakes have been made because the problem should have been settled within an hour or two ... Units were sent out without proper armament before, but now they have been given war ammunition ... This is a state of emergency ... Everyone who does not submit to the soldiers, I've given the order to be shot. People should be challenged, and if they do not comply with the order, they should be shot ... I have ordered the troops to fire ... They made the mistake before of turning the other cheek ... Humanism does not mean joining the enemy. Humanism means the defence of socialism.'

After an exchange with Ion Coman, the member of the political executive committee whom he had sent to Timisoara on his behalf, Ceausescu concluded the teleconference by saying, 'You must take firm steps right away.' He had no idea that he was on the road to ruin.

The massacre of Bloody Sunday in Timisoara started about 5.30 p.m. as darkness fell on the city. There are eyewitness testimonies which suggest that in the early afternoon there had been a number of isolated shootings, but after 6 p.m. there was undoubtedly a qualitative shift in events as the security forces opened up indiscriminately against the masses of people roaming the streets in inchoate protest.

Some of the great events of Romanian history have become tangled in a web of claim and counter-claim, myth and reality. Timisoara 1989 is no exception. Controversy still reigns about these events. How many people died, and exactly who killed them, are at the heart of the debate. There were greatly exaggerated reports emerging from Timisoara at the time. On 20th December, the august newspaper *The Times* reported on its front page: 'Romania deaths may reach 2,000', and the *Financial Times* followed the next day, quoting the official East

German news agency, ADN, that 'security forces had killed between 3,000 and 4,000 demonstrators in Timisoara'. It seems that the initial estimates were exaggerated by the nature of the firing from tanks and even helicopter gunships which gave the impression of wholesale slaughter.

The official count is now 128 dead and about 400 wounded, although the body count may be slightly underestimated because it is known that many bodies were cleared and disposed of by the killers. The police militia and Securitate men were responsible for the greatest percentage of these deaths, but any objective assessment has to apportion some of the blame to the army also. Eyewitness reports carried in the British press at the time quote accounts of people being crushed under tank wheels, soldiers bayoneting people and soldiers opening fire on demonstrators. The generals are still reticent about this, to say the least.

In the discussion at the political executive committee in Bucharest, Ceausescu said, 'If one soldier had fired, they would all have scattered like partridges', but reality proved him wrong. People fought back, often with bare hands, and paid the price.

Claudiu Iordache was in the Opera House Square early that Sunday evening, and can still describe the scene vividly:

> The town centre had been burned and looted ... I watched a fire truck putting out a fire in a shop beside the cathedral. As they were doing that, others were setting a shop alight scarcely fifteen yards away ... I did not approve of such things, but disorder creates its own rules; it does not operate by the laws of normal society ...
>
> As I watched all this, there was a burst of automatic fire from the direction of the Opera House. A man called out to me about a boy beside him, 'Look, he is

shot ... Look, he is shot,' he yelled. This was the beginning of the so-called cathedral incident, where people told of masses of children being shot.

This incident became part of the folklore of the events, where a group of school-children supposedly emerged from the cathedral carrying candles and were mown down by automatic gunfire from the adjacent rooftops. Perhaps the panic of the times created this hyperbole. The only death commemorated on the Timisoara Cathedral steps is that of Sorin Leia, whose name is carved on a white stone plaque at the right-hand side of the cathedral doors. Leia was shot on the steps by persons unknown, on 18th December, while carrying a Romanian flag and singing 'Romanians Awake'. Speaking of the cathedral shootings, Iordache says, 'I was there at the time, standing at the left-hand side of the cathedral. I heard the shots, and the crowd scattered in all directions. Immediately afterwards, there were no bodies on the steps of the cathedral.'

One who did fall, however, was a French journalist, Jean-Louis Calderon, whose body lay on the ground opposite the cathedral steps after this shooting. A white marble plaque still marks the spot in the Opera House Square. Another was Traian Orban, who went to the aid of a man shot in the head. He was then shot in the left leg. It was with a dum-dum bullet which shattered his left femur.

If controversy about how many died and who killed them remains, there can be little doubt about who was killed in these first brutal armed clashes. It was the downtrodden poor of Timisoara, the sans-culottes of the Romanian revolution. Lorin Fortuna says, 'Those who took a chance were desperate ... Those who went in the front lines had nothing further to lose ... They were the poorest of the very poor.'

Thus the lumpenproletariat of Timisoara were the first to rise, and this coloured the character of the early days of the revolt. It explains partly their somewhat chaotic nature, and the indiscipline which manifested itself in widespread looting and destructiveness. There are numerous stories of bands of demonstrators reaching the outlying areas of Timisoara as evangels of the revolt, but then actually coming into physical collision with the people from these localities when they began to destroy property and set shops on fire, and so on. This analysis of the class composition of the first revolutionaries seems more convincing than the xenophobic assertion that they were all Hungarians. But this recklessness also had a consequence for the short-term prospects of the revolt. These people of the abyss, precisely because they had nothing left to lose, would not listen to reason, and this fearlessness provoked the state authorities into going too far in their acts of suppression. In turn, this caused division among the army leaders about how far to go in repressing the people, and fear of what it could lead to produced a revolt in the ranks of the conscripts and decisively brought out the disciplined ranks of the ordinary organised working class to protest at the extent of the savagery of that repression.

A visit to the offices in Timisoara of the Association of 17th December supported some of these contentions. The Association takes care of the welfare of the bereaved and the wounded from the Timisoara revolt. It has 270 cases on its books. Its offices, maybe paradoxically, are the old rooms of the Young Communist League, for almost all who frequent them are vehemently anti-communist. Many of those involved with the association have the marks of degradation and deprivation on their faces, tributes to lost battles of the body and spirit. The first official we were introduced to was drunk, and demanded money for his story. The waiting-rooms were full of people whose lives are a continuing testimony to poverty: women, old and obese long before their time, screaming babies in their arms, with unwiped noses or unwashed waifs running around them; men with the odour of stale alcohol about them, broken shoes on their feet.

Mariana Mariuta, a tall twenty-year-old volunteer with the Association, was an exception to these general impressions. She was arrested on the evening of 17th December and held for three days. In detention, her stomach was jumped on and her arm was twisted repeatedly until eventually it broke. She was forced to stand in freezing water for hours on end. Her best friend, who was arrested with her, has never been seen again. Since the revolution, Mariana has had two miscarriages and has never regained the power of her left arm.

At around 9 p.m. Claudiu Iordache was still in the town centre amid the rattle of machine-gun fire. 'When the troops continued to advance, we fled into the park behind the cathedral and then into the Boulevard Republicii. There was shooting there also. It was terrifying. At the junction of the Boulevard and Paris Street the firing was indiscriminate ... It seemed that all the main streets were patrolled by soldiers shooting, and there were still multitudes of people out there. When we reached home, I went out on to the balcony. There were shots ringing out all over the town. It was too much for me. I broke down and cried.'

CHAPTER 10

Towards the Revolution – 18th, 19th and 20th December

The street skirmishes continued in the centre of Timisoara over the next two days, although the crowds diminished because the butchery of the 17th had cloaked the city in fear. But the pendulum of revolution was swinging away from the dictatorship. On the morning of Monday 18th there were sporadic strikes in the factories on the outskirts. 'We heard about that, but we could do nothing because the place was like a military camp,' Claudiu Iordache says.

Lorin Fortuna says, 'I was beside myself with desperation ... I thought that everything that had been done ... all the sacrifice ... would have been in vain unless the big battalions of the factories were involved.' He feared that Timisoara was about to become another Brasov, where a rising in 1987 had been drowned in blood. He says he spent most of the Monday in the factory areas trying to find out what was going on. He had no success, since everyone was in fear of those they did not know, due to the spectre of the Securitate. Fortuna spent the evening listening in to the Securitate radio network, which he had been able to crack some time before because of his skill in telecommunications.

On the evening news that night, Romanian TV devoted more than fifteen minutes to a report of Ceausescu's visit to Iran. It included a transmission of the ceremony to herald his departure, during which he received more than twenty handshakes, four bunches of flowers and five kisses on the cheek, including an embrace from Elena, his wife.

That Monday morning, Ion Ratiu, who later became the Peasants' Party's presidential candidate, was in his luxury flat in the 15th arrondissement of Paris, in the André Citroën district near the Eiffel Tower. The phone rang. It was the foreign editor of *The Times*, speaking from London to ask Ratiu if he had heard about the shootings in Timisoara from the night before and to commission him to write a piece on it for the following day's paper.

On the 17th, Ratiu had heard about the disturbances associated with the Tokes demonstrations, so he agreed to write the article. He was a millionaire businessman by this time but had a journalistic background, having worked for the BBC as their Romanian correspondent for seven years, among others. Ratiu spent more than an hour trying to phone contacts of his in Romania. He gave that up, and rang sources in Belgrade and then in Budapest before he eventually got through to Jimbolia, a small Romanian town on the Yugoslavian border about twenty-five miles west of Timisoara. 'That is when I got complete confirmation that they had shot people in Timisoara . . . I was absolutely convinced then that the balloon was going up . . . Until I got through to Jimbolia, I was not quite sure . . . but when I heard about the shootings in Timisoara, I knew this was not just another Brasov uprising . . . I said to myself then, "A ajuns cutitul la os" (The knife has reached the bone) – It is too much to bear. This time it won't wash.' Ratiu reflected some of these sentiments in his *Times* article, but the prevailing mood of newspaper comment at the time was that Romania would remain outside the Eastern European revolution. For example, the *Independent* on 19th December declared, 'Despite the disturbances, and their evidently brutal repression, it may be that the Eastern Europe "domino theory" will prove, at least for the time being, invalid in Romania.'

As the first copies of *The Times* with Ratiu's article in it were being bought from the news-stands in London on the morning of Tuesday 19th, the workforce of Claudiu Iordache's Institute were assembled before their director, Joseph Roth, for a special meeting. Roth was a leading Party official in the town and a member of the Grand National Assembly. He told the meeting that he wanted to warn them about what had happened in the last few days, that the people involved in the disturbances were hooligans who wanted to destroy the town and that the security forces had had no option but to shoot to restore order.

Claudiu Iordache remembers: 'I am a temperamental man. I was outraged. I rose and asked the meeting to stand in respect for a minute's silence for those who had died. They did. Then I spoke. I said that everything that had happened in the previous days was the responsibility of the authorities. I referred to our national hero, Nicolae Balcescu, and said that when he cut the cloth from the throne of Louis-Philippe, he was not a hooligan, and that neither were those who had died in the street the day before.'

Roth yelled in response, 'Iordache, you are an agent provocateur!' but just then the rattle of automatic gunfire was heard outside and Iordache shouted, pointing out of the window, 'Here is your answer, Mr Director. Here is the truth!' Everyone in the Institute went home early that day, and Iordache says he spoke that night to his wife and family about his likely arrest.

It did not come. The security forces were too busy

making preparations to try to contain a likely general strike the next day. In his rigged listening-post that Tuesday, Fortuna had heard the Securitate message: 'I must go now. There is a gathering of people at the back of the Elba factory ...' Fortuna hastened to the scene. There had been a demonstration on a bridge leading into Timisoara near the factory, and a woman had been shot dead. When the factory workers heard about it, they downed tools in protest against the killings and sent messengers to the factories near by, asking them to strike in protest, too. From these beginnings a general strike call went out over all Timisoara for Wednesday 20th December at 10.30 a.m.

The next morning, there were security cordons round most of Timisoara's major factories by 10 a.m. But in many cases the troops and policemen were locking a stable door when the horse had already bolted. Anticipating such actions, thousands of workers had gone on strike an hour before the agreed time and were marching towards the city centre before the major detachments of security forces arrived to prevent their doing just that.

Lorin Fortuna met one such proletarian column on the edge of town that morning. He stopped his car, jumped out, and asked the leaders, 'Where are you going and what do you want to do?' The reply came: 'We are going to the town centre to ask the authorities for the bodies of the dead and to demand to know who was to blame for the killings.' Fortuna advised them that some of the streets around the town centre were blocked and that a re-routing was necessary. They asked him to join them, and he told them he had only come to give advice. The workers were chanting 'Romanians, come with us', when one of those at the head of the demonstration said to him, 'Ah ... you come only to give advice, but not to follow it, my dear friend!'

Fortuna agreed to join them, but first he would go to his workplace to make placards for the demonstration. He left knowing they thought he would be too scared to return. Hastily at his workplace he made four placards with four separate slogans, which he remembers even now: 'The Romanian Democratic Front', 'This is Timisoara! Where is the Rest of the Country?' 'Down with the Dictatorship!' and 'We Want Democracy!' He managed to rejoin the marching workers, who immediately hoisted the makeshift placards at the front of their demonstration. It was nearing noon as they reached the town centre. Fortuna estimates that the total by then numbered anything between 10,000 and 20,000.

Iordache recalls: 'On 20th December, when I reached work, all the talk was of the demonstration called for that day at the Opera House Square. I argued vehemently that we should all join the demonstration. When the allotted time came, around 1 p.m., I left the Institute with four other men and forty women. I have to say that throughout these days the formidable courage of the women had to be seen to be believed.'

The contingent marched together hesitantly towards the town centre. 'Platoons of soldiers blocked the way into the Opera House Square, but we could see it was packed full; all the workers had come from their industrial areas. It was the moment that transformed an uprising into a revolution. This is not to overlook the heroic role of the young people, but it was these workers who delivered the decisive blow. This was the moment that communism died in Romania, vanquished at the hand of those it claimed to represent for all these years. The sight of the square packed full of workers overpowered me,' he says.

Iordache pushed his way through the crowd to the top of the square, where ranks of soldiers blocked the way. He moved remorselessly forward, unable to stop himself, determined to break a way through to the Opera House and the precious vantage-point of its balcony. He issued his stirring appeal, now famous in the annals of Timisoara. The soldiers' ranks gave way. History might judge it as the moment in Timisoara when the ranks of the army divided and the balance of power swung decisively in favour of revolution.

Iordache met Fortuna for the first time in his life moments later. They were both seized by the necessity of reaching the balcony. Fortuna went to the back of the Opera House and broke a window to try to gain entry. The technical director opened the door immediately, and pleaded with him, 'Please ... Please don't destroy the Opera House!' Fortuna replied, 'We have no such intention, my friend, but it is now about to be put to a more important use than ever before.'

It was between 1 and 2 p.m. when Fortuna spoke from the balcony, using a loudspeaker system improvised from equipment in the Opera House. He appealed to the crowd that there should be no more attacks on the army, that all vandalism should cease and that from now on they should press for their demands by organising the general strike in the Opera House Square. When he asked if they were all in agreement, more than 50,000 voices yelled 'Da!' ('Yes!') in approval. He went on, 'We have to have a political organisation if we are to continue to resist the Government. So, as a start, can each factory here send three delegates to the platform so that we can make up a co-ordinating committee!' Voices in the crowd began to demand, 'Who are you?' and Fortuna told them he was a university teacher and where he worked.

Then Iordache moved to the microphone. He says that it must have been about 3 p.m. 'The view from the balcony was spellbinding – there was just a sea of faces. There must have been 80,000 people there.' He spoke few words. 'I am Claudiu Iordache, the Romanian writer. I am afraid. We are all afraid. But if we remain together, we cannot be driven from the square.'

When Iordache retreated from the balcony, there were more than fifty workers milling around awaiting advice. Fortuna was speaking to them, urging them to return to their factories and bring more people to the square and to organise in their areas to bring their factories out on strike the next day. Many of the workers' leaders left immediately. From those left, a committee of twelve was formed on an *ad hoc* basis.

Things began to get more and more chaotic as increasing numbers of people came into the building to get to the balcony to speak to the crowd. In the early evening, after more than four hours of speeches, the crowd was bigger than ever and a deputation from another demonstration, at the Communist Party county offices in Boulevard 23 August, arrived to seek the creation of a joint committee. They explained that Constantin Dascalescu, the Prime Minister, and Cornel Pacoste, one of the secretaries of the political executive committee of the Communist Party, had come to Timisoara, to the communist HQ, to negotiate with the protestors on behalf of the Government.

Ceausescu returned from his three-day visit to Iran late in the afternoon of the 20th. He was briefed on the general situation and the particulars of the visit of Dascalescu and Pacoste. That evening he made the first official Government response to the events in Timisoara, in a simultaneous television and radio broadcast to the nation.

He spoke totally uncompromisingly. He referred to the anti-government demonstrators as 'groups of hooligan elements' and continued in exemplary Stalinist wordspeak: 'Considering the information that is at present known to us, it can be said with complete conviction that these actions of a terrorist nature were organised and unleashed in close connection with imperialist, irredentist, chauvinist circles, and foreign espionage services in various foreign countries.' He defended the security forces resolutely, saying, 'The military units were obliged to defend themselves and to protect order ... They have shown great patience, and in the actions they took have fully fulfilled their duty towards the homeland, the people and our socialist achievements.' There was no mention of the numbers shot, of course. His speech ended on familiar themes, with an appeal to the people to 'defend socialism' and show 'patriotic and revolutionary spirit in defending the gains of the Socialist Republic in strengthened co-operation and unity', and then he announced a demonstration in support of the Government the following day outside the Central Committee building in the capital.

Isabela Prina was with 'what seemed like all of Timisoara' in the Opera House Square when the Ceausescu speech was relayed there that evening. She remembers: 'It did not matter what he said then. By then, we knew it was life or death. Us or him.'

The committee at the Opera House, headed by Fortuna and Iordache, had received delegates from the secondary demonstration at the county buildings in Boulevard 23 August throughout the day. There had been a division of opinion as to who should be on the committee to unite the respective forces, and consequently both Fortuna and Iordache had been reluctant to go to the City Hall to discuss terms with the Government representatives, in case they would exploit these differences to weaken the unity of the protest. The two relented about 11 p.m., and walked the half-mile between the Opera House and the City Hall. When they reached the City Hall, there were still some 5,000 or 6,000 people demonstrating, although none of the leaders of the protest had remained. Mircea Muresan, a professor of history at the university who had spoken and organised many of the speeches there on that day, was never seen again.

Dascalescu, the Prime Minister, had departed for Bucharest after Ceausescu's speech, its tenor having convinced him that there was no longer anything to talk about. Fortuna and Iordache went to the City Hall balcony and addressed those protestors standing outside. They both made calls for the revolt to continue, and urged support for a further strike demonstration the next day, at the Opera House.

When they left the balcony, Pacoste, the secretary of the political executive committee of the Romanian Communist Party, and Radu Balan, the secretary of the Timisoara County Communist Party, were waiting for them in the adjacent ante-room. Arguably, Pacoste was one of the most important men in the entire country, and Balan was the most important man in the local province. Fortuna, flushed with the success of the day and maybe even slightly intoxicated with it, treated them with utter contempt. He asked them immediately, 'Are you here on a mission for Ceausescu? If so, you are wasting your time.' The bureaucrats were astonished that Fortuna had the audacity to address them in this manner without a shred of the slavish formalities demanded by the hierarchies of communism. With a valedictory wave of his hand, he added, 'Look, we have only one thing to ask of you. If we win, we shall take care of your children. If you win, we want your word that you will take care of ours.' Then, speaking directly to Balan, he said, 'Mr Balan, there may still be hope for you ... Come with us now, and you can enter history. Otherwise ...'

CHAPTER 11

21st December

Most of the time the incidental can be overlooked in politics. Not always. At half-past five on the morning of 21st December, General Victor Stanculescu, one of Ceausescu's Deputy Ministers of Defence, says he walked into the emergency ward of the Municipal Hospital in Timisoara. He was wearing his uniform. He asked to see the doctor on duty.

The previous day, Stanculescu had refused to proclaim further decrees of the state of emergency from the balcony of the county Party HQ in Boulevard 23 August as the demonstrations grew in strength. Under army regulations, he had immediately applied to his superior officers for discharge from the army, after refusing to carry out an order. In the circumstances, he says, he felt this refusal to obey orders was 'virtually signing my own death-warrant'.

Explaining his 'case history' to the doctor, the General asked for an injection that would put him to sleep for the rest of the day. Stanculescu was playing for time, hoping for the best but preparing for the worst. If a firing squad came for him, he would be 'unconscious in hospital'.

These actions were not incidental. They were like the first raindrops that foretell the coming of a thunderstorm, the first feeble flurries that herald the avalanche.

Stanculescu's action meant that the enormity of the events of the revolution would break the reliability of the army high command as ineluctably as it won over the ranks. At the time he asked the doctor to put him to sleep he was also saying in a way, 'My friends, this uprising cannot be shot to death.'

Even as the General was taking off his uniform and preparing to get into bed, the Opera House Square was filling to substantiate this point. Lorin Fortuna said, 'At 7 a.m. the square was full to the cathedral. It was the happiest moment of my life. I knew then there was no way back. The demonstration had become a revolution.' For Fortuna and Iordache and the tumults of Timisoara, it would be a day of waiting. 'Our eyes were on Bucharest the whole day,' Iordache said.

Ceausescu emerged from the Central Committee building on to its first-floor balcony to address the huge multitude, more than 100,000 strong, gathered there. The Securitate had done its work as thoroughly as ever. The loyal masses had mobilised in confirmation that Ceausescu was still their great 'Conducator', their 'Genius of the Carpathians', their 'Treasure of Wisdom and Charisma'. As he stood on the white stone-faced balcony in front of the eight brown marble pillars supporting the three upper storeys of the building and gazed down, he saw that the front ranks of the crowd held photographs portraying himself and his 'Comrade, academician, doctor, engineer' wife, taken in the early 1960s but still the vogue, raised high. Beside these, masses of red banners proclaimed the virtues of socialism and paeans to the pair of them.

Ceausescu was wearing the dark blue fur-lined coat he would be shot in, and his favourite black Astrakhan fur hat. He was flanked on each side by the toadying members of the political executive committee, but Elena stood the closest, at his left side. The microphone system boomed out his first hoarse greeting across Palace Square (or Republic Square, as it had been called practically since the days when the Red Army swept into it). 'To begin with, I would like to extend to you warm revolutionary greetings,' he said. The multitude chanted in unison in reply, 'Ceau-ses-cu! Ro-ma-ni-a!'

Viorica Butariu was there. Like almost all the rest, she had been part of a forced mobilisation from her workplace, a watch-making factory. Her story was recorded in the London *Observer* on 31st December 1989. She says that when she went to work that morning, the factory director told the workers: 'You have to exclaim your joy at the way we crushed the bandits at Timisoara.' Viorica was one of the twelve who were selected to do so.

Ceausescu began to develop well-worn themes in his initial remarks: the need for national unity, the necessity of safeguarding the independence of the country and of socialism, and the need for vigilance in the face of foreign-inspired provocation. He was soon into his usual stride, hectoring the assembly, emphasising his points with rapid up-and-down movements of his clenched right hand. At each pause for breath, there was dutiful applause and even some cheering, a tribute to the schizophrenic gap in the politics of public and private life in the People's Socialist Republic.

At 11.30 a.m. he was saying, with typical syntactic difficulties, 'The best thing to do in these circumstances is to show the unity of the people and the Party and the people, without doing anything that will endanger our independence, and ...' when it happened. It was almost imperceptible initially, then it grew clearer and clearer. Some of the people were booing Ceausescu. Then, as the technical director of the live TV broadcast was panicking, it was indisputable that there was a section of the crowd chanting, 'Jos Ceausescu! Jos Ceausescu! Jos Ceausescu!'

When the booing started, Ceausescu continued his peroration, pumping his right fist up and down, but when the chants of opposition could be heard, he stuttered to a dumbfounded halt. He held his hand up as though to stop them, a King Canute trying to stop a verbal tide flowing in. Elena moved forward, and was heard to say, 'Stay calm, please,' before the live TV transmission was cut and television sets all over Romania went blank. It was too late. The spell of invincibility was broken. The revolution had announced its arrival in Bucharest, shouting it in the face of the dictator himself. And the whole country knew it. Mioara, the wife of Petre Roman, was in their flat in the Calea Victoriei watching the broadcast. She said, 'I can put a time on it ... 11.30 ... The words "Jos Ceausescu!" were heard for a minute ... It was a signal to the people.'

There are many different explanations of how the booing and chanting started. Some say a lamp standard collapsed and its fall sounded like gunfire, and that the jeering began then. Others say a group of students at the rear of the crowd simply began it, and repetition rolled it to the front of the demonstration. It matters little. What does matter is that in the dynamics of quantity and quality, twenty years had been eclipsed in a minute.

Order was restored, and Ceausescu completed his speech with a tirade against the 'terrorist acts in Timisoara'. But as the demonstration dispersed, people were chanting, 'Timisoara yesterday, Bucharest today!', 'Jos Ceausescu!' and the strains of the anthem, 'Romanians Awake', were soon swirling round University Square, at the end of Nicolae Balcescu Boulevard, which was to be the focus of Bucharest's evening of revolt. Banners and portraits were hurled to the ground, spat on and trampled on. If the Ceausescus had any choices left now, they were only about which road to take to ruin. The streets of Bucharest, Brasov, Braila, Cluj, Sibiu, Oradea, Tirgoviste and Timisoara would manifest that throughout the day.

Even by the bizarre standards of political life in Ceausescu's Romania, Cornel Pumnea makes an unlikely revolutionary. He was one of the leading sports commentators in Romania, and, like all journalists in high positions, he had got there by keeping his critical eye closed, his mouth shut, doing what he was told to do and saying the same. He might not have been one of Ceausescu's apostles of the personality cult, but he was certainly no dissident either. On 21st December he was in a restaurant with a group of friends, enjoying the run-up to Christmas. When he told his story, he was candid about his privileges. 'The old regime was difficult for almost everyone, but for me, life was easy ... I was privileged, a sports reporter ... I did not have problems getting things for my family.'

At about 4 p.m. a man came into the restaurant and said that there was serious trouble at University Square, near the Intercontinental Hotel. Pumnea thought to himself, given all that he had found out about Timisoara, 'It's now or never.' He said to his friends, 'We must go', drained the remains of a large brandy and, leaving the devil to take the hindmost, made for the door.

At the Tineretului underground station, he found that the Romana and University stations were closed because of the demonstration, so he and his friends, a group of about ten or twelve, took the train to Union Square. There were about fifty people gathered in the street when they disembarked there. Pumnea found voice to say that they should all go to University Square. While he was telling his story, he chain-smoked and his hands were shaking, even nine months after the revolution.

As they marched along the road, the group increased to about two hundred. 'There were lots of people standing at the side of the street, watching. When we got to St George's Church, we started to shout, "Come with us, Romanians! Come with us!" Suddenly everyone watching responded, and hundreds became thousands in a flash,' he said.

It was dark when they reached University Square, which was 'filling to capacity'. People had lit rolled-up newspapers to act as impromptu candles. The chanting was dominated by 'Jos Ceausescu!', 'Jos the Dictator!' and 'Jos the Illiterate Academician!' The ranks of soldiers stood by impassively as they were appealed to: 'Soldiers, soldiers, you are our brothers! We are the people!' Pumnea says that in these early evening hours the crowd was made up of all types of people, and 'not just students; anyway, most of them were on holiday'.

The crowd stood firm, chanting and singing, about 5,000 or 6,000 strong, according to Pumnea. It was about 9 p.m. when the fire trucks moved in, six of them spraying high-pressure foam in all directions. 'Everyone there was soaked to the skin, including me,' he said. He headed for home then, because he had to look after his young son when his wife went out to work a night shift.

When his wife answered the door, she looked at the state of her husband, and exclaimed, 'Look at the state you are in! Are you drunk? Where in God's name have you been?' Pumnea told her he had been to the square. 'Are you mad? Don't you know we have a child whose future must be always taken into consideration?' she continued. 'Yes, dear, that's why I went to the square,' Pumnea answered.

Petre Roman was in University Square from the early evening of 21st December until the early hours of the next day. He had gone back to his flat in Calea Victoriei three times that night to let his wife know that he was all right, and on two of those occasions to beg her to allow him to take his younger daughter with him. 'I told her that this was a historical night in the history of Romania, and that I believed our daughter should be able to say in later life that she was there and saw what happened,' he said. When the bullets started to fly and blood flowed in the street, he saw the wisdom of his wife's refusals.

Roman was there when the fire trucks came to break up the demonstration. 'It was striking how many young people were there – I mean really young people, twelve, thirteen and fourteen years old ... I remember when the fire trucks came, it was incredible, because the young people climbed on the trucks and tried to dismantle the hoses or cut them, or smash the windows and attack the drivers.' After this sweep by the trucks, the barricades of burning buses and cars were broken up and the crowd diminished in size to around 2,000 or 3,000, according to Roman. But then a dangerous cat-and-mouse game began with the militia forces advancing little by little and the demonstrators giving ground and then regrouping.

Late in the evening, after 11.30, the most serious assault began. The sky was lit with tracer bullets, and then the army began to press forward again in a formation of armoured cars. Roman recollects:

> They entered with armoured cars, shooting, first with tracer bullets in the air but then it was with live ammunition ... Everybody fled ... I saw people falling down injured, others shot ... Of course there was great panic, but somehow I was not frightened. I knew it would come to this; that after Timisoara, Ceausescu was prepared to kill thousands to preserve his rule ... The young people were absolutely determined to fight ... even with bare hands against the armoured cars ... I ran in the direction of the Architecture Department and I remember standing there watching one boy, about one hundred metres away, blocking the advance of an armoured car ... just standing in front of it.

Cries of 'As-sa-si-ne!' and 'Ti-mi-soa-ra!' rent the night air. The blood of Timisoara had not been spilled in vain: Bucharest had joined battle, but at great cost.

The Ethiopian Ambassador, who was an eye-witness of the shootings from his top-floor suite above Nicolae Balcescu Boulevard, told the *Independent* later: 'The troops began shooting from their tanks ... Then they fired tear gas, and the machine-gun fire became more intense.

You couldn't see everything, but when the fumes cleared, the bodies were there.'

Gelu Voican was a technician in building construction who had long been considered to be an unstable man by the regime, and was dogged constantly by the Securitate. He is a mystical man, which partly explains that at one time he was a leading light in the Transcendental Meditation sect in Romania, before it was banned by Ceausescu. He also went to University Square on 21st December. He says he knew he was being watched by the Securitate, but felt 'mysteriously drawn to the place, even though I did not believe that victory was possible.' He too thought that 'Ceausescu would repress the rebellion with all the force at his disposal.' He says:

> When the shooting started for real, many of the young people just stood before the guns shouting uncontrollably ... The odds against them were so great ... I thought that victory would be a miracle. But little by little I was consumed by the fires of revolution ... I stayed until around 1.30 in the night ... when the machine-gun fire from the tanks was so terrible that it would have been suicide to remain there.

He says he walked home, his heart breaking with the humiliation of death and defeat. The day had changed him, and he decided at that point, 'that I would return the next day to help start things again, no matter what the consequences ... There was no way back.'

He was a living example of what Petre Roman was hoping for. When he went home that night, he said to his wife, 'Maybe all this will be the match ... the light for the consciousness of hundreds of thousands in Bucharest that this is it. Now or never.'

After the killings in University Square, Nicolae Ceausescu phoned the Minister of Defence, Vasile Milea, to tell him:

'Have two rows of tanks deployed round the Central Committee building before first light tomorrow. And in the first row of tanks put eighty flame-throwers ... and men who are prepared to use them.'

——— *CHAPTER 12* ———

22nd December

Revolutions take history by surprise. In normal times, making history is left to kings and queens, parliamentarians, politicians or even the army generals of the day. In revolutions, history is made by the mass of the people, generally on the streets of capital cities. In 1989, all Europe watched agog as the people marched in Warsaw, Berlin, Budapest and Prague. The question by the year's end, as the world's news agencies told of the blood flowing on Timisoara's streets, was, what would happen in Bucharest? Would the capital join battle to provide the momentous hammer-blows to break down the walls of Ceausescu's prison-house?

It did, the first blows being struck on the evening of 21st December. But as the warnings of Timisoara showed, this was to be no 'Velvet Revolution' like Czechoslovakia's. In Romania, the old would not shake hands politely to usher in the new, as they did eventually in Poland. Bucharest would not see the dancing in the streets enjoyed for weeks in Berlin. Instead, in Romania, there would be bayonet stabbings and mass murder in Timisoara, lynchings and shootings in Sibiu, and blood and butchery on the streets of Bucharest.

But the Romanian revolution was subject to the same

laws of development as everywhere else – it had quantity and quality. Its quantity was excoriating misery, suffered year after year; its quality the volcanic venting of chronic rage on the streets, when that misery could be endured no longer.

It might have been so different if the 'crivat' had come as usual. The 'crivat' is the wind from Siberia that swirls into Romania at the end of each year. It sends the thermometer plunging below zero and throws a blanket of snow over the country long before December is out. The 'crivat' never blew in from Siberia in 1989 until after Christmas. That was a critical climatic factor that allowed the people to gather in the streets for hours, even days, certainly haunted by the prospect of death, but not fearing frostbite.

Iftene Pop, who became one of the leaders of the Peasants' Party after the revolution, saw the results of Bucharest's first evening of revolt early the next morning. At 5.30 a.m. on the 22nd, the streets of Bucharest were deserted. Gangs of old women cleaners were washing blood off the street in University Square and Nicolae Balcescu Boulevard.

Pop had spent his vacation in the Sisesti monastery in Maramures the previous summer. He says he smelled the unmistakable sweaty breath of revolution there. He talked with 'peasants, teachers, priests, miners and workers, and all wanted Ceausescu to go … The first secretary of the Party, army men and policemen told me the same.' Pop had listened to Radio Free Europe, like the rest of Romania, on the evening of 20th December and thought, 'He's finished,' but as he watched the cleaning women go about their work, he concluded, 'It has all been in vain.'

He walked from University Square up Nicolae Balcescu Boulevard to the Piata Romana. There was no one there. Then, tiring of the eerie silence, he went to Union Square after walking through Palace Square past the Central Committee building of the Communist Party. Pop returned home, where he stayed with his mother, at about 6.30 a.m. He told her sadly, 'Nothing has happened.' But history would disagree. Something had happened: a historic avalanche had begun.

In Palace Square, whose emptiness had filled Iftene Pop with disillusion at 6 a.m., hundreds of thousands gathered little more than three hours later, and the white marble Central Committee building there, in the heart of old Bucharest, would be the focus of the day's events. They came in their multitudes to protest against the old order and ended up forging the new, transforming the building into a symbolic latter-day Bastille, exactly 200 years on.

Palace Square already had the echo of history about it. In 1940 King Carol II announced his abdication from the State Palace, which stands about 300 yards opposite the baroque pillars of the Central Committee building. This was after Romania had lost 40,000 square miles of territory, in Bessarabia and Transylvania, in the ravages of the Second World War. The fascist Iron Guard marched round the square in those days, celebrating the demise of the king and the coming of the military dictatorship of General Antonescu. Then the cafés of Bucharest, the Paris of the East, had tittered with jokes parodying the King's procrastination and his earlier defiant, 'Eu nu abdic' – 'I'll not abdicate' – speech. But he went, his going personifying the Romanian proverb: 'Capul ce se pleaca, sabia nu-l taie' ('The man who bows his head doesn't get it cut off').

The King ended the royal dictatorship, keeping his head. The Ceausescu regime did not heed the proverb; it stayed too long. There would be blood, fire and thunder in Palace Square on this day as a result, and at the end of it only the domed Atheneum of Galeron adjacent to the Central Committee building would stand unscathed. Battles would burn, batter and pock-mark the rest. The nineteenth-century Gottereau library would be a smouldering ruin, almost all its half-million books destroyed by fire. The red volumes, *On the Way of Building Up the Multilaterally-Developed Socialist Society* – the collected speeches and writings of Nicolae Ceausescu – would burn too.

Petre Roman left his flat in the Calea Victoriei early in the morning. He had stood shoulder to shoulder with the protesters in Nicolae Balcescu Boulevard the previous evening before returning home in the early hours, machine-gun fire and the cries of 'Ti-mi-soa-ra!' and 'As-sa-si-ne!' ringing in his ears. The next morning he went to work at the Polytechnic, and at a staff meeting made an impassioned plea to his fellows that they should join the protest in Palace Square, in front of the Central Committee building, that morning.

Roman spoke in a broken voice, hoarse from the chanting of the previous evening. He was not well dressed for a man who would be the provisional Prime Minister less than twelve hours later. He was wearing a green casual jacket, a green woollen sweater and a dark blue checked shirt which did not match. By 9.30 he was in the throng of thousands making their way down the Calea Grivitei. As they entered the Calea Victoriei, he recalls, 'I looked back down the Calea Grivitei, and I could not see the end of the crowd, and I looked to the front, down the Calea Victoriei, and I could not see its beginning ... They were dominantly workers,' he added, in contrast to the crowds of the evening before when young people were preponderant. As he marched, he dwelled briefly on the events of the previous night and the terror of it all. Now, the soldiers were firing in the air and joining the demonstration, to the jubilation of the crowds yelling: 'Armata e cu noi!' – 'The army is with us!'

In the Central Committee building, Nicolae Ceausescu was taking the last step which would ensure his downfall. In a rage, he ordered that General Milea, the Minister of Defence, be shot for treason on account of his failure to carry out Ceausescu's express orders to ring the building with tanks and prevent the demonstration from massing. Whether Milea was shot by others or forced to take his own life remains one of the conundrums of the revolution. General Stanculescu says he knows that Ceausescu told his guard, when he was held in custody at Tirgoviste after the revolution, that he had had Milea shot. Another variant of this story is that Ceausescu ordered Milea to command the army to fire on the crowds and, rather than do that, Milea took his own life. This may be true. Stanculescu believes it is: 'My own opinion is that he was pushed to take his own life by the dictator ... both the post mortem and the coroner's report gave a suicide verdict.' If, however, this is the case, Milea is among the few army men who have committed suicide without putting his uniform jacket on and by shooting himself in the chest.

Milea was denounced as a traitor when his death was announced on TV and radio between 10 and 11 a.m. General Victor Stanculescu, then Deputy Minister of Defence, heard of Milea's death at 10.20 in the Central Committee building. The General's elaborate plans to avoid this circumstance had failed. After sleeping most of 21st December away in the Timisoara hospital, he had returned to Bucharest at 2 a.m. on the 22nd, having sought Milea's advice as to whether it was safe to do this. Then, undaunted by the failure of his first evasive action, he proceeded to the Central Military Hospital in Bucharest and had his leg put in plaster.

He explains: 'I anticipated the coming events and wanted to avoid any responsibility for attacks on the people. I decided to "break" my leg so as to be incapacitated. So I had it put in plaster to prevent my participating in the slaughter planned by Ceausescu, but it was not to be.' Ceausescu had him summoned from home to take charge of the army. He was ordered to appear at the Central Committee, 'irrespective of his medical condition'. There was little to laugh about as events unfolded that day, but Stanculescu certainly cut a strange figure among the dignitaries of communism, an army man with a plaster cast on his right leg.

A special escort was sent to his home to ensure that he was brought to the Central Committee to see Ceausescu. Stanculescu thought it might be taking him to face a firing squad, but once there, he was taken to the Ceausescus. Nicolae Ceausescu told him, 'The army must not surrender. Take all necessary measures.'

Stanculescu says: 'People said that Ceausescu was mad, but the deliberate ambiguity of this order demonstrates that he had not lost the power to reason. If a massacre were perpetrated against the people, he would absolve himself by saying that his orders had been misinterpreted, and if strong enough measures were not taken, he would have my head in a noose for not obeying orders.'

General Gheorghe Voinea, the army commander for Bucharest, heard of Milea's death when he was also summoned to see the Comrade President. Voinea also feared he was going to be shot. On his way to the building he removed the bullets from his pistol and put them in his boots to avoid the soldier's dishonour of being shot with his own gun.

He says: 'When I entered the Central Committee building, it was full of Securitate men in civilian clothes, all startled. You could see the fear in their eyes.' He went to the Central Committee meeting-room, where he met General Stanculescu, Deputy Minister of Defence, and General Eftimescu. All the miscreants of the era were present – Dascalescu, Bobu, Dinca, Postelnicu, Curticeanu and others. Nicolae Ceausescu and Elena Ceausescu were standing in front.

Ceausescu was now demented with rage. He demanded that they do something. He stamped his feet and yelled, 'Why doesn't the army do its duty? You must take all the necessary measures, do you hear me, all the necessary measures to stop them marching on us.' Voinea's shirt was sticking to his back with the sweat of fear. He said bravely,

'Comrade President, the situation cannot be resolved.' Ceausescu waved them out, yelling, 'Do something!' and as they left to go to the army command-post in the building, he started to go out on the balcony to speak to the crowd. He was booed and jeered as he stood behind the microphone preparing to speak. As the protests grew louder, he waved his hands in exasperation, and retreated, consternation and fear showing on his face.

The three generals were taken to the command-post by chiefs of the Securitate. Voinea says, 'We looked at each other; we did not say a word ... We lifted the telephones and dialled some numbers, because they were watching us, to give the impression that we were commanding units of the army, but we did not move a single soldier ... The demonstrators were at the walls of the building ... any movement would have started a slaughter.' Curticeanu entered and said, 'The ignorant mob are upon us ...' Stanculescu yelled at him, 'Shut up! We will take the necessary measures.' Curticeanu left, but soon returned in a state of panic, shouting, 'They are in the building ... You have to come to the President!'

As they entered the Central Committee meeting-room again, General Vlad, chief of the Securitate, and Tudor Postelnicu, the Minister of the Interior, were standing before the Ceausescus. Nicolae Ceausescu was screaming at Postelnicu, 'You are a traitor! ... You are a traitor! You lied to us!' Postelnicu besought him obsequiously again, 'Comrade President, I have devoted my life to you, I have served you.... I shall always serve you ... I have done what I can ... all that I could ...' Ceausescu raged: 'You ... You ... serve me? You are a pig, and you, Vlad, you bastard ... you only told me lies also!'

Then Elena shouted as the three generals joined the line: 'You pigs! You traitors! You fuckers! You have loved yourselves more than you loved the cause!' As bricks and stones were shattering the windows, she stepped forward. She spat in Vlad's face, and moved up the line. 'You garbage!'

Spit. 'You fuckers!' Spit. 'You bastards!' Spit. 'You pigs ... You traitorous bastards!' Through spit-splattered spectacles, Voinea saw them turn to flee to the waiting helicopter on the roof.

Some fifteen minutes before this, the Ceausescus' last message to the people of Bucharest had been delivered as leaflets cascaded down on the startled masses from helicopters flying over the central area of the city. They read: 'Workers, do not let yourselves be dragged from the path of truth by enemies of our people! Be vigilant, and expose those who are trying to cause panic and disorder! Citizens! Stop and think! Don't play into the hands of our enemies! The country is in danger. The future is in your hands!'

It certainly was. Minutes after the Ceausescus had fled, unknown heroes were covering the huge metal sign on the roof of the Central Committee building which read 'Traiasca Republica Socialista Romania' ('Long Live the Romanian Socialist Republic') with flags. When they had finished, only 'Traiasca Romania' could be seen. Their flags had holes in the middle where the communist hammer and sickle had been cut out as had first been done in Hungary in 1956. In the square, they were singing 'Ole, Ole, Ole, Ole, Ceausescu nu mai e!') ('Ceausescu is no more!'). The tune had first been adapted from a football chant by Solidarity supporters in Poland. The knots of history were being retied, as piles of the red books of the *Collected Works of Ceausescu* were thrown from the balcony into the square.

The first members of the Ceausescu household to perish were their two black Labradors, bludgeoned by the first revolutionaries who came on them in the Central Committee building. There was no room in the helicopter for the dogs. They had been gifts from Queen Elizabeth II and the British former Liberal leader, Sir David Steel.

Petre Roman stood in the square and watched the Ceausescu helicopter take off. 'Everybody knew from that moment on that he was gone ... I said to my colleagues that we had to do something,' he said. He made his way to the front of the crowd, where there was a lorry with loud-speakers on it. When he told two students who were in the lorry he wanted to speak to the crowd, one of them suggested that it would be better to do it from the Central Committee building's balcony.

So Roman and two of his colleagues pushed forward to the entrance of the Central Committee building. 'We entered the building. No one tried to stop us – in fact, the contrary. We saw a line of guards – Securitate – with their guns lying at their feet ... I went to the top floors to see what was happening,' he said.

The building was now swarming with people. General Voinea was on the sixth floor when he was grabbed by a man, a gypsy, who said, 'You bastard! You killed my brother in Timisoara.' The General replied that he had not been in Timisoara, then felt someone tugging at his sleeve. It was Petre Roman, who said, 'Mr General ... I am Petre Roman, a university lecturer. Is the army with the people?' Voinea said, 'If the army were not with the people, you would not be standing here now.' Roman then suggested that they should go to make a declaration to the people in the square that the dictator had fallen and that the army supported the revolution.

They went to the balcony, where a line had been rigged up to connect a microphone to the loudspeaker van below. Roman says, 'The loudspeakers were really strong ... I think I was the first to speak to the crowd ... Others had chanted slogans, but I was the first to speak ... I said simply, "We today now say the dictatorship of Ceausescu is abolished. We, the people, now proclaim the power of the people!"' Roman had just stepped into history, although he probably did not know it. He said later, 'I doubt if anyone in the crowd knew who I was!'

They retreated from the balcony and made for the special TV studio in the building that Ceausescu had used for his broadcasts, which they intended to use to make

Ceausescu's last speech, Palace Square,
21 December 1989

The break-up of pro-Ceausescu demonstration,
21 December 1989

The Ceausescus fleeing from the Central Committee Building, 22 December 1989

Major Vasile Malutan – the Ceausescu's helicopter pilot

Female student confronting soldiers, Bucharest, 22 December 1989

Passersby running from terrorist sniperfire at the Romanian
TV centre, Bucharest, 22 December 1989

Ole, Ole, Ole, Ole, Ceausescu Nu Mai e, Bucharest,
22 December 1989

Petre Roman addressing the
crowd in Palace Square,
22 December 1989

The mortuary at Brasol,
23 December 1989

First television pictures of Iliescu proclaiming provisional
government, 23 December 1989

Romania's first 'free' newspaper, Bucharest,
24 December 1989

Candles being lit for the martyrs of the Revolution
in Timisoara

The 20 May 1990 Elections: Nicu Ceausescu votes

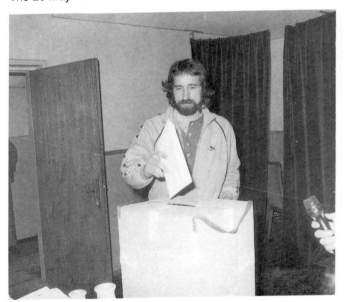

Valentin Ceausescu takes his turn

Zoia Ceausescu casts her vote

Vigil for the martyrs of the Revolution – Bucharest

Ion Iliescu, President of Romania

A great debt is owed to Udroiu Neagu and Florin Nicodim at
ROMPRES who gave the authors access to the photo library at
ROMPRES, and to Razvan Theodorescu who allowed them to view
film from the Revolution at Romanian Television. All photos are
copyright © *Rompres*

their declaration to the nation. On the way, Voinea said to Roman, 'It is perhaps better for you to make the proclamation. If I make it, it may be seen as a coup d'état ... You make the declaration, and my being there with you will assure the people that the army is with you.'

Roman wrote the declaration in the TV studio while they were waiting to see if the technicians could make a transmission possible. It declared in favour of democracy and pluralism, and proclaimed the fall of Ceausescu, communism and the one-party state. He said later, 'I wrote the declaration there and then. I am really pleased with it still ... even if I had had a couple of hours more, I don't think I could have done better. It was really what we wanted to say.' It was signed 'Front of the Unity of the People', and written on four light-blue 'Post-it' notelets – the type with a gummed edge for sticking 'Remember' notes to the wall.

When they discovered that it would not be possible to transmit from the Central Committee building, they went to the TV centre through the crowds out on the streets in one of the cars used by officials of the regime. 'I remember the car was a black Dacia of the [Party] apparatus, and so as to be recognised by everyone, I waved a flag with a hole in it out of the window all the way. Everyone was yelling, "They have the declaration! Let them pass!", and people parted ... like Moses and the Red Sea!' Roman said.

In the studio at the TV centre, just before transmission, General Voinea pulled off his army boots, with some difficulty, and bullets jangled to the floor. Roman watched in amazement. Voinea laughed, and said, 'I'll tell you about this later!' Roman was flanked by General Voinea and General Chitac when the TV director told them to prepare to speak to the country. The drama of the day, and indeed the hour, had left them parched. Voinea remembers, 'Our mouths were dry ... The only thing available at the time was a vase of flowers ... We drank from it, and Petre Roman made the proclamation ... When he had finished, he said to me, "I think we should go back to the Central Committee and create a government".'

On the way out of the TV centre, Roman and Voinea met Ion Iliescu, who had been at work in the technical-scientific publishing house on the outskirts of Bucharest that morning. Roman and he were acquainted, since the publishing house had printed books he had written, and Roman's father had collaborated with Iliescu in their earlier days together in the Communist Party. Roman said, 'Mr Iliescu, the General and I are going to the Central Committee to form a government.' Iliescu asked them to wait. He said later, 'I have known Petre Roman since he was a young boy ... I knew his father ... I knew him too as a young professor of hydraulics through the publishing house, through printing his books ... but I never gave him a thought when I was going to the TV; far less that he would be the Prime Minister of Romania one day!'

Iliescu had been in touch with the heartbeat of events in Timisoara because his firm were scheduled to publish a book written by someone in the city. He says:

> I spoke with them until the 16th because there were some problems with the book ... They told me the details of what was happening, so I rang again on the 17th. All the lines were cut, so I knew that it was serious ... Everyone knew it was something big ... I was surprised when Ceausescu went to Iran and then committed the monumental mistake of the address on the 21st ... It showed how blind he was.

At around 1 p.m. on the 22nd a publishing colleague of Iliescu came to his office on the seventh floor and said, 'Come to the TV on the second floor ... There is something important happening.' Iliescu took one glance at Mircea Dinescu, the poet, speaking to the nation and declared, 'That's it, boys! I'm off ... Who's for the TV centre?' He went with three of his colleagues, first dropping his own car at home.

Unknown to Iliescu as he made his way to the TV centre, they were chanting his name hundreds of miles away in the Opera House Square in Timisoara. The general strike had held fast into its third day, and the square was packed to capacity for the third time. The revolutionary committee at the Opera House received a surprise visitor late in the morning: General Viorel Dancea, commander of the army in the Timisoara area. 'General Dancea came to the Opera and announced that he was joining the revolution and that his men were with us. A great cheer went up in the meeting-room when he told us this ... We were jubilant, although it did not last; for shortly after this, when he returned to his unit, we heard that he had been arrested,' Claudiu Iordache reported.

Nevertheless, the renewed fears for the future were short-lived. The news of the flight of the Ceausescus and the overthrow of the dictatorship reached Timisoara. 'There was uncontainable joy on the streets ... The news was acclaimed by the people ... They were dancing in the square ... Fortuna spoke of our victory from the balcony. He yelled, "Traiasca Ion Iliescu ... Traiasca Ion Iliescu!" and the name was echoed round the square ... We decided that Fortuna should go with two others to be part of the new situation.'

Colonel Zeca, chief of the garrison in the Timisoara area, arrived at the Opera House shortly afterwards. Soon he was on the balcony, speaking to the masses below. Iordache says he helped the Colonel to write his speech. Its most important statement was: 'The army is with the people.'

Back in Bucharest, Iliescu had little trouble in getting through the revolutionary security cordon surrounding the TV centre, since his face was well known to many in the capital. But when he reached the doors of the fourth-floor studio, the eager young guards there would not let him pass. The lugubrious Gelu Voican watched this scene from inside the studio. True to his avowals in the early hours of the morning, he had gone to the streets again to protest, and was in Palace Square when the Ceausescu helicopter took off. He had gone to the TV centre from Palace Square at around 2 p.m. 'Don't ask me why I went there; I felt something telling me to go,' he said. It would have irrevocable consequences for him. After he gained entry to the main TV building, he 'walked the empty corridors' that led to the fourth-floor studio. He says:

> After I had been allowed to speak on the TV, I stayed around the studio for about thirty minutes. There was indescribable disorder ... I was contemplating this troubled vacuum of power when I saw Iliescu appear at the doorway ... Without ever meeting him or knowing him, I knew everything about his reputation ... Here is the man of Providence, I thought, and I leaped across to the doorway and pulled him into the studio ... From that moment on I never left his side for days and days.

Once in the famed studio, Iliescu made a proclamation appealing to the nation for calm, and suggesting that there should be a meeting at the Central Committee building at 5 p.m. to create a structure for organising a new government. He made this proclamation between 3.30 and 4.30, by which time there had already been two serious attempts to create a new government from the chaos in the Central Committee building corridors. Ilie Verdet and Constantin Dascalescu, Ceausescu's Prime Minister, were the principal movers in this, but their efforts were doomed to fail.

After Roman had spoken from the balcony of the Central Committee building, a procession of people had come to speak in the following hours. Many were eager to have their say in history: the known, such as Colonel Pircalabescu who underlined General Vionea's message that the army was with the people; the unknown, such as

the bearded man who had to be dragged from the microphone after endlessly intoning 'Ceausescu has gone', or
the beautiful blonde girl who passed into newsreel history
standing on the wooden plinth in a tight light blue blouse,
waving a huge holed flag as the crowd below chanted 'Liber-
ta-te' as their interpretation of her revolutionary semaphore.

Now, inside Room 229, behind the first-floor balcony,
there was a cacophony of argument. Revolutionary youth,
communists, ex-communists, actors and film directors
were to the fore among those trying to bring order out of
anarchy, and, in some cases, have their inherent place-
seeking ratified by the emerging new order before it had
taken its second breath of life. About 3 p.m. Ilie Verdet
came forward to take his bow, just as demonstrators next
door, in the room of Ceausescu's adviser Constantin
Uitea, were displaying hard-core pornographic photos
taken from Uitea's desk drawers.

Verdet, who was a key figure in Ceausescu's cabal in
the Party in-fighting that took place in the struggle for the
succession to Gheorghiu-Dej in the late 1960s, had long
fallen from grace. But the fact that he was now an anonymous president of an agricultural co-operative collective
did not mean that he did not have an eye for the main
chance. He was introduced to the meeting by the bearded
Alexa Vissarion, a film director who was chairing the
proceedings.

Verdet put himself forward as a possible leader for the
new government with the opening declaration: 'Comrades, please note that I am using this form of address and
not "Mr" ... I believe we are all entitled to our own
opinion ... I have been a communist all my life. I shall find
it difficult to adjust, but I am willing to lead if you will
allow me ...' Few were convinced, although Verdet was
the first to have commanded almost total silence when he
spoke. The passage of time would validate the accuracy of
his words. Eleven months later became the president of the
Socialist Party of Labour, the reconstituted Communist

Party of Romania, after a vote-rigging fiasco to take over the Democratic Party of Labour. Manolache, who was the Party secretary at the Party academy in Bucharest when Verdet was making his bid, finished beside him as secretary of the Socialist Party of Labour.

Not even the presence of General Iulian Vlad, chief of the Securitate, at Verdet's elbow made any difference to the scepticism that greeted his appeal. The grey-haired Vlad, moving confidently and effortlessly in these waters like a white shark in search of unknowing prey, shifted allegiance and began to lobby for Dascalescu, Ceausescu's prime minister, to be given the job of putting a new government together. At 4 p.m. the alleged black-marketeer Dan Josif went to the balcony after Dascalescu had addressed the crowd and shouted, 'Do you agree that Dascalescu should be Prime Minister?' Hundreds of thousands yelled 'No!', and the Dascalescu government fell.

Minutes later, Dascalescu signed a proclamation in the name of 'The Government of the Socialist Republic of Romania' to release all political prisoners and those arrested during the days of demonstrations. He wrote at the bottom of the page, 'I have signed in a state of freedom, forced by no one'.

Sergiu Nicolaescu, the famous film director, was now part of the proceedings, handsome in his grey herringbone jacket, his grey hair swept off his forehead, his age betrayed only by the older man's habit of keeping his spectacles in the breast-pocket of his jacket. A gang of youths recognised him and insisted, 'We don't want Dascalescu!' 'As I am alive, there will be no nomenklatura in the new government,' the urbane director replied, then called to Vissarion, 'Where are the representatives of the youth? They made the revolution!' He was beginning to command the proceedings now. He turned to a Party hack, the deputy mayor of Bucharest, and said, 'Sorry, you are no good.' Suddenly, Vlad, Dascalescu and Verdet were noticeable by their absence.

*

The shock-waves of these events reached the Holy Grail of communism, the Stefan Gheorghiu Party Academy, about an hour after Ceausescu fled. For months the professors of communism had been troubled by dissension within their own learned ranks as the Young Turks of the Academy had charted the changes in Eastern Europe and had argued, even to the point that some of them were being threatened with disciplining and dismissal, that Romania, too, would have to change. The professors had not been able to recognise one of the fundamental precepts of Marx – that, in revolution as in nature, the wind blows at the tops of the trees first – even where every word of every lecture given at the Academy was scrutinised by thought policemen for deviationism. Now the mob had come forward into the streets, their twisted fury a worse nightmare than the professors could ever have imagined in the days when they were driven to obsessive paranoia by the polite questioning of the younger members of their corps.

At about 1 p.m. there was a spontaneous gathering of all the senior members of the Party Academy, from the professors down, in the Party committee meeting-room as the news of the revolution was broadcast on the radio. Most of the congregation, especially the professorial elite, the high canons of Ceausescu's church, had eyes bulging with panic. The sans-culottes had arrived to put all their pedagogical theorising about the Golden Age of communism in jeopardy, to say nothing about their privileges. A few of the younger men exchanged knowing 'What did we tell you?' looks, and it was one of their number who suggested that the TV be switched on.

The proceedings from the TV studio were being broadcast live. Speaker after speaker indicted communism, the *raison d'être* of most of those gazing at the TV in the Academy, hands over mouths in perplexity, eyes wide in disbelief. Then an announcement was broadcast on behalf of the revolution: 'Academics skilled in the following disciplines are required to come to the TV centre and make themselves known ... Economics ...' As the word of the discipline was uttered, two or three in the room raised their hands hesitatingly in a volunteering gesture, whispering 'Me' in apparent relief. And as the announcer continued with further academic demarcations: '... International Affairs ... History ... Law ...' so his requests were met with increasing numbers of volunteers. Then the hammer-blow fell. The announcer finished with the valedictory qualification: '... only non-members of the Communist Party will be considered.' At this, the chief of the Philosophy Department at the Academy – Marxist–Leninist philosophy – gasped into the stunned silence, 'My God, we are done for!'

As the learned professor was making his exclamation in the capital, another man, Nicolae Croitoru, was drawing a different conclusion at another spontaneous meeting, not in the hallowed halls of communism, but in the bowels of the earth at the bottom of the pit-shaft in the Vulcan mine, in the Jiu Valley, 250 miles away. Croitoru had been a face-worker for twenty-two years, the top of his left-hand thumb missing as a testimony to his 'working jail sentence', as he puts it. The miners waiting for the cage at the bottom of the shaft were in a state of agitation. As Croitoru trudged towards them, one approached and exclaimed, 'Nicolae, do you hear that they say Ceausescu has fallen?' 'Is it true?' yelled another. 'It is rumours, rumours!' 'Ceausescu has gone!' and 'It's a trick!' all swirled in contradiction.

But there was no doubt when he reached the surface. Everyone there waiting to go down on the afternoon shift was telling the disbelievers: 'Ceausescu has gone!' 'We heard it on the TV!' Croitoru had been waiting for this for a long time. 'At last it has happened ...' he thought. 'Communism is finished.' Then he took the action that would later see him elected as the leader of the miners of

Vulcan. He summoned his mates from the shift, and said, 'Right, let's empty the offices.'

The pictures of Ceausescu were the first to go, and in minutes anything in the mine connected with communism was burning in a bonfire near the main gate as the 'Hurrahs' went up. Then, emboldened, Croitoru led his fellow avengers, still in their pit clothes, to the Communist Party headquarters in the town. They met no resistance. The red books of Ceausescu's collected works fuelled bonfires in the streets outside offices where they had been kept. However, not for the miners the niceties of draping flags over the offending metal signs of communism on buildings, as in Bucharest. Up they went to the roofs, and down into the street clanged the rusting remnants of the 'Traiasca Republica Socialista Romania' icons, broken by brutal bare hands.

Valerica Matei was the commander of the Patriotic Guard in Petrosani, the largest of the mining towns in the Jiu Valley, when the revolution came. He had been a member of the Communist Party purely from personal necessity. Like many now he says, 'Well, I was a member of the Party, but I was never a communist.' On the morning of the 22nd he was summoned to the offices of the first secretary of the Party in the centre of Petrosani and told that he would have to appear before officers of the Securitate later that morning, in the office, because complaints had been received about his openly discussing the recent broadcasts of Radio Free Europe in the office, and with members of the Patriotic Guard.

Matei says: 'This sent a chill down my spine because, if they knew this, I wondered if they knew that some of us in the Guard had discussed that if we were given the order to fire on the people, we were for turning our guns on the chiefs and fomenting an insurrection.' He need not have worried, for by the late morning in Petrosani, the offices of the Party and the county council were besieged by 'a sea of people'. When he heard this, Matei decided that it was now or never. He collected a detachment of the Guard and proceeded to the Party HQ and arrested the first secretary. Three hours can be a long time in politics. Then they headed, arms in hand, in a large detachment for the police and Securitate building. An astonishing sight met them there. All the main body of police and Securitate officers were standing outside it behind a white flag. Surrender had become the better part of valour.

Militia units were then created as the arms from the police headquarters were distributed among the people. Petrosani became a garrison. There would be no serious terrorist counter-revolution here. 'By the end of the day, the Jiu Valley was a stronghold,' Matei says. 'The miners organised armed guards at all the strategic points, and by 4 o'clock nothing could get in or out of the valley without the permission of the miners' militia.' The first decree of the new power in Petrosani was to send messengers to all the local mines, and delegates to Timisoara and Bucharest. A miner from the Lupeni mine who went to Bucharest perished in the street shootings there, a day later.

As General Voinea and Petre Roman waited for Iliescu at the TV centre, Voinea suggested that they should go first to the Ministry of Defence to check on the situation there and follow on to the Central Committee building later. At the Ministry of Defence, one of the more astonishing exchanges in a day of them took place. Voinea and Roman were shown to the office of the Minister. General Stanculescu, now without plaster cast and in full military uniform, was there with Ilie Ceausescu, the dictator's brother, who was head of the Political Council of the Ministry of Defence.

Roman was flabbergasted. He says: 'Stanculescu was standing politely talking to Ilie Ceausescu as though nothing had happened. I said to him angrily, "What is this man doing here?" Stanculescu sheepishly replied, "Well, nothing. We were just waiting ... eh ..."' Roman stormed at him, 'For God's sake, arrest him immediately and throw him in jail!' Ilie Ceausescu offered Roman his gun immediately, and asked if he could keep his personal effects from his desk; then he was taken to another room. Roman and Stanculescu exchanged looks. Roman shook his head in incredulity.

Iliescu arrived at the meeting-room behind the balcony of the Central Committee building at 5.19, according to a video film of the day's events. In a contemporary account, the news of the capture of the 'Sinisters' – Ceausescu and his wife – had been given to those there about one hour before, from the telex in the building. Iliescu pushed his way purposefully through the crowds in the corridors, followed by Roman, Lupoi, the white bearded Voican and Mircea Dinescu, ever the poet, looking slightly ridiculous in a long woollen jersey down to his knees. Dumitru Mazilu brought up the rear, his face like a haunted house.

Sergiu Nicolaescu introduced Iliescu to the crowds in Palace Square at about 5.30. Iliescu spoke powerfully, but briefly, shouting into the microphone. He announced the fall of the Government, said that the army supported the revolution and that a proclamation for the people would be established 'in a short time'. Then there was another remarkable exchange as the front ranks of the demonstration began to chant 'Free Elections! Free Elections!' and a dialogue ensued between people and platform. Iliescu recalls:

> We went to the Central Committee building, and frankly it was in a state of disarray. Many people there knew me and there was a general consensus that I should organise things ... so I tried. I went to the balcony and spoke, and the crowd demanded that we organise free elections immediately. There was a discussion there and then with the crowd ... We suggested May, and they yelled that that was too late, and

proposed March. We said that was too early. Ion Caramitru, who was at my side, suggested April to mark our people rising from the dead, but then it was generally agreed that May would do.

Iliescu left the platform and adjourned to one of the rooms off the main corridor, where one of the most important meetings of the day was beginning. In the chaos of the Central Committee building there was much to-ing and fro-ing in the meeting-room, but Iliescu had with him a core group who later became decisive on the committee established to create a provisional government. The army generals Militaru, Guse and Moraru were there, with Silviu Brucan, Birladeanu, Mazilu, Voican, Roman and Iliescu.

The meeting opened with Iliescu in the chair. Then there was personal acrimony between Brucan and Roman. Brucan asked him, 'What are you doing here? Who are you?' and Roman replied, 'I am a nobody, but that is not a problem. You do not represent the young people from the street who conquered this building, and they have to be represented here.' After this sharp exchange, there had to be a decision on what the committee was to call itself.

Roman put forward the idea of 'Front of the Unity of the People', since that was how the first proclamation had been signed. There was then lengthy discussion, during which Iliescu suggested 'Front of the National Salvation of the People', since 'the people need to be saved', and from further discussion the name 'National Salvation Front' emerged, but there was a problem. Roman explained later: 'Militaru said that the name already existed, that it had been used by a dissident professor of the university. But we passed on from that. It was not considered important.'

Then the shooting started. Four days of counter-revolutionary terror, based on Ceausescu loyalists from within the ranks of the Securitate, the hated secret police, had begun. The shots came first through the windows of the room where Iliescu and the rest were meeting. Someone yelled that the lights should be switched off, but another contradicted that, shouting that darkness would create the best conditions for infra-red sightings. Then it was clear that there was firing inside the building on its upper floors. The building was in chaos, with people running for their lives.

Remarkably, a large number of the people in the square below held their ground, lying flat in the hail of fire. Many paid for this with their lives, before the army organised a counter-attack. Inside the Central Committee building, as the army counter-attacked, those who had picked up the mantle of leadership of the revolution were making a run for it.

Iliescu left, together with Voican and Mihai Ispas, a young curly-haired revolutionary he had met at the TV centre. Iliescu says, 'We were looking for an exit, but everywhere we went there was shooting ... not only from the upper floors but from the lower floors as well ... We managed eventually to get out of the back exit at the "D" door, and went out on to Onesti Street. There was an armoured car there, and we took cover behind it ... They were shooting down from the Palace, and the bullets were zinging off the street.'

'The escape was a miracle. We were running in panic, plunging down dark corridors, glass shattering around us, guns rattling everywhere as we went,' Voican said. From Onesti Street they scuttled into Nicolae Balcescu Boulevard and, incredibly, hailed a passing taxi, which they took to the Ministry of Defence. The driver would not accept any money for the fare. 'I have never seen that young taxi-driver again, although I tried for a while after the revolution to find him ... I owe him a lot,' Iliescu says. Meanwhile, Roman and Brucan had accepted the offer of army assistance as they left the building and clambered into a nearby armoured car. However, it would not start, so they made their way in Lupoi's car to the TV centre.

General Stanculescu and Gelu Voican say that before that afternoon, when Voican came with Iliescu to the Ministry of Defence, they had never met. They struck up an immediate rapport, which was to have a decisive influence on the short-term course of events. Stanculescu says of Voican in those days: 'He had a penetrating look about him and a quasi-military manner, and somehow I did not hesitate to put my trust in him, especially since he seemed to be in the confidence of Iliescu.'

At that meeting in the Ministry of Defence, Stanculescu took Voican aside and told him, 'I know where the "Sinisters" are. We have them in an army barracks in Tirgoviste.' This was before any of the others knew. Voican replied, 'How quickly can we kill them?' and the plot was hatched. Before this, Stanculescu had considered the option of the summary execution for the pair and had even arranged a secret call sign for Colonel Chemenici, commander at the army base in Tirgoviste. The cryptic message, 'Resort to the method', was the agreed order to proceed with the immediate execution of the Ceausescus.

Stanculescu and Voican felt that the execution of the Ceausescus was a vital part of the strategy to defeat the counter-revolution, and agreed that the explanation could be offered that they had been 'shot while trying to escape'. The two then arranged that Voican would later attempt to secure Iliescu's agreement, and that if that was achieved, a telephone message from Voican to Stanculescu saying, 'Resort to the method', would indicate that the plan should be put into action. Voican took Stanculescu's direct-line telephone number – his short number – before leaving for the TV centre with Iliescu.

Later that night he talked to Iliescu there. He told him: 'They have to be killed, otherwise the counter-revolution will go on and on ... We can say they were shot trying to escape.' Iliescu replied, 'It is inconceivable ... There has to be a trial. How can we begin democracy with a crime, killing them, and a lie, saying they were shot trying to run away?' These arguments held sway with the leading group, Roman, Brucan, Ionescu and others, at the TV centre.

Voican says, 'Iliescu was idealistically humanitarian. He was in favour of a large-scale process to indict the whole Ceausescu dictatorship, not merely on the level of the recent genocide, but on the so-called "Golden Era" as a whole ... At this time everyone was in favour of a "Nuremburg trial", but that was before the extent of the killings of the terrorist counter-revolution was clear ... I had to tell Stanculescu that Iliescu and the others were not persuaded. I felt: how could I spoil Iliescu's reputation?'

As 22nd December passed into the 23rd, the most important meeting of the day was drawing to a close in the presidential suite on the eleventh floor of the TV centre. Iliescu had brought together those from the meeting at the Central Committee building, as well as others, to draft the declaration to the country and announce the provisional committee of government. They talked for a long time. Petre Roman remembers:

Now, at the meeting at the TV centre I had been on the go for a straight fifteen hours, but I never thought about the fact that I had left the house that morning as a protester and now here I was with these men discussing the plans for the new government ... I was absolutely determined to fight for my ideas, for the renewal. To bury the old system once and for all was my sole idea, not to have the same thing, not to conserve the old regime in any form.

It was clear to me that Iliescu had the same position, as did Birladeanu, but obviously Militaru and Brucan were not thinking exactly like us ... Militaru said at one stage that the Front had to be an organisation of the Party and state, which was the old concept of Ceausescu ... and Brucan spoke all the time about people, not ideas ... He was very eager to put up the names of the men he thought should rule. He had a scenario, I think.

Thus, through discussion, the platform was elaborated. Roman says:

The platform had ten points, but they were all connected to the central idea of democracy. It was really a charter of human rights, a democratic declaration. It was a platform of a democratic society, without any ideological direction ... the platform even clearly explained that ... It was only at the end that we realised that we would have to sign it. Somebody said that we should just sign it as the Council of the Front, but then we agreed that we needed more names. So in a hurry we drew up the names of the first Council of the Front. There were thirty-one or thirty-three, I don't remember exactly.

Ion Iliescu's recollections of the critical meeting are similar:

In the evening and night of the 22nd we drafted the ten-point call to the country concerning democratisation, the market economy and so forth. Then we hastily put together a list of names with people from the first lot from the Central Committee building discussion, the first group that assumed responsibility for power and decision-making. Then that was improvised from among those that were at the TV centre that night, to which we added the names of known dissidents like Doina Cornea, Mircea Dinescu, Ana Blandiana, Corneliu Manescu and others that I don't recall exactly.
  This list was written in the presidential room on the eleventh floor ... People came there with suggestions ... On the spot I called for some young people, students, and I said that the list should remain open to

be completed by representatives in other categories and then completed with the presidents of all the county councils of the Front formed in the country.

And so we proclaimed the abolition of all the state bodies, ministries of government and the State Council and so forth, and their replacement by the Council of the National Salvation Front and the councils of the Front at county and local level.

Thus in the early hours of the morning of 23rd December, in front of the sign in the fourth studio of the TV centre which read 'Televiziunea Romana Libera', flanked by Roman, Voican, Mazilu, Brucan and a host of young people, Iliescu announced to the country that indeed the dictator and communism were gone and a new provisional government was born. It would be a child of controversy from its birth. As the broadcast ended, Iliescu looked at the unkempt appearance of most of those around him, and said to Roman, 'I have a government of *golani* [tramps].'

CHAPTER 13

The Flight of the Ceausescus

Nicu Ceausescu knew it was going to be a long and perilous day. At 5.30 a.m. he was standing shaving in the bathroom of his Party villa. He had never turned out to the office without shaving, in the two years and two months he had been the first secretary of the Party in Sibiu, despite his binge drinking. Today would be no exception, although he felt as though the pale green walls of the bathroom were closing in.

As he shaved his heavy stubble, he considered what he should take with him. He knew things were bad. Yesterday's demonstrations had been a terrible warning of what was to come. Walking on the streets then, among the demonstrators, he had thought that things might have been different if his father had resigned at the November congress. But it was too late. Now it was 'Jos Ceausescu!' and six dead in Sibiu since the afternoon, on top of the Timisoara toll. He had consoled himself then that the crowds did not molest him before he sought refuge in the Party office behind a cordon of Securitate men with

Kalashnikovs. 'At least it's not "Jos Nicu Ceausescu!",' he joked with the two Securitate guards with him. But he knew now that when his father went, he would go too. That is why he took his gun from the drawer in the bedside cabinet and put in his belt.

Daniela Vladescu, who had been Nicu Ceausescu's lover for two years, was combing her hair at the dressing-table mirror. They had made a plan the previous night to flee together if necessary. So he began to put a few of his things in his small travelling-case, and Vladescu added some of hers. She had been staying at the villa recently. Since 19th December she had been singing in an operetta in nearby Brasov.

Nicu looked at the Bible on the bedside cabinet, and put it in the case, although later he would not admit he believed in God, saying, 'I have nothing against God, and I hope He has nothing against me.' As usual, he took only a glass of milk for breakfast before leaving for the Party offices in town about 6.30.

One hour after he reached there, the street demonstrations started. The troop of Securitate officers with machine guns was still in place from the day before, but that would not last. Ceausescu talked with his Chief of Security and loyal bodyguard, Camil Sever, about leaving. Sever said that it would be better if they did not go together. Nicu Ceausescu knew why. Two hours later, his administrative secretary, Ioan Preda, deserted the building. Nicu Ceausescu knew things were definitely slipping then. That was about 9.30 a.m. He spent the next two hours pacing the floor 'like a caged lion', trying to find out what was happening in Bucharest, before fleeing by car.

In the Central Committee building in Palace Square in Bucharest, his father Nicolae was pacing like a lion too. But he was also roaring like one. He was in a ferocious rage about the demonstration in the square, which was already mustering tens of thousands. And this, despite his orders that the demonstrators should be prevented from marching there by shooting them, if necessary!

Ceausescu, like his son, had feared the worst. He had put his personal helicopter on alert ready to fly to rescue him at any moment. At 11.20 the commander of Ceausescu's flight, Lieutenant-Colonel Vasile Malutan, received instructions from General Lieutenant Opruta to proceed to Palace Square to pick up the President.

Malutan had been told to land in Palace Square, but as he flew over it, he saw that was 'clearly impossible'. He was flying in formation with four others, which he ordered back to base, and began the difficult manoeuvre of putting down on the terrace roof of the Central Committee building. It was a fitting climax to Malutan's five years in the service of Ceausescu. He had been ordered to defy meteorological reports on countless occasions, flown blind over mountains with his windscreens frozen over, flown in gales and snowstorms, 'all because Ceausescu could not be told "It cannot be done".' Malutan landed his white Dauphin, no. 203, on the terrace at 11.44. A man brandishing a white net curtain from one of the windows waved him down.

He kept the engines roaring, now desperate about his predicament. If he took Ceausescu, he might be shot by the revolutionaries; if he didn't, he might be shot by the Securitate. He asked the chief of Ceausescu's Securitate bodyguard, General Neagoe, what was happening. 'Some of the demonstrators have broken into the Central Committee building ... The Comrade is talking to them,' he was told. Malutan says:

> Then Stelica, the co-pilot, came to me and said that there were demonstrators coming to the terrace. Then the Ceausescus came out, both practically carried by their bodyguards ... They looked as if they were fainting. They were white with terror. Manescu [one of the Vice-Presidents] and Bobu [Secretary to the Central Committee] were running behind them.

Manescu, Bobu, Neagoe and another Securitate officer scrambled to the four seats in the back ... As I pulled Ceausescu in, I saw the demonstrators running across the terrace ... There wasn't enough space. Elena Ceausescu was in the front with the co-pilot, and Ceausescu and I were squeezed in between the chairs and the door ... We were only supposed to carry four passengers ... We had six ... The Dauphin dropped like a stone after take-off ... It dropped about fifteen or twenty metres before it gained sufficient power to climb away. It was lucky we took off from such a height, otherwise we could not have got airborne.

According to Malutan's military punctiliousness, it was 12.08. Ceausescu, the leader of one of the most powerful police states in history, had been reduced to fleeing, the wolves of retribution snapping at his heels, in an overloaded helicopter. And he did not know where to go. As the Dauphin rose, Malutan asked, 'Where now?' 'Dimbovita, maybe, or Arges or Dolj counties ... Where do you think?' the beleaguered Ceausescu replied, trickles of sweat running down his forehead below his peasant-style Astrakhan hat.

At about this time, Nicu Ceausescu got through to the Ministry of Defence. He was told his father had fled. 'I knew then it was all over,' he said. Nicu left Sibiu with Daniela Vladescu in her metallic blue Oltcit car at just after 12.30. He, also, was unsure where to go – to Bucharest or to Brasov, where Vladescu had a flat. When he left, the death-toll in Sibiu was seven. By the end of the day, the unofficial estimates would be ten times that.

Malutan landed the Dauphin in the meadow beside the palace at Snagov, some twenty miles north of Bucharest, at 12.18. The Ceausescus were running across the lawns into the palace before the rotor-blades had stopped turning. Ceausescu took Malutan into the presidential suite and ordered him to get two helicopters filled with soldiers for an armed guard, and a further Dauphin to come to Snagov. Malutan's unit commander told him on the phone, 'There has been a revolution ... You are on your own ... Good luck!'

Malutan pretended to make a few more phone calls, then told Ceausescu that he had to return to base to raise help and get a replacement helicopter since his own was damaged. Elena Ceausescu seemed to accept this, but Nicolae said, 'Just whose side are you on? Are you abandoning the cause?' and then ordered Malutan to make ready to leave. Malutan told his co-pilot that if the second engine was warmed up before their passengers had made it to the helicopter, they should 'make a run for it'. But the six arrived in time. He told them that he could not take all six. 'Manescu and Bobu insisted they should stay ... They were like men who had slipped their heads out of the noose ... Manescu kissed the dictator's hands as they left,' he said.

Ceausescu commanded Malutan to head for Titu, a small town six miles from Pitesti, which had a military airport. Malutan was determined to get his head out of the noose as well, so he headed for the air force base at Otopeni, near Bucharest. Ceausescu realised this, and again demanded through clenched teeth, 'Whose side are you on?' The Securitate officer took his radio earphones from him and threatened to kill him if he did not obey orders.

Near Titu, Malutan says that he made the helicopter dip up and down. He lied to Ceausescu, saying that this was to avoid anti-aircraft fire, since they would now be in range. The dictator panicked, and told him to land. He did – in a field next to the old road that led to Pitesti. Malutan then told his four passengers that he could do nothing more. The Securitate men ran to the roadside and began to flag down passing cars. The Ceausescus followed them. Then Nicolae walked back to the helicopter with Ivan Marian, the other Securitate officer. 'So you are deserting the cause?' Nicolae asked. 'What cause and whose cause?' Malutan replied. Ceausescu made to turn away, waving his hand dismissively, then, surprisingly, he shook Malutan's hand. Ivan Marian said to Malutan, 'You will have to answer for this one day.' 'My friend, we shall all have to answer for what we have done one day,' he replied. It was 1.45.

Despite his stern words to Malutan, Marian himself had decided to 'jump ship' at the earliest opportunity. It came almost immediately. He flagged down two passing cars, one of a forestry official and one a red Dacia of a local doctor. Marian packed the Ceausescus into the Dacia with the doctor, and said he would follow them. At the first chance, he told his commandeered driver to turn in the opposite direction.

The doctor, Nicolae Deca, drove the Ceausescus and General Neagoe in the direction of Tirgoviste. He, following in Malutan's footsteps, was desperate to get rid of his passengers. Outside a village some miles on, Deca pretended to have trouble with the carburettor, stopped the car and got out. A bicycle repair man was next for the Keystone Cops routine. He would be their last driver, however.

The repair man, Nicolae Petrisor, took them to Tirgoviste and drove round the town while they deliberated what to do next. Neagoe had got out of the car at a junction to decide which way to go when a group of passers-by recognised the pair, and Elena Ceausescu ordered Petrisor to drive off. It was reported in the Romanian press that they then tried to seek refuge in a nunnery before Petrisor convinced them that they could hide successfully in an agricultural technical institute on the edge of town.

Petrisor knew one of the staff at the institute. When he got there, the director showed the Ceausescus into a room, and then locked them in. They were arrested by the local police about 3.30 p.m. Twenty-three years of unrivalled power had come to an end in the hijacking of the cars of a village doctor and a bicycle repair man. Just twelve hours earlier, Nicolae Ceausescu had had the power to call for eighty flamethrowers to be put at his disposal. How were the mighty fallen!

Nicu Ceausescu was caught much later. The Oltcit was stopped in the dusk of early evening at a road-block manned by revolutionaries and soldiers near Baneasa airport, north of Bucharest. The soldiers recognised him, and started to take him to an armoured personnel-carrier. But when the revolutionaries realised who he was, he was attacked and, in the mêlée, was knifed.

Doctors said later that his habit of having only a glass of milk for breakfast and eating dinner at night saved him. The blade narrowly missed his spleen. If his stomach had been full, he would have died. The last Nicu Ceausescu ever saw of Daniela Vladescu was her being bundled towards the armoured car. Henceforth, she would desert him.

The revolutionaries took him bleeding, to the TV centre, where his capture was broadcast to the nation about 10 that night. His reputation in Sibiu for doing his best for the people there had not travelled with him to Bucharest.

Nicu Ceausescu had tried to escape the inevitable for most of the day, but from late morning he knew really that this was all in vain. 'When I left Sibiu on the 22nd, I knew that it was finished ... I had phoned one of the army leaders earlier, and he told me that my parents had fled ... and there were people in the Central Committee building. I knew then that it was all over,' he said.

CHAPTER 14

The Days before Christmas

One of the most evocative pieces of journalism in the British press concerning the events of the revolution was written by Michael Sheridan of the *Independent*, who now works as their correspondent in Jerusalem. Recounting the evening of 22nd December, he wrote:

> At about 7 p.m. I was in my room on the fifteenth floor of the Intercontinental Hotel when a sound like popping firecrackers echoed across the rooftops. About one minute later came the nauseating rumble of heavy machine-gun fire, a sound like a stack of steel chairs crashing over.
>
> Only 200–300 yards away, the hated Securitate, Mr Ceausescu's 'anti-terrorist' Praetorian Guard, had emerged from its sewers – the network of secret tunnels it built long ago – to open fire on the crowd around the Party Central Committee offices. I ran outside in the darkness. People were screaming, jeering and whistling. Incredibly, though, they were not running away from the source of fire, but towards it ...
>
> Indifferent, the security men blazed away from one

of Ceausescu's monumental follies. Armed soldiers, standing amid the crowd, began shooting back, while the people, maddened by tiredness, alcohol and euphoria, bellowed their hate. Within minutes everyone in the city centre could see and hear that a concerted counter-revolution by the secret police was in progress. This was phase one: pitched battle. By about 8.30 p.m. the speakers on the national television were pleading for help at the radio and television stations, not far away to the north, 'Bring the army units! We appeal to the people to come!' they said.

Shots began whistling down Nicolae Balcescu Boulevard, short bursts of automatic weapon fire that rang much closer in the ears than the mayhem just around the block at the Central Committee. This was phase two: random sniping attacks to sow terror and chaos . . .

By 10 p.m., battle was raging all around. Outside the Intercontinental Hotel and in the square the army was firing tank rounds and machine guns. Astonishingly, people stayed put, their defiance carried on the national television . . . The thud of tank cannon came from the radio station. More muffled reports resounded from the direction of the TV station where foreign journalists were trapped with the people calling themselves the National Salvation Front . . .

By 3 a.m. Saturday there was nothing for it but to venture back upstairs and try to sleep, head wrapped between two pillows to muffle the incessant banging . . . Towards 5 a.m., the army began a ferocious bombardment of the Central Committee building. Even above the noise of it, I could discern the sharper crack of automatic weaponry just a few balconies away. Evidently the 'terrorists' were still in residence. . . . By daylight, the army had won the battle of Bucharest through sheer firepower, but the terrorist attacks went on.

*

These killing-fields of Bucharest were replicated throughout Romania. The renegade elements of the Securitate, the 'terrorists', as they became known throughout the country, had national co-ordination, and operated in a similar fashion in most of the main towns. Claudiu Iordache remembers, 'It was cold on the 22nd in Timisoara; until then, the weather had been extraordinarily mild. It had been like an extra five divisions in our victory ... In the evening, by 8 or 9 p.m., it was cold and the crowd was dissipating. We had announced the 23rd as a Feast Day. I thought our troubles were over. Then the shooting started from the rooftops of the Opera House Square.' Mayhem followed. Isabela Prina said, 'It was like Beirut here for days after that.'

All over Romania there were shootings, snipings and murder. In the seaside town of Constanta, for example, most of the sixty-nine martyrs of the revolution died struggling to defend the power of the new order, not fighting to take it from the old. These were the killing-fields that took the official death-toll of the days of revolution to 1043, although that is probably an underestimate since many bodies were disposed of by the Ceausescu death squads. When time was taken to remember the dead, it was found that the coffins of the revolution were most commonly filled with young soldiers. They repaid the debts they owed, with interest, in those days of slaughter.

Romania's first post-revolution government and political party, to herald the new democracy, were born in these circumstances. Iftene Pop, who had walked the empty streets in despair in the early morning, had met three or four of his colleagues in the late afternoon after being at the TV centre, and founded the 'Christian National Peasants' Party'; hours later, they composed the first proclamation of the Party programme and stayed up all night to print it in a broadsheet they called 'Renasterea' ('Renaissance'). Five thousand copies of it were on the streets the next morning.

As Pop, Alexandru, Neagra, Petrina and others were drafting 'Renasterea', as Sheridan reports above, 'the people calling themselves the National Salvation Front' were under siege at the television centre. To be absolutely precise, they were under the table in the office of the former president of the television station.

Maria Borza, who had been the president's secretary, reports:

> The shooting started around 10 p.m., just after the arrest of Nicu Ceausescu was broadcast on the TV. There was panic, because the firing was coming through the windows. Iliescu, Roman and the rest of them crawled under the table. The first instructions they issued were done lying on their bellies! The firing lasted throughout the night. At 5.30 a.m. a grenade-launcher hit the floor below and a fire started ... The troops were fighting the terrorists then, but they were better equipped. It was like hell ...

The grenade explosion meant that the upper floors of the TV centre were without water for the next days. Maria Borza recalls that she was received like the Madonna when she brought a tray of sandwiches and cigarettes to the president's office on Christmas Eve morning. Food, cigarettes and water had been scarce. One of the more famous who took one of the cigarettes was Zoia Ceausescu, held captive there, sitting on the floor of the corridor outside the offices for hour after hour.

'In those days I lost six kilos in one week through dehydration, my lips were cracked, and for four nights I had practically no sleep at all,' Iliescu said. Roman said:

> You could say that the government started to operate from the TV centre in the first days but that would be inaccurate really because we were only issuing appeals by the telephone, keeping in contact with military units,

and liaising with similar councils that had been formed in towns all over the country ... Every town had formed its local Front Council, and they called us for advice on this point and that point ... That was the only sense at this stage that the Council ruled anything ... When I was phoning, I had to present myself, so I used just to say, 'I am phoning on behalf of the Front', 'Imputernicit al Frontului', that was my only rank or title.

Despite Roman's qualifications, it is true to say that the committee at the TV station became the centre of decision-making. There were committees operating at the Central Committee building and at the Ministry of Defence, but their authority was subservient to the Council of the Front at the TV centre, now led by Iliescu and Roman.

In the circumstances of this kind of dual power, the emerging government power under assault from the counter-revolution, Romania became Rumourania: 'The water supply has been poisoned. Don't drink it'; 'The terrorists have been sent from Yasser Arafat to defend Ceausescu'; 'The terrorists are sending a squadron of sixty helicopter gunships to attack the new provisional government'; 'There are only a few terrorists operating from a secret location, detonating machine-gun fire using electronic devices'; 'Ceausescu loyalists have taken control of the airport', and so on, as the killing continued.

Gelu Voican was convinced he was right. He was firing verbal bullets at Iliescu, Roman and the rest, as the murder went on unabated. With fresh news of incidents and casualties, he would approach Iliescu and insist that this would not stop until the Ceausescus were dead and their followers knew that their counter-revolution was leaderless, and restoration of the old order a vain hope.

Then, in the early morning of Christmas Eve, the TV centre came under heavy bombardment; so heavy, that it was decided that an evacuation was necessary. According to Petre Roman, when the leading group reached the first floor as they made to leave the building, they came under direct fire from a Securitate' terrorist, the survivor of a group of eight who had breached the defences of the building. Only the armed guard accompanying Iliescu and the others saved them. Then, as they came out of the armoured cars that took them to the Ministry of Defence, that location came under heavy fire. Machine-gun bullets zinged off the tarmac as the leaders of the Front scurried, heads down, to the shelter of the Ministry.

Voican cornered Iliescu in one of the meeting-rooms immediately. He said to him, 'This is the fourth or fifth time you have come under fire; how long do you think you can escape the bullets? These people are madmen. We caught one of them last night, and he told us, "We have an oath of allegiance to Ceausescu, not to the country, and until he is dead, the bloodshed will continue. The others will not stop." It is clear in my mind that we have to deal with the Ceausescus. How long are you going to delay facing up to reality?' For the first time, Iliescu exhibited hesitation. Then he insisted that here would still need to be a trial.

Stanculescu and Voican began a pincer movement on the rest, developing the same arguments. As a supreme irony, the state of emergency that Ceausescu had instituted allowed for ordinary citizens to face summary trial under military laws. Thus the legal pretext for Ceausescu's summary execution derived from his own draconian statues. 'Shot' by his own petard, you might say.

Voican says, 'Brucan and Roman came towards the position first, and then with the others coming round, we could assault the idealism of Iliescu.' A plenary meeting was called in the cabinet room of the Ministry of Defence just before midday. All the leading members of the Council of the Front were there: Brucan, Roman, Militaru, Mazilu, Cazimir Ionescu, Stanculescu, Voican and Iliescu. Before the meeting started, Voican drew

Iliescu aside into the bathroom off the cabinet room. In a whisper, he told him, 'I remain convinced that the fanaticism will die with the Ceausescus. They are all agreed next door. And there is a legal basis for proceeding under the regulations of the state of emergency which allow the trial of civilians under military conditions of summary trial.' Iliescu replied, 'What does Stanculescu say?' Voican replied, 'He agrees.' 'Very well,' Iliescu conceded.

So about midday they agreed that the Ceausescus should face a summary trial under military conditions. It could have only one verdict. Stanculescu agreed to make the arrangements for the trial and execution. Someone else from the Council of the Front would have to attend. All eyes turned to Voican. After all, it had been his idea.

The fate of the Ceausescus was thus sealed. The preparations started after the plenary meeting. Had the resolve needed for this decision required any stiffening, it came in the early evening with news from the military barracks in Tirgoviste, where the Ceausescus were being held. Colonel Chemenici, the commander at the barracks, phoned the Ministry of Defence to inform them that the base had come under serious machine-gun assault. He was told to remove the couple from the base to a place of safety.

So on the evening of 24th December Ion Iliescu, the chairman of the Council of the National Salvation Front, wrote the decree authorising the summary trial of the Ceausescus. He hand-wrote it for fear that a typed script might be copied and fall into the wrong hands.

At about the same time as Iliescu was putting pen to paper for this decree, Maria Borza at the TV centre was typing another, annulling the abortion laws of the dictatorship which had made Romania the septic abortion capital of Europe. At least 25,000 women had died of this condition from the time abortion was made illegal in 1967, according to authoritative medical opinion.

Iliescu and Roman slept on the floor of the cabinet room of the Ministry of Defence that night. The buccaneering Voican and the young revolutionary Mihai Ispas, stood guard all night outside the room; Voican with a gun in his belt in case the counter-revolution knew of the day's decisions and made a last desperate attempt to save their doomed dictator, by murdering Iliescu and Roman.

— CHAPTER 15 —

The Trial

After their capture, the Ceausescus were taken to the army barracks in Tirgoviste, the main town of the Dimbovita region ninety miles north-west of Bucharest. The headquarters of the barracks, which used to be a cavalry school, is a rather grand old building in the centre of town. Today you can see the bullet-marks on its front from the onslaught of the Securitate troops on Christmas Eve, when they made their last desperate attempt to free their leader. When that assault took place, the commander of the barracks had the Ceausescus bundled into an armoured car and secluded in a remote part of the base. They spent their last night there, unaware of what its portents were.

General Victor Stanculescu carried out the preparations for the trial with military precision and punctiliousness. In fact, if you speak to him now about it, he is prepared to say that some of the precautions taken then might seem excessive, but 'that would only be from hindsight, because there was great apprehension about the power of the counter-revolution at the time, and understandably so.'

Colonel Gica Popa, a military lawyer, was selected as the prosecutor, with Colonel Ion Nistor as his supporting prosecutor. Major Dan Voinea was enlisted as chairman of the tribunal. Stanculescu then used the good offices of people who worked in his advisory team to carry out other important tasks: Colonel Ion Baiu filmed the proceedings, Major Mugurel Florescu and Sergeant-Major Trifan Matenciuc went as military magistrates on the tribunal, the full tribunal board being made up by three other military personnel from the Tirgoviste barracks, and Sergeant Jan Tanasa made the written record.

The chief defence lawyer was Nicolae Teodorescu, with Constantin Lucescu as his assistant. They were chosen not for any particular noted brilliance of reputation but purely from the expedient reality that they lived in the residential area of Drumul Taberei in Bucharest that is adjacent to the grounds of the Ministry of Defence.

Teodorescu and Lucescu, the civilians, sped the ninety miles to Tirgoviste by road under military escort. The arrangements made for Voican and Virgil Magureanu, the other civilian who attended, and the military personnel, were more elaborate. On Christmas morning three helicopters took off from the Steaua Bucharest football pitch in the Ghencea stadium near the Defence Ministry. One of the helicopters took the officials for the trial and the other two carried members of the elite Parachute Regiment whose number would provide the guard and firing squad for the execution.

These three helicopters were joined by a further two just north-west of Bucharest to complete the formation that flew to Tirgoviste. This allowed the main group of three to fly near ground level, in zig-zag formation, with the other two providing air cover from above. If you want something done properly in Romania, speak to Victor Stanculescu! As the formation flew into the army barracks,

Stanculescu held a yellow scarf out of the lead helicopter's cockpit as a sign to the army commanders there that this was not an enemy attack zooming in.

Ceausescu gasped as he bent double to emerge from the armoured carrier. He took off his familiar black Astrakhan fur hat and ran the fingers of his left hand through his greying hair, showing the gold Rolex on his wrist, before entering the headquarters. He had not shaved, and looked bemused when examined by an army doctor before the trial commenced. This bemusement is understandable, given that until the two were told at this moment that they were being examined to establish their physical fitness to stand trial, they had been told that they were being held at Tirgoviste for their own protection.

Although outwardly quite calm, Ceausescu was in a state of high anxiety, as demonstrated by his blood pressure, which was 170 over 150. He said nothing during the examination. Elena uttered her only word, a curt 'No', when she was asked if she was hungry.

They wore the same clothes as three days previously, when they had stood on the balcony of the Central Committee building before fleeing from its roof in the helicopter. He was in a dark suit with a blue fur-lined jacket over it. She wore a light fawn wool coat with a brown fur collar, perhaps having hurriedly eschewed her penchant for all-fur efforts; a blue head-scarf of modern design was tied below her chin. In a few hours it would be bloodied, as the firing squad's bullets ripped into her body.

The tribunal was in place in a lecture-room of the head-quarters when the Ceausescus were brought in. Two brown formica tables set at right-angles in the corner of the room formed the makeshift dock for what was to be a makeshift trial. The accused sat down at the chairs behind the table; the video film of the proceedings catches pale yellow walls and a dirty white floral net curtain as their backdrop.

The chairman of the tribunal began the proceedings by asking the defendants to stand to hear the charges against them. Ceausescu immediately spat out, 'Read the country's constitution.' The judge replied, 'You want us to read the constitution? We know it better than you ... you who never observed it.' This exchange was to be typical of all that was to come.

Teodorescu, the defending lawyer, then rose to explain his role as Counsel for the Ceausescus, but was violently rebuffed by the dictator, who yelled, 'I do not recognise you!' Unbelievably, Teodorescu meekly played little further part in the proceedings.

So with the Ceausescus seated in defiance, Gica Popa, the Prosecutor, read out the charges. He said: 'Today we have to try Nicolae Ceausescu and Elena Ceausescu, who are guilty of serious crimes against the people, incompatible with human dignity. They have behaved as despots towards the Romanian people, and for these crimes we consider the two guilty, and ask the tribunal to sentence them to death.'

The charges were then read out. They were:

1. The genocide of more than 64,000 victims.
2. Organising armed rebellion against the people and the state.
3. The destruction of public assets, buildings, etc.
4. Sabotage of the national economy.
5. Attempting to flee the country with funds of more than a billion dollars deposited in foreign banks.

The number of deaths listed in the first charge was an entirely arbitrary figure. It had been reached by Gelu Voican estimating that 60,000 would be an adequate estimation of the number of people who had died in recent years of cold and hunger, added to 4,000, the number of conjectured deaths in Timisoara after a Yugoslav newspaper had published this estimate a day or two earlier.

Prosecutor: Have you heard this? Please stand up.

Ceausescu: Everything that has been said is a lie. I do not recognise this tribunal ... I recognise only the Grand National Assembly.

This was to be Ceausescu's mantra of defiance throughout the trial, in what was to become a successful attempt to cast his prosecutors as vengeful persecutors who never gave him, or his wife, a fair hearing. Whether this was a conscious strategy or a product of Ceausescu's false hopes that he would be rescued from his captors does not alter the fact that his refusal to recognise the court robbed the provisional government of the legitimacy it desired in executing the pair, even if the whole country agreed with the verdict.

Voican said later: 'We lost the legal process because the prosecutor and the defence lawyers lost the place, they cracked under the strain ... Although, because it was a summary trial, it would not have made any difference anyway to the verdict ... that would have remained the same.' Iliescu also admitted later: 'I regret that we could not do it properly, but it was a necessity at the time.'

These final hours were Ceausescu's personal history turning full circle, in a manner of speaking. His refusal to recognise the tribunal of the National Salvation Front could be compared to his defiance of the courts of the royal dictatorship of King Carol II, when Ceausescu was a young communist agitator in the 1930s. However, then he spoke with determination born of hope in the future; now with a stubbornness born of despair. If the last stand is some form of mirror image of the earlier days, then it is a distorted one, through a prism of light that has been cracked top to bottom by the passage of history.

Prosecutor: You know the drastic situation that prevailed throughout Romania before 22nd December?

Popa then makes reference to the 'dawn of freedom'. Ceausescu laughs, raises his eyes to the ceiling and blows out his cheeks incredulously. Then he says, 'I leave all reply to the Grand National Assembly. Those who have organised this *coup d'état* were in the service of capitalism and the western powers ... I don't reply.'

Prosecutor: Who ordered the army to shoot the crowd at Timisoara? You say you don't know, but do you know that in Palace Square in Bucharest people were killed, shot, and it is still going on? There are people dying, old people, women and children ... Who are these madmen who are killing them, who paid them, who trained them?

Ceausescu: I don't reply to any questions ... I never gave any order to the army to shoot the mob in Palace Square.

Elena Ceausescu is becoming animated now and looks to be drawn into the argument. Nicolae maintains the protective role he has taken from the beginning, taking her hand in his, and asking her to calm down, while shaking his head each time her mouth opens to reply in anger. He tells her quietly not to speak on several occasions throughout the trial. She becomes more assured, patting her bun of brown hair, her head-scarf down round her neck.

Prosecutor: And what about her now, the guilty woman? ... Thousands have died as a result of your orders at the time when your husband was in Iran ... Who gave the orders to shoot in all the towns? Who ordered the destruction of these towns built by the people and not by you, with your lack of culture and intelligence? ... Who are the foreign mercenaries who are shooting now?

At this stage Gelu Voican passed his first note to Popa, telling him to get on with the proceedings and avoid further personalisation of the charges.

Ceausescu (answering for his wife): This is a provocation, and I don't reply to any questions. I will answer only to the people.

Prosecutor: Who recruited the foreign mercenaries who are committing acts of terror at the present time?

Elena Ceausescu, you are usually so talkative, our academician who does not know how to read ... (a reference to the fact that Elena Ceausescu had to be addressed always as 'Comrade, academician, doctor, engineer Ceausescu').

Elena Ceausescu (with her head supported on her cupped hand, her elbow propped on the table, says dismissively): Only the intellectuals of this country will hear you ... You have denied me my rights.

Prosecutor: What is preventing you from speaking?

Ceausescu: I repeat that I will reply only to questions in front of the Grand National Assembly and the representatives of the working class ... I don't recognise you. (He is angry now, and bangs his fist down on the table after this riposte.)

Prosecutor: The Grand National Assembly no longer exists ... The people have created the Council of the Front for National Salvation, the people with their sacrifice ... that is who they recognise. Why is there still shooting?

Ceausescu: This power was established with the help of foreign agents. In time I will speak publicly about this, but I do not recognise your authority ... I shall tell the truth, not work to destroy Romania, as you are.

Prosecutor: I have to make a point, from the legal side of things ... I hope you understand that you have lost all positions you held, you have been stripped of the Presidency and your position as Head of the Party ... I hope your wife, Elena Ceausescu, realises she has lost all her positions also ... Are you clear that you face trial as ordinary citizens, that your government has been overthrown?

Ceausescu: I am the President of Romania and the Chief Commander of the army ... and I do not recognise any of the capacities you claim. I recognise you only as simple common citizens ... I am the President of the Socialist Republic of Romania. I will not answer to those who with the help of a foreign power carried out a coup

... This is a nonsense! I am still the President of the Republic.

Prosecutor: Why did you reduce the Romanian people to the state of humiliation they suffer today? People had to come from all over the country to buy food in Bucharest ... Why did you starve the people?

Ceausescu: I will not answer your questions. You are simple common citizens, but let me tell you that for the first time the co-operative farmers have been given 200 kg of wheat per person; not per family, but per person ... (He begins to look really tired now, his sentences drifting, his voice hoarse.)

Prosecutor: You are telling lies ... If this was the truth, why did the peasants have to come to buy bread in the towns?

Ceausescu: Let one citizen come and ask me these questions and I will answer ... one citizen ... But I will not answer to you.

Prosecutor: You have talked of the wonders of your achievements, your programmes, but in fact you signed the death notice of the Romanian peasantry ... You destroyed the villages.

Ceausescu: Never! Never have the villages of Romania seen such development ... We have built schools and hospitals, and not just schools and hospitals, but we have ensured everything that is necessary for a dignified life for the citizens.

Prosecutor: Well, if we are all supposed to be equal, why did I see your daughter on television weighing out meat for her dogs on golden scales?

Elena Ceausescu: This is not true! How can you say this? (Nicolae tells her again not to speak.)

Prosecutor: What about the 4,000 million ... transferred to Swiss banks? (The signs of strain are evident in the Prosecutor, who still has not formally presented the charges. He screams this question in a stream of otherwise indistinguishable invective, his spectacles slipping down his nose as he emphasises his points with downward sweeps of his left arm.)

Elena Ceausescu: What! What fund?

Prosecutor: The fund of 4,000 million dollars.

Elena Ceausescu: The proof, the proof. Where is the concrete proof?

Ceausescu: No member of my family has deposited dollars in any foreign bank.

Prosecutor: If you are proved wrong, will you agree that the money should be brought back to the people of Romania?

Ceausescu: I will discuss only with the Grand National Assembly.

Fierce argument then breaks out between the prosecutor and Ceausescu, each hurling insults at the other. Voican passes Popa a second note, telling him to get on with it and present the charges formally, since this is all that is required.

Ceausescu (shouting): I have no part in any other country ... This is a tribunal of insults, and I (to prosecutor) will see that you face the judgment of the workers ... I don't recognise this tribunal and I gave no orders to the police to shoot the people ... I refuse to answer your questions. The taking of power was organised by foreign powers ... I am the President and the Supreme Commander ... I do not accept that I made the people hungry, or took land from the peasants ... I did not pull down the villages of Romania ... I sent no dollars abroad ... I do not recognise your authority.

Prosecutor: Will you sign the statement of guilt?

Ceausescu: I refuse to sign any statement of guilt.

Prosecutor: The guilty man refuses to accept his guilt.

Ceausescu: I have never heard of the Council of National Salvation ... There cannot be another body of power in the state without the approval of the Grand National Assembly.

Prosecutor (speaking to Elena Ceausescu): Do you know about the genocide in Timisoara?

Elena Ceausescu: What genocide?

Prosecutor: ... Are you trying to tell us you never knew about Timisoara? ... Of course, you are a woman of science, you can speak of polymers, you told us you had volumes published abroad, so if you can say this, you can say you never knew about Timisoara ...

Ceausescu: We refuse to answer before you.

Prosecutor: Why not let her answer in her capacity as the Deputy Prime Minister? As Deputy Prime Minister you had collective responsibility for the regime, you gave orders ... So I ask: who gave the order to shoot in Timisoara? Who shot the young people of Ploesti? Are the terrorists from the Securitate?

Ceausescu: No! No!

Prosecutor: I'll put this another way. Who demoted General Milea? Who shot General Milea? Why did you say that General Milea was a traitor and committed suicide? You are responsible for his life.

Ceausescu: Who told you that Milea was a traitor? ... He was given orders which he did not carry out ... The officers on duty that day told me he had committed suicide ... instead of doing his duty.

Prosecutor (to Elena Ceausescu): You were involved in all these things ... It would be better if you co-operated with the court ... For instance, can you tell us who paid for the publication of your selected works abroad (to Ceausescu), and the so-called books of science of the Academician?

Elena Ceausescu: Have you taken away my title of 'Academician'?

Ceausescu: You have said that I ate only meals prepared from abroad ... I had only 1,100 calories per day and 60 gm of meat.

Prosecutor: I want to know who gave the order to the army to shoot in Timisoara.

Ceausescu: I don't reply ... I will answer only to the Grand National Assembly.

Prosecutor (to Elena Ceausescu): Do you think you could be described as irresponsible, from a psychological point of view?

Elena Ceausescu: Only with the stupidities that you are bringing before me ... How can you say such things? (She then resorts to village slang.)

Prosecutor: ... You have learned nothing even from today's proceedings ... Do you have a defence statement?

Defence Counsel (Teodorescu): We want to make a last attempt ...

Ceausescu: I don't want to say anything ... Please leave me ... I recognise nothing here.

Teodorescu: Please note for the record that they refused to co-operate with their defence counsel.

Prosecutor: You will sign the statement?

Elena Ceausescu: No ... I have worked and fought for the people since I was fourteen years old ... (She thumps the table in anger, and again Nicolae stretches out a restraining hand to take her arm.)

Prosecutor (clearly now in a rage): How much were your wages? ... Because we cannot tell from the books ... the accounts ... Really, Mr President, I consider the debate to be finished. Nicolae and Elena Ceausescu are guilty of the charges quoted at the beginning ... We request that they be found guilty and sentenced to death, with the confiscation of all their goods and wealth.

Teodorescu: The defence lawyers travelled from Bucharest today to ensure that the due process of law was observed ... irrespective of the identity of those involved. We want to put that on record ... but we have to register the absolutely obstructionist position adopted by the chief accused ... He has continually referred to the calling of the Grand National Assembly ... Only the President of the country has the power to do that, and he is no longer the President ... The powers he refers to have been taken over by the National Salvation Front ...

They have therefore been tried here as ordinary citizens, and the norms of legality have been observed for this ... It is an error for the two accused not to accept defence ... I have come here to help them, and all they say is that the case is an act of provocation ... When a man is ill and is visited by an experienced physician and decides not to accept his help, it has to be accepted that he takes such a decision responsibly, recognising the consequences. The decision of the accused not to accept legal defence here today has to be seen in this light ...

The state decision brought here today should not be seen as having the character of a vendetta, nor should further tribunals of this nature. If this were not a legal process, we would have been first to say so. They refer to the constitution, but they do not know its contents. The tribunal was and is legally constituted.

(In the entire proceedings of the trial where his defendants were badgered continuously by the avenging prosecutor, this is the only lengthy statement by the defence lawyer. History might judge that he supported his clients the way the rope supports the hanging man. During this diatribe Ceausescu sat quietly, turning his Astrakhan hat over in his hands, again and again.)

Prosecutor: As regards the punishment provided in Article 162 ... I cannot make any objections. From the material put at our disposal, they are guilty of these charges ... So also the details of Article 165 and most seriously Article 350. If you impose these punishments, it would not be seen as an act of revenge but as the correct decision ...

The members of the tribunal must realise that those they sit in judgment over today, in their refusal to recognise the tribunal are also refusing to recognise the crimes they perpetrated against the people; not just those in Timisoara or Bucharest, but the crimes of decades ... the crimes of cold, of houses without heat, the crimes of poverty, of people starving, of imprisoning the soul of a nation ... and the crimes of the killings in Timisoara ... the murder of the young students ... (He loses control here, and starts to rant at the defendants. Ceausescu laughs at him and then looks down at his watch, as though to say 'How long to go?')

Prosecutor (continuing): ... And then in the basements you hid the Securitate who emerged to do more of your killing ... Romania has paid a great price for your rule, for the homage you demanded to the last ...

You do not recognise the tribunal ... but what you do not recognise in reality is that your Presidency is over. You stole power in 1947, you robbed the people of their dignity ... On some of your foreign trips, you should have stayed abroad ...

Ceausescu: No, never.

Elena Ceausescu: What are they saying?

Prosecutor: ... You two have had an odious collaboration in leadership, but you made three catastrophic errors ... The army would never agree to obey your order to shoot the workers ... You killed young people. What have you done to our children, what a price we have paid for our freedom? We have paid in blood ... You are a guilty man, Nicolae Ceausescu. What do you have to say? (He puts the questions, not managing to add the third error to the two he has already mentioned.)

Ceausescu: I am not a guilty man. I am the President of the Republic. I shall reply in front of the Grand National Assembly and to the representatives of the working class, and with this I have finished ... Everything you have said is lies from those who made the *coup d'état* to destroy the independence of Romania.

Prosecutor: What do you have to say, Elena Ceausescu?

Ceausescu: When I went to the factories, the people stood and cheered. Have you not seen that? ... No, I am finished with you.

Chairman of the Tribunal: Stand up!

Elena Ceausescu (to Ceausescu): Not here ... No, dear. We are human beings; we sit down.

Judge: In the name of the people, meeting in secret, we condemn Nicolae Ceausescu and Elena Ceausescu to the death penalty for their acts of genocide, their subordination of the state power in armed actions against the state ... and the sabotage of the national economy ...

Elena Ceausescu (with sneering disdain): Just look at them ...

Judge: ... pronounced today, 25th December.

Teodorescu: Please allow me to take the floor.

Ceausescu: I don't recognise you.

An announcement is then made by the chairman to close the proceedings, and the tribunal members leave the room. Teodorescu departs without exercising his right under the rules of summary trial to lodge an appeal, which would have delayed the execution by a further five days.

Ceausescu (yells): I don't recognise you ... Romania will live for ever ... Romania will deal with all the traitors as many as there will be. Romania will live in freedom, not with traitors! (Then he rages) A great injustice has been done ... (This is followed by a stanza from a revolutionary poem: 'Better die in the struggle with glory, than be slaves on the old land ...')

Nothing in his life became him like the leaving it, as Malcolm says in *Macbeth*.

Elena Ceausescu (yells almost simultaneously): We have had them so near us ... The traitors have been next to us all this time!

Captain Ion Boeru of the Parachute Regiment from Boteni, who was in charge of the execution, then motioned to them to come forward. Elena Ceausescu screams, 'We want to die together! Together we have fought; together we will die!'

Hurriedly their hands were tied behind their backs. They both resist this stubbornly. Elena Ceausescu wept briefly when she was being tied. As Boeru led them outside, a young soldier approaches them. 'You killed my brother in Timisoara. You are in big trouble now,' he says. Elena Ceausescu spits in rage, 'Go fuck your mother!'

CHAPTER 16

The Execution

Lieutenant-Colonel Mares had been responsible for guarding the Ceausescus since they had been brought to the Tirgoviste barracks. Now his responsibility passed to Captain Ion Boeru of the Parachute Regiment from Boteni, the commander of the firing squad.

When they left the headquarters, the Ceausescus made to go towards the helicopter stationed on the parade ground which had brought the army officers to the tribunal, as though not knowing what was coming. Boeru, who was in a terrible panic about his responsibility as hangman, guided them in another direction, to the yard where they would meet their ignominious end in front of a whitewashed brick wall, which was fading to yellow.

Exactly one month before, on 24th November, 3,308 delegates to the Romanian Communist Party Congress had unanimously elected Ceausescu as its leader, and President of the country, for a further five-year term. During the Congress, the 'outstanding champion of the communist and working-class movement' had been given sixty standing ovations by the lickspittle assembly. When asked by a journalist at the Congress if the wave of reform sweeping Eastern Europe would ever wash up on Romania's shores, Ceausescu reportedly replied, 'Yes, when there are pears on the poplars and the reeds of the marshes have flowers blooming on them.'

The day after Ceausescu's election as Party leader in November, Dennis Deletant, the renowned Romania expert from the University of London, had written in *The Times*: 'He will continue to dominate his country because the conditions for change in the rest of Eastern Europe ... do not apply in Romania's case.' On 20th December Mark Almond, also writing in *The Times*, said: 'Perhaps Ceausescu's system of dynastic socialism will collapse, but the odds are against it ... The Ceausescus may still rule in Romania when perestroika is as fond a memory as the "Prague Spring".'

Four days later Ceausescu was walking to meet his firing squad, alone in the world except for his beloved Elena. The crunch of Captain Boeru's boots on the gravel of an anonymous Romanian army base was really the sound of the tumbrils.

There were three soldiers from the Boteni Parachute Regiment in the firing squad. Behind them stood an assembly of soldiers from the barracks in a large semi-circle, waiting to witness the end. Women in the near-by flats stood out on their balconies, watching – the Romanian equivalent of the tricoteuses of the French Revolution.

Gelu Voican and General Stanculescu had made thorough preparations for the execution. It was arranged that a party of five would follow the firing squad on to the parade ground. These were Popa the prosecutor, Major Voinea the chairman of the tribunal, Tanasa the recorder, a doctor, and Voican. Tanasa was to ask the Ceausescus if they had any last wish and Voican if they wished to talk to a priest before their execution. The well-laid plans did not bear fruit.

Boeru arranged the Ceausescus before the firing squad: Ceausescu to their right, with his wife next to him on their left. The paratroopers of the firing squad took three steps back and stood to attention at the ready. Voican's party were making their way towards the two when Captain Boeru's nerve went. He pulled his revolver from his holster and, without giving any command to the firing squad, opened fire on the Ceausescus who were standing less than two metres away. His first shot hit Elena Ceausescu on the right side of her forehead. Voican swears he watched astonished as a fragment of bone sheered from her head, followed by a spume of blood. Then the startled members of the firing squad opened up. After their first volley, Elena Ceausescu was dead, shot through the head at least twice, her right shoe twisting off as she crumpled to the ground, her right leg splayed in front and her left leg folded behind. Nicolae Ceausescu sank to his knees with the first shots, and as the firing continued to riddle his body with bullets, his torso fell back, doubling over his heels. When Boeru moved forward to check the corpses, there was a pool of blood flowing from Elena Ceausescu's right temple, and Ceausescu's corpse was a stump, looking as if he had been beheaded and had his legs cut off below the knees.

It was just after 3 p.m. when Boeru gave the command to stop. The wall behind where they had stood had blotches of blood all over it. The corpses were holed with the bullets from more than a hundred rounds used by the firing squad, and quite a few of those in the crowd with a gun had taken a pot-shot too. But apart from Elena Ceausescu's head wound, their blood did not flow on the parade ground; it was mainly soaked up by the thick fur linings of their coats. It is a fable that Ceausescu sang the Internationale as he went down or cried out 'Long live a free and independent Romania!'

The film crew recording these events missed the execution because of Boeru's unexpected panic firing. This missing footage would inspire thousands of rumours about the demise of the 'Sinisters'. A short excerpt of the film was shown on Romanian television late on Christmas night. Of course, the sequence of the execution was missing. The TV version had been prepared by the film-maker, Sergiu Nicolaescu. In the TV station when it was shown, he and Voican were almost shot dead by an enraged paratrooper captain, Ion Chiranescu, who yelled at them as he advanced across the studio, his finger on the trigger, 'You have manipulated us! They are not dead!' Voican's display of colour photographs of the corpses pacified the captain in the nick of time.

The provisional government could not decide what to do with this precious record of events before a fuller showing on Boxing Day. Petre Roman eventually took responsibility for looking after the precious proof of the demise of the dictator and his wife. He slept that night with the master videotape taped to his body.

Roman remains convinced of the actions taken:

I have absolutely no doubts about the trial and execution. It was necessary for the people to see them charged ... The people wanted to see them charged with what they had done ... the poverty, the hunger, the genocide. Of course the defence lawyer did not perform at all well, and that was unfortunate, but we were victims of circumstances. If we had not executed Ceausescu, the killings would have continued ... There was no alternative to their execution at the time. As long as they were alive, there was the possibility of the terrorists organising against the revolution, at a great cost to human life and to the danger of the revolution itself ... I am absolutely convinced that all Romanians were keen to see the Ceausescus dead ... as quickly as possible ... Dead.

He says that he would do the same again if he had the chance to relive history.

General Stanculescu was, naturally, just as resolute:

It was the guarantee of the future of the revolution. Only their death gave us the assurance that a weak democracy could become a reality from just the promise of it. Those who assumed responsibility for this decision deserve great merit, despite all the accusations from all places about the legality of the trial. The victory of the revolution was only secured after 25th December. Secondly, it is an incontestable fact that the execution of the Two stopped the bloodshed, saving innumerable lives. It was the best Christmas present Romania could ever have had ... Tragic, with blood, but a Christmas present.

After the execution, the bodies were wrapped in green army tent sheets and flown to Bucharest by helicopter. Then the first of a series of bizarre happenings concerned with the death of the Ceausescus took place: the corpses disappeared. The helicopter landed at the Steaua Bucharest football field. Voican and Stanculescu went into the sports complex at the stadium and sought the help of members of a handball team to move the bodies and other effects into the awaiting armoured car. When they came out of the stadium, the bodies were missing. Voican and Baiu returned immediately to the Ministry of Defence with the video-cassette and the record of the trial. There was understandable consternation among Roman, Iliescu and company when Voican, ever the joker, told them, 'Everything went to plan, apart from the fact that the corpses are missing.'

Stanculescu groped around in the dark looking for them. 'I could not believe it! The bodies were not there. I was half worried and half embarrassed to death. How could two bodies go missing? All sorts of dark hypotheses were swirling in my head,' he recalled. His perplexity was more than matched by that of the others. They had executed the tyrants at great personal risk, and now they could not prove it!

Stanculescu left the football field in the armoured car with Teodorescu the lawyer, Sergeant-Major Matencuic, and his driver Lieutenant-Major Pancea. The tank had been requisitioned especially for this work from the militia. As they drove along the road to the Ministry of Defence, the tank drove over a dangling trolley-bus wire in the wreckage of the vicinity which had been the scene of fierce terrorist attacks. The electric wire short-circuited on the armour of the tank, which was not immediately recognisable as army equipment. The spark and report startled the defence units around the Ministry, who opened up with 14.5 mm shells.

The tank driver, Lieutenant-Major Pancea, was killed instantly and slumped over the machine-gun button in the tank, causing rapid fire. All hell broke loose as an attack on the Ministry of Defence was apparently confirmed. Teodorescu was wounded in the head in the volleys of return fire. Stanculescu, the Deputy Minister of Defence, was almost blown away by his own troops! Sergeant-Major Matencuic saved the day. He threw the turret open, and climbed out, shouting, 'Don't shoot! Don't shoot! There's a fucking General in here!' It had been a long day for Stanculescu, to say the least.

Things are never so bad once you have slept on them. Stanculescu found the bodies in the stadium the next morning. A passing patrol had discovered them and put them behind an earth mound, not knowing that they were the corpses of the Ceausescus. They were then taken to a military morgue to await the next stage in the bizarre story: the burial.

The burial took place on 30th December. Voican

organised that also. It had been delayed because, in the interim, a provisional government had been put together. Voican was one of the Deputy Prime Ministers by this time.

The bodies were brought out of the deep-freeze in the military mortuary on stretchers to be prepared for burial. They had not been properly prepared: their hands and legs were still tied, and there was no funeral shroud. Cerasela Demetresu, a young woman accompanying Voican, had the unenviable task of checking the bodies while Voican looked for a white sheet to cover them. When she checked Ceausescu's body, his gold Rolex watch was clasped in his right hand.

The two empty maroon coffins Stanculescu had brought were lying waiting, filled with yellow polystyrene bubbles. Voican got two white sheets from the morgue, but when the last faltering steps were taken to wipe the memory of Nicolae Ceausescu from history, his corpse refused to co-operate. It seemed too big for the coffin. An ungainly wrestling-match ensued between the corpse and its bearers. It was taken out of the coffin, and most of the polystyrene bubbles had to be removed before it was squeezed inside in a macabre pantomime. Just before the lid was put on, a soldier, ignorant of the follicle biology of death, whispered, 'His beard is still growing!'

When both lids were closed, the coffins were transported to a military cemetery at Ghencea in Bucharest. They were put in graves about a hundred yards apart. The grave-diggers were told that the graves were for two colonels killed by the terrorists. It was snowing heavily when Ceausescu's coffin was interred. It was covered with spadefuls of concrete, and two large concrete slabs were put on top. Everything was done in a hurry so as not to attract attention. There was no priest and no service. When they went to put the two simple maroon crosses on the graves, they discovered there were no crosses either. They had been left at the morgue.

It is the tradition in the Romanian Orthodox Church that, as earth is thrown on a man's grave before it is closed, someone says, 'Let the earth be light on him.' Despite the burning hatred that existed for Ceausescu, Voican still threw a handful of earth on the grave before it was closed. But, as he turned away, a soldier said to him, 'No one said: "Let the earth be light on him".'

The list of the uncanny was not yet complete. The icy hand from the grave still had a bit further to stretch. Less than two months after the automatic fire of Kalashnikovs had blasted the Ceausescus to their graves, the prosecutor who had sent them there was as dead as they were. Gica Popa committed suicide in February 1990. He had had a troubled personal life, but the memory of the trial of the Ceausescus seems to have been the factor which made his susceptibility to depression fatal. Plans were made for him to emigrate, but he never needed the tickets. The deeply superstitious Romanians say very little about this. Least said, soonest forgotten.

Arguably, Voican paid a price, too. His wife suspected that Cerasela Demetrescu, the attractive young woman who accompanied him at the funeral, was having an affair with him. Subsequently the film of the proceedings was seen by Voican's wife, Sanda, and not long afterwards she left Romania. Mrs Voican got her revenge on her husband by posing nude in the French magazine *Lui* in its September 1990 edition. This was, as she put it, to 'attract his attention' to her message that she considered him a 'revolutionary cowboy' who was consorting with a government that had destroyed the revolution and 'shattered all the hopes of the people for democracy'.

The whole list of the macabre makes for interesting reading for any with an interest in haunted houses. As Voican said, 'Who can say, but, beyond death, did the spectres have their revenge?'

PART III

The June Days

CHAPTER 17

From January to June

The national unity inspired by the revolution in Romania lasted twenty days before it evaporated. The new administration of Petre Roman, in place by the end of December, ruled in conjunction with the Council of the National Salvation Front headed by Ion Iliescu.

The first serious demonstrations against the new power took place on 12th January, after marches to commemorate the fallen in the revolution. These demonstrations were the first of a series of mass actions demanding the resignation of the Government and key figures in it. Serious disturbances followed on 28th January, 18th February and 20th March, which hindsight allows us to see as a continuum which led, eventually, to the bloody settling of accounts in June.

By the end of January the Council of the Front was replaced by the Provisional Council of National Unity, an all-party affair although dominated by the members of the Front; Iliescu was elected its chairman on 9th February. Similar councils were appointed, usually on a consensus, in the localities. But compromise and concession made no difference: the opposition to the Government and its executive authority, the PCNU, was born. The honeymoon was over. It had never been much of a love affair in the first place.

The schism in society and its development was affected by the nature of the Ceausescu regime and by the nature of the revolution that overthrew it. These two characteristics reflected the existence of the hated Securitate, the secret police. Ceausescu became Eastern Europe's most effective policeman outside the realms of the KGB and arguably achieved a type of totalitarianism that could only be compared historically with the police terror of Stalin, even if Ceausescu did not finally perpetrate murderous purges on the Stalin scale.

However, his police state ensured that in Eastern Europe Romania was alone in having no coherent organised circles of opposition. This meant that there was no nascent Civic Forum in Romania, no Solidarity that had the confidence of all the people mirroring their credentials of anti-communism. Instead, Romania emerged in the days after Christmas with many fingers pointed in accusation.

The nature of the revolution was unique in Eastern Europe's freedom march also. It was bloody. But because of the counter-revolt of the 'terrorists', it was also short. This reality robbed Romania of the rhythm of national unity which accompanied all the other revolutions. Poland had Solidarity for nearly a decade. In East Germany what started in Leipzig took weeks to bring the Wall down in Berlin, and in Czechoslovakia there were days and days where each succeeding general strike was bigger than the last. In Romania it all started in Timisoara on the 16th and Bucharest had an evening and day of joyous revolt before the guns of reaction made the future a bloody fight to the finish.

Nevertheless, in essence, the split reflected class divisions. The ordinary workers and the peasants supported the Front, even if this was a critical support. The intellectuals, the middle class, were the heart of the opposition. This description is a generalisation which holds good: the opposition had Ion Ratiu's bow tie and the Front wore a miner's helmet. Bogdan Balthazar, who later became press spokesman for the Prime Minister, said that one of the reasons the Government got such a bad press internationally was that the opposition in Romania informed the existing class prejudices of most foreign reporters.

But the opposition cause was organised around a starkly simple syllogism, which had an immediate appeal and had the Government of Iliescu and Roman permanently on the defensive. Privately, opposition leaders said that whoever had inherited the mess, it would take years to clear it up, but publicly their syllogism of defiance was: 'Nothing has changed'; 'The National Salvation Front is the old Communist Party' and 'Down with Iliescu!' These latter two calls were immortalised in the street slogans and graffiti of the towns of Romania as 'FSN = PCR' (the National Salvation Front equals the Romanian Communist Party) and, of course, 'Jos Iliescu!'. For political convenience the forces of the opposition ignored the fact that in their own ranks there were many who had been members of the 3.8 million strong Romanian Communist Party – and not merely local activitists, but leaders!

For their part, the Front were operating in conditions which made it difficult to demolish these ideas by economic deeds: the communist system could not be transformed overnight, because of the immediate lack of capital and capitalists, and, most importantly, the enormous social inertia that the continuation of the old communist bureaucracy represented at all levels of state society. In addition, their case was not helped by the evolution of a free press, which never sought to inform but instead proselytised opinion, its view of the world and interpretation of events being a reflection of where the papers stood politically in relation to the great divide; the opposition

Romania Libera being every bit as guilty of this as the pro-Government *Adevarul*.

The politics of the street, in this period, deepened the divide. When thousands mobilised to chant anti-Government slogans every single Sunday outside the Government headquarters in the Piata Victoriei, the nerves of tens of thousands were fraying. When things went too far on 28th January and 18th February, the miners arrived in Bucharest the next day – seemingly mobilised in the way Ceausescu had used them, as a warning. In fact, 29th January was more than a warning. The level of physical intimidation then was a portent of June.

Romanian society was genuinely unstable in these days; the army remained at best equivocal when confronted with unrest, the police incapable; both sets of commanders living under the shadow of the trials of their former leaders indicted for their resolute action against the people in the earliest days of the revolution.

Two issues emerged as central to the ideological debate: Had Romania had a coup or a revolution? and Who were the terrorists? The opposition case was strengthened by linking the two, since it allowed the suggestion that Iliescu and co. were somehow in league with the terrorists; their attacks were described as part of a grand design supporting the panic installation of Iliescu. Given the detail of the days of the counter-revolution recorded here, this may seem fatuous, but its survival in polemic continues, and not only in Romania. In a BBC drama documentary shown in late December 1990 on the anniversary of the revolution, the accusation was given life in a film scene where the main counter-revolutionary Securitate man in the drama focuses his rifle-sights on Iliescu on the balcony of the Central Committee building on 22nd December, and then is refused permission to shoot by his superior officer when he rings him on his portable telephone. So we asked Virgil Magureanu, the former professor of philosophy from the Communist Party

Academy, and now the Chief of the Romanian Intelligence Service, who were the terrorists?

His reply was discursive. He said, 'There are various suppositions. Some of them may be true but there is as yet no definitive answer. It has been told that Ceausescu had an understanding with various Arab regimes, according to the agreement that in case of need there should be mutual assistance. Hence the theory of Arab, or Palestinian, terrorists after the revolution, although there is no evidence of that. It is also told that Ceausescu had an elite guard, key trained fighters who were provided with high technology equipment … yet whose bodies were never recovered. This is still an open chapter. There also existed loners and desperadoes who wanted to defend the regime and undertook such actions. We have to find a way of clearing such things up because there are those who have used the uncertainty to suggest that the "terrorist" outrages were a diversion to legitimise the grasping of power. There is no ground to support that, but this is Romania.

The Intelligence Chief was much more definite when he was asked about what happened to the former Securitate officers. He read from a report he had just finished for presentation to parliament: 'On 22nd December 1989 the ex-Department of State Security accounted for 14,259 military personnel … Out of these, 8,376 officers and under-officers were involved in operative activities; the rest belonged to the security troops. Out of the total personnel of the ex-Department of State Security, 2,841 were removed by the dissolution of some central and territorial units, some 2,769 were retired, 2,869 belonging to the ex-security troops were handed over to the Ministry of the Interior and 449 given to the Ministry of Defence for communications work.' That leaves 5,331 unaccounted for, presumably the strength of the current RIS. The impeccably polite Mr Magureanu would, of course, neither confirm nor deny that.

There are facts and opinion here. And in Romania the

two are subject to infinite interpretations.

Marian Munteanu, President of the League of Students, expressed his opinions on the revolution in a five-minute interview with the authors in September 1990. He said, 'The 16th and 17th in Timisoara and the 21st in Bucharest were the real revolution. On the 21st, at the end of the day we were 5,000 strong, and that was a spontaneous movement. The 22nd! The 22nd was the disaster!'

Dr Emil Constantinescu, one of the Vice-Rectors of the University of Bucharest, took up where Munteanu finished:

> A *coup d'état* was probably prepared ... The current Government thus represents the development of a party that came to power illegally ... The plot existed, that has been publicly recognised by General Militaru and Silviu Brucan ... It was organised by cadres in army circles and cadres of the Securitate troops, including the chief of the Securitate. They recognise now that Iliescu participated in the plot; the plan being to preserve communism without Ceausescu ... although the psychological pressure of the opposition prevented a return to communism, because of the effect it had on the country at large ... What we have now is not communism but a kind of dictatorship; power in the hands of one man, a kind of totalitarianism.

These opinions represent the extreme right in Romanian politics and they were too crude an interpretation to be acceptable to the opposition as a whole. The more erudite of the opposition, men like Iftene Pop of the Peasants' Party, would have nothing to do with these arguments that denigrated the sacrifice of the revolution, and thereby their arguments were more sophisticated and had a wider appeal in opposition circles. The central thesis became not that there was a *coup d'état* but that after the revolution political power was stolen from the people by the emergence of the clique around Iliescu and Roman, who used the structures of the old communist state to safeguard their hegemony. Pop told us:

> It was a real revolution of the Romanian people, indisputably ... There was a plot, some people gathered and planned as we did, but until now there is little evidence to suggest that that had a role in the revolution ... There was a spontaneous insurrection of the Romanian people; those who plotted did not lead the revolution, they did not expose themselves, but after Ceausescu ran away they put themselves at the front of things ... In a sense they confiscated the revolution.

The political logic of this position dictated the development of opposition strategy which became a crusade against what they perceived as the weakest link in the new Government: Ion Iliescu and his communist past. This had as its aim the removal of Iliescu and a hope that the deluge would follow. Thus emerged what would evolve as the key political demand of the opposition and its focal point: point 8 in the Declaration of the Timisoara Society.

Claudiu Iordache was the first president of the Timisoara Society which, he says, was 'originally developed as a society for the security and integrity of Romanian writers'. That was before a night in February 1990 when political in-fighting saw Iordache removed from his position because of his continued support of Iliescu, whom his opponents described as 'a member of the nomenklatura (the privileged communists) ... and a coward who for twenty years did not say a word against communism'. Iordache resigned, and one week later the Timisoara Declaration was published.

It claimed Timisoara as the hearth of the Romanian revolution, defined the movement there as separate and differently defined from the movements elsewhere, and argued vociferously for the privatisation of the economy. It said of the revolution, 'It was a genuine revolution, not a *coup d'état*. It was definitely anti-communist, not only anti-Ceausescu. In Timisoara, people did not die so that the second- and third-rank communists should go to the front line, or that one of the participants in the mass murders should be promoted by the latter as Minister of the Interior.'

Point 8 declared:

We suggest that the electoral law should deny the former Party workers and Securitate officers the right to be nominated as candidates on any list for the first three running legislatures. Their presence in the country's political life is the chief source of the tensions and suspicions that worry Romanian society today. Their absence from public life is absolutely necessary until the situation has been settled and national reconciliation has been effected.

We also demand that in a special clause the electoral law should ban former Party activists from running for the position of President of the country. Romania's President ought to be one of the symbols of our divorce from communism. To have been a Party member is an offence ... The Party activists had been those people who gave up their professions in order to serve the Communist Party and to benefit from the uncommon material privileges it offered. A man who had made such a choice is no longer morally worthy of being a President ...

On 18th February the Piata Victoriei was crowded by about 3,000–4,000 demonstrators protesting, as usual on these Sundays, against the Government. 'Jos Securitate!' 'Jos Iliescu!' they chanted. At some time just before 6 p.m. the crowd surged forward and the single line of soldiers stood aside after token resistance. The crowd invaded the

Government building in their hundreds. On its balcony, young people waved the Romanian tricolour with the hole cut in it and chanted, 'We'll die before we come down!' Inside the building the mob rampaged, setting fire to green volumes containing the collected records of the affairs of the Romanian Communist Party. In a frenzy, individuals pointed out Iliescu's name in a list of members of the Central Committee from the record book of the early 1970s. Gelu Voican, the only Government minister in the building, was beaten before he retreated to the safety of a locked room.

At 8 p.m. the demonstrators came down from the balcony very much alive, and people went home to get ready for work the next day. We spoke to Paraschiva Ionescu, a woman in her late forties, about why she was there. She is a hospital dentist, and was well groomed, wearing a purple checked wool sweater, a gold cross dangling from her neck, under a light brown fur jacket. 'We did not simply want to get rid of Ceausescu ... We wanted to get rid of communism, that's why I am here today ... I have been here every Sunday since 21st December ... Iliescu helped us to get rid of Ceausescu but he is still a communist ... No one elected them; they have taken power ... Ceausescu asked us all his life to be revolutionaries, and now we are!' she said.

The next night, the same square was full of miners from the Jiu Valley. They made an awesome sight: 7,000 or 8,000 miners' lamps glowing in the dark. As speeches from the Provisional Council of National Unity were broadcast live to the crowd, they cheered Iliescu to the echo and booed Radu Campeanu, the Liberal leader, and the Social Democratic Party. None of them spoke English. But a cameraman translated briefly when we asked two miners their opinion of Iliescu. One said: 'Iliescu? He is as good as bread!'

The stage was set for the elections, although there was ethnic rioting on 20th March between Romanians and the minority Hungarians on the streets of Tirgu Mures, with six deaths. Afterwards, the people put the politics of the street behind them, if temporarily, and marked their crosses on their ballot paper on election day, 20th May.

When we asked Iliescu for his view on the swirling currents of opinion in Romanian politics, he replied:

I personally do not agree with the simplistic manner in which it is suggested that the fate of the revolution was determined by conspiracy ... especially the recent suggestions of Brucan and Militaru that the revolution was determined by their conspiracy ... In 1984 I discussed with them the possibility of a revolution without bloodshed, either through involving people at the top or the military, but after much analysis we concluded that it would be impossible to create the necessary organisation to overthrow the structure, and from then on I told them that there was only one solution – a common explosion ... It would be a very big mistake in political thinking and maturity to explain this popular explosion as the consequence of the work of one group or another ...

And the issues surrounding point 8 of the Timisoara Declaration?

There were two basic slogans used by the opposition in the period of the elections. The first was an attempt to hinder the elections or to postpone them, on which the PCNU had already ruled, and the second point was the so-called point 8 of the Timisoara Declaration, which was also an attempt to stop me from standing in the elections. This precise point had been debated and decided in the parliamentary debates on electoral law, where the Liberals put forward a similar formulation which was taken into account, with the proposal that no one who had not stayed in the country for the last ten years could stand either. If this had been passed, along with the Liberal anti-communist motion, we would have had all the candidates for the Presidency disqualified from standing because the other two, Ratiu and Campeanu, had been absent from the country for fifty years and for seventeen years respectively.

The army men, General Voinea and General Stanculescu, share Iliescu's view of the *coup d'état* theories. In particular, General Voinea was adamant that the army was not involved in any conspiracy. 'A *coup d'état* is out of the question. The army rallied to the people without stealing the revolution. If the army had wanted power, we could have taken it any time ... We could have surrounded the Central Committee and torn it to pieces ... Then we would have had our hands on power.' General Stanculescu was equally dismissive. He said, 'Conspiracy? Ah, the delirium of the plot! ... Let me offer you a spectacular revelation ... We belonged to a conspiracy so secret that we did not know each other!'

Hindsight, that most precious of political qualities, shows that the opposition made a gross miscalculation in directing their campaign against Iliescu. He, in reality, proved to be a huge asset to the Front's victory, gaining an even more convincing personal victory in the presidential vote than the Front did in the parliamentary election. Before the poll, the authors of the Timisoara Declaration, in their most modest claims, said that they had more than four million signatures supporting it. The combined vote secured by the Peasants' Party candidate, Ion Ratiu, and the Liberal candidate, Campeanu, was 2.1 million votes compared with Iliescu's 12.2 million. Iliescu took a massive 85 per cent of the poll. The Front took 66.3 per cent of the parliamentary poll, against the Liberals' share of 6.4 per cent and the Peasants' Party's 2.5 per cent, fewer than the Ecology Party. (See the full results of all the elections contained in Appendix 1.)

The scale of this victory can only be interpreted as the Romanian people giving a vote of confidence to Iliescu and the Front as the custodians of the revolution, combined with the fact that the Front's programme, for a measured move towards capitalism, reflected accurately their outlook. The opposition yelled 'Ballot-rigging!' and 'Intimidation!', but they have to face up to the reality that most of the international observers considered the elections 'flawed but fair'. Despite the fact that the American Ambassador left for home in protest against the conduct of the elections the very day that the opposition threatened to boycott the poll in a similar protest, most of the American contingent agreed with the general verdict. Republican Governor Garrey Carruthers of New Mexico, who headed the White House team of observers, called the poll 'a good election' and 'a very giant step towards democracy'. 'In our view, it was a proper election. We were unable to discover anywhere in our observations obvious, systematic fraud in the electoral process,' he said in the *St Louis Post-Dispatch* on his return from Romania.

After the election, the Vice-President of the Timsoara Society, Vasile Popovici, declared, 'Iliescu was elected democratically by a majority of the population: a population in which Mr Brucan, who was the chief ideologue of the National Salvation Front, said that 20 per cent of the people were intelligent and 80 per cent were stupid. Well, the 80 per cent he said who were stupid had 5 per cent who actually were stupid and 75 per cent who were fooled by means of a well-prepared election campaign.'

Doina Cornea, the doyen of the western press coverage of opposition affairs in Romania, went even further. The day after the election, 'Romania's best-known dissident' told the *Independent*'s Isobel Hilton, '... I have come to the conclusion that universal suffrage – at least when you are moving from a dark night into daylight – is not fair. It's not the majority who are right. There are a few people who have maintained moral values and who see that we are threatened with another night. The rest don't see it.'

Only in the Byzantine politics of Romania could such an election result be interpreted in such a way. Only in Romania, too, could such a result resolve nothing. The Ides of June beckoned.

CHAPTER 18

The Days Leading to 13th June

In the calendar of the events that led to the thunder of miners' boots on the pavements of Bucharest, Sunday 22nd April is an important day. The occupation of University Square in the centre of Bucharest began then. The protesters' chief demands were the postponement of the presidential and parliamentary elections, and the disqualification of former leading communists from eligibility to stand for election. Both these issues had been debated at length in the provisional parliament when the law for the elections had been agreed; the latter proposal was a direct attack on Iliescu, who was the National Salvation Front presidential candidate. On the 22nd, the small group who started erecting barricades at the bottom of Nicolae Balcescu Boulevard in the late morning were later joined by students from the university area, and a large contingent of well-heeled intellectuals who came after attending the Peasants' Party demonstration and rally that afternoon at the Piata Aviatorilor. The students and the intellectuals, in concert with sections of Bucharest's low life, would be the main constituents of the protest occupation from then on.

However, by Monday 11th June, almost three weeks after the election and seven weeks after the protest began, when its leaders went to see President-elect Iliescu, the numbers at their tent-city occupation had dwindled to fewer than two hundred. They had been largely forsaken by the intellectuals and students, and the main active supporters of the continued occupation were elements from Bucharest's lumpenproletariat. This meant that on most evenings the tent city, situated mostly on the grass area between the concrete slabs of the Intercontinental Hotel and the neo-classical portals of the National Theatre, became a gaggle of pimps, prostitutes, drunkards, petty thieves and money-changing swindlers. This was not the least of the reasons why public opposition to it was becoming more vociferous day by day.

This is not to say that all those still supporting the protest were in this category; there was still a significant element of drop-out students, but the declassed and desperate poor of Bucharest were predominant. So Iliescu might not have been polite to call these 'guardians of democracy' golani (tramps), but he was accurate. An hour's stroll round the encampment on the evening of the 11th testified to that: there were people staggering drunkenly between the tents; refuse-bags were overflowing and the area was malodorous, indicating that sanitary conditions were in a state of deterioration. Importuning for prostitution was commonplace, the rates being a quarter of what was demanded by the queens of Bucharest's whoredom in the adjacent Intercontinental Hotel. Strangely, these characteristics of the protest seemed to be overlooked in most commentaries on it in the foreign press.

Thus it was the leaders of a demoralised rag-tag army who went to Iliescu that Monday to demand the creation of an independent television station. It would require an almost impossible leap in the imagination to conceive of the Prime Minister of the time in Britain, Margaret

Thatcher, receiving a deputation from London's down-and-outs to discuss their homelessness, far less sitting and listening while they informed her that, in their opinion, some of her policies were insufficiently democratic. Even Marc Champion, the *Independent*'s correspondent in Bucharest, was forced to admit, however reluctantly: 'In any other country, one would have to say that the government had shown great patience. President Ion Iliescu allowed the golani protesters to occupy University Square, the heart of Bucharest's traffic system, for seven weeks.'

Of course there was a hidden agenda, and the leaders of the occupation knew that. Their real constituency was not that of the scavengers of Bucharest society, now inhabiting the swards surrounding the Intercontinental Hotel, but the editorial offices of New York, London, Paris and the like. This was a constituency the newly elected government could not afford to ignore.

But, on 11th June, Iliescu's patience ran out. He says that after the financial and technical difficulties of creating another TV station were argued out with the protesters, they signed an agreement to end their occupation and associated hunger strike. After that, however, when the leaders returned to the occupation, there was factional discord and disagreement about the ending of the protest. This culminated in bands of protesters from the site making further attempts to invade the government headquarters and force entry to the TV station, to demand, under menaces, that the director-general, Razvan Theodorescu, broadcast their demands for the government to resign.

These demonstrations took place on 11th and 12th June, the first of them occurring hours after the accord had been signed. It was then that Iliescu succumbed to the insistent pressure he had been under from some of the acting ministers of the government, particularly General Mihai Chitac, the then Minister of the Interior, and other sources to allow the police to clear the square, using force if necessary.

The main argument used by those who favoured this course was that the government had been given a mandate by the electorate, and to fail to exercise its authority was displaying weakness, although in Iliescu's councils and in the National Salvation Front (FSN) at large there was not unanimity on the subject. On the very eve of the police moving into the square, a discussion with Adrian Manole, the FSN leader from the port of Constanta, revealed this. He urged further caution, and was against clearing the square when the question was put to him. 'It is better to let them rot where they are. Day by day there are fewer of them. I fear that if we clear the square it may cause an explosion. The situation is still combustible. We might reap a whirlwind, so why take the risk?' Prophetic words indeed.

On the evening of 12th June a crowd of maybe several hundred from University Square finished its protests of the day by again marching up Nicolae Balcescu Boulevard towards the government headquarters at Piata Victoriei. They were chanting their usual demand, 'Jos Iliescu!', and combining that with their latest Romanian rhyming rubric: 'Sound asleep, you voted in a dictator!' Retribution for these months of illegal protest came about eight hours later. The militiamen made their co-ordinated assault against the '*golani*' in the square at 4. a.m. on 13th June. The police militia blocked all exit points from the square, and then snatch-squads moved in to arrest those who were captured within the security cordon created by the sweep. The roughness of justice then meted out to the 263 arrested, including six hunger-strikers, has been disputed ever since. The square was cleared in just over thirty minutes.

Radu Campeanu, leader of the Liberal Party, says, 'The level of brutality used against the people in University Square was totally unjustified. The movement there had lost its way. It was practically without support at large, so the excessive brutality that was used to take the demonstrators out was totally disproportionate. People were badly beaten, and a reaction to that followed ... So the clearing of the square was either a provocation or a serious mistake.' Ion Ratiu, the parliamentary leader of the Peasants' Party, says '... how totally disgracefully they behaved ... how violently they cleared the square.' On the other hand Liam Jeory, a journalist with New Zealand TV who was to scoop the world with the first television pictures of the miners' assault, expressed a different eye-witness opinion. He said, 'Well, when the miners came it was altogether different ... it was terrifying ... terrible ... frightening, but I have to say that the clearing of the square was done professionally. In fact, I've seen much worse police action at home.'

Despite these differences of opinion about the brutality or otherwise of the police moves, hindsight informs us that the die was cast. Three days of mayhem followed which would alter the short-term course of Romanian history. About 9 a.m., the government had every reason to believe that the remove-and-arrest operation had been a success. The illegal political embarrassment had been dealt with, and the white traffic lines had been repainted on Nicolae Balcescu Boulevard.

But the electric tensions jarring Bucharest's body politic became evident about 11 a.m., when workers from the IMGB giant engineering factory marched to the doors of the Institute of Architecture, where six months before Petre Roman had sheltered from army bullets, and sought to confront the students. Nerves seemed to have snapped, but behind locked doors the students avoided confrontation. Then, to the rear of IMGB workers, a counter-demonstration assembled, chanting that the workers were 'paid by Iliescu'. Scuffles broke out as the police looked on and did nothing. The scene was set for the day.

About an hour later the first attempts were made by a

large crowd emerging from the university area to reoccupy the square, which had been cordoned off by the police. Most of those arrested in University Square that morning had been charged, and by this time released. It is not known how many of them, if any, took part in this challenge or subsequent assaults on the square. Be that as it may, there then followed a series of charges against the police in the square, which the forces of law and order could not sustain. By 1 p.m. the square was back in the hands of the '*golani*'.

Suddenly the crowd was growing exponentially. News of the retaking of the square was spreading like wildfire through the warrens of Bucharest, and hundreds became thousands. The police countered. A column of two hundred policemen, six abreast, armed with riot sticks, dressed in white helmets and carrying riot shields marched on the square. They were repulsed in a barrage of stones, bottles and the first flaming Molotov cocktail. One or two of the less agile policemen were cornered and beaten. The militiamen regrouped, and returned some time later with tear gas. There was now a massive crowd in the university area.

Hundreds upon hundreds of rolled newspapers were lit to mitigate the effects of the tear gas as the decisive battle loomed. The police ranks advanced, but now evincing a palpable trepidation. A hail of debris rained down on them, and leaders in the mob urged them to advance on the police. That changed the balance of forces as the barrage continued to fall on the police. Then the first ranks of police turned to retreat and tumbled in disarray into their colleagues advancing behind. The leaders of the mob were advancing on them as riot sticks and shields fell, and the first turning became a full-scale retreat. The police had been ignominiously routed. They ran away like school-children confronted by a gang of bullies.

Later in the year at another 'Jos Iliescu!' demonstration, we persuaded a man with a gap-toothed grin to talk to us about this battle. For understandable reasons he would give only his first name, Ioan. He said, 'I remember it. I was at the back of that crowd. I could not believe it when the police ran for their lives. The crowd went into a frenzy after that.' The frenzy had its initial celebration in the torching of the buses, lorries and vans that the police had used to cordon the square. Soon seven buses were ablaze, and huge clouds of dense burning diesel smoke billowed into the warm summer sun shining down on the capital. What William Waldegrave, the then Minister of State at the British Foreign and Commonwealth Office, later described verbally as 'a no doubt inconvenient challenge' to the government, and the White House called 'legitimate dissent', had begun in earnest.

Ioan Pascu met Vasile Secares in the corridors of the parliament building early in the afternoon that day. Pascu still has a broad-shouldered athletic look about him from the days when he was captain of Romania's water-polo team. He moves too in the waters of politics with the same compelling urgency that one imagines he exercised in the pool. Pascu and Secares were both members of the bureau advising Iliescu on foreign relations. 'Have you heard about the trouble at University Square?' Pascu asked Secares. His colleague nodded in affirmation. 'What about the police? ... I smell a rat, Vasile. There is going to be hell to pay now,' Pascu told him. They both agreed to finish their immediate tasks and go together to Iliescu's office in Piata Victoriei.

Riot, by its very nature, does not have exact parameters, so it is difficult to reconstruct a precise, incontestable report of the times, places, events and people involved. What can be said is that the torching of the buses, vans and lorries in University Square ignited around ten hours of anarchy in the capital, during which frenzied mobs consecutively stormed, burned and looted the key locations of the offices of state security to Romania, largely as the forces of law and order looked on, seemingly powerless to take retaliatory action, as later evidence will testify.

The whirlwind of anarchy engulfed the police head-quarters, the Ministry of the Interior, the offices of the Romanian Intelligence Services and the TV centre, roughly in that order, although there was not necessarily a single contiguous mob moving from one place to another. Rather, there was a core contingent of hooligans and ne'er-do-wells who did that, while other contingents joined the fray at different times, sometimes attacking premises that had already been attacked earlier in the day, and at other times unifying with the main mob.

Three certainties can, however, be stated in this account. By the late afternoon Bucharest looked, from the air, as though it was a city on fire, as smoke belched, black and billowing, grey and engulfing, from the locations mentioned. Second, the zenith of the apocalypse of riot that day was the storming of the television centre, which, viewed by the nation, lit the fuse for a further spiral of riot and retribution that would be visited on the capital the following day – the nemesis of the miners. Third, although it can be disputed whether Bucharest teetered on the brink of mob rule, even *coup d'état*, it is indisputable that for a considerable part of the day, from the initial imbroglio with the police in the square, Molotov cocktails materialised as though by magic.

By the time the mob left the university area, their number was anything between 5,000 and 6,000. They headed for the police headquarters, ostensibly in search of their leaders, whom they thought were still imprisoned there. On the way, they chanted the familiar 'Jos Communismu!' but also another rubric rhyming with the 'Ole Ole Ole Ole' introduction, that the Front was the Romanian Communist Party. At the police building, the front doors were broken down by youngsters in their teens who drove at them in hijacked police vans. The watching crowd chanted, 'Only one solution – another revolution!' before hundreds swarmed into the building and ransacked it. Documents, letters and papers fluttered in the air and then furniture crashed from the windows into the street before Molotov cocktails set the place on fire.

It is reported that the first death occurred then, when police sniper-fire hit a man in the head. He crumpled on to the street, his brains blown out by a high-velocity bullet. This drove the mob to new heights of frenzy, and they marched on to the Ministry of the Interior. Outside, they chanted, 'We want Chitac!', the Minister of the Interior, whose reputation among these denizens of disorder had long been tarnished by the rumour that he had machine-gunned revolutionaries in Timisoara before the revolution, before he was judged culpable for the clearing of the square. General Chitac was not to be found, by anyone, for most of the day.

The Interior Ministry was defended by sporadic rifle-fire from inside, so the rioters did not manage to gain entry there, but soon their bravest had got close enough to hurl their Molotovs and set the building ablaze. Here another of their number died instantly, shot through the head, and Gheorghe Dunca, a thirty-nine-year-old, was fatally shot in the stomach, dying of his wounds two days later. The adjacent brick building, which was the offices of the old Securitate, went up in flames next. So far, not a soldier was to be seen as the rampage continued.

About the time the flames were licking the Intelligence Services buildings, Ion Iliescu was in his cabinet room in the government headquarters building in Piata Victoriei, which had been the Ministry of Foreign Affairs in Ceausescu's time. On their way from the parliament building to Piata Victoriei, Ioan Pascu and Vasile Secares had had to run the gauntlet of a detachment of some 300 or 400 anti-government protesters heading for the same destination. When they entered the cabinet room, Iliescu was pacing up and down the wine and white floral carpet, agonising over whether to make a call to the people to come and defend the government and its institutions.

Petre Roman was there with his chief adviser, the former film-maker Adrian Sirbu, Virgil Magureanu, chief of the Intelligence Services, and others whom Pascu was not acquainted with. Iliescu said, in greeting Pascu, 'It seems that they got guns from the police headquarters and we cannot get any news now from the Ministry of the Interior ... It was attacked, and Chitac has been out of reach for hours.' Sirbu presented Pascu with a draft appeal to the people to come and defend the government institutions to support the army and police.

Pascu says he was concerned about the strident nature of the appeal, and said so. He asked about the army, and was told that Stanculescu, the Minister of Defence, was on a visit in Berlin to a Warsaw Pact meeting to celebrate its thirty-fifth anniversary, and that the First Deputy Chief of Staff, Vasile Ionel, had been spoken to about army reinforcements, but nothing had happened. The army wanted a confirmative order, from Iliescu, to give them the right to shoot demonstrators if they entered defined military areas, but he refused to give it. He told Pascu: 'I refused to give it ... But in any case it seems these CADA people have got a real grip on things with this idea that the army should not intervene in any events on the street and only defend the borders ... It's bloody ridiculous!' CADA was a committee of army officers who had campaigned widely in the army after the revolution for it not to have a civilian role – partly in reaction to the role the army had been forced to play in the early part of the revolution, and partly because they feared that army action in any civil circumstances faced them with the future possibility, in the flux of Romanian politics, of being charged later as 'enemies of the people'.

For almost an hour the argument went back and forth about the appeal to the people to come and defend the government. Eventually those in favour of it prevailed, and at about 5 p.m. Adrian Sirbu, Roman's adviser, left the room grasping the communiqué, signed by Iliescu, for broadcasting on television and radio. Petre Roman recalls the decision being taken: 'The absolutely critical moment was when it was realised that the army could not stop the violence. We did not want them to shoot, and without that, the situation got further and further out of hand … Then there were further attacks, and that … decided us that the President should make an appeal to the people.'

As Sirbu left the cabinet room with the President's appeal, Marian Munteanu, the leader of the League of Students, was putting forward an appeal of a different nature from the balcony of one of the buildings in University Square. He made an impassioned plea to the fresh forces of demonstrators gathered there to march again on police headquarters 'to free the prisoners there'. Munteanu was the hero of the golani, who actually called him 'Jesus Christ' because his pale, gaunt features, long bedraggled hair and wispish beard made him resemble popular depictions of Christ's image.

Munteanu was a strange anti-communist 'Saviour', however. His conversion to become a 'Christian Conservative', as he describes himself, had been as quick as Paul's on the road to Damascus. Before the revolution, he had been the leading Communist Party propagandist in his third year faculty at the university, and ran the communist student association. This perhaps explains why he played no leading role in the revolution despite the reputation of the students as a whole; although, after it, he emerged as the most clearly identifiable accuser of Iliescu as a neo-communist, because of Iliescu's past. Remarkably, as Iliescu became the 'bête noire' of the foreign media as 'another Ceausescu', Munteanu became their doyen. It would be a feature of British media coverage of events in Romania that the first time Munteanu's anti-communist credentials and authoritarian style were questioned was in the *Independent*, exactly one year after the revolution.

As he made his appeal to the demonstrators to march on the police headquarters, Munteanu ended with the caveat: 'Fara violenta' (Without violence). He would have been as likely to have had a call heeded as the Securitate were to torture people gently in his old days. William McPherson, a former Pulitzer-Prize-winning journalist, heard Munteanu make his call and recorded it in his eye-witness story of these events published in the British literary magazine *Granta*, volume 33. He followed the crowd, and noted:

> Hundreds, maybe thousands, thronged the street that led to the headquarters entrance, but the street in front was relatively clear: a man had been shot in the head there an hour before ... I went into the courtyard for a quick look. Six or eight young men were lounging on the steps, passing beer bottles among them. They did not look like students ... Where were the police? Where were the army? They had run away, I was told. Strange.

Nicolae Croitoru, leader of the miners of the Vulcan pit in the Jiu Valley, came off shift on 13th June about 1 p.m. After he had bathed, he went up the stone steps of the administration offices of the mine, passing the Stakhano-vite mural on the wall that dated from the Ceausescu era. This is a three-times-lifesize picture of a miner, clenched fist raised, which calls for ever greater production, with a space at its base for the insertion of the name of the coal-hewer of the month. Croitoru spent some hours in his office, but less than usual; things were quiet these days. The televising of the World Cup at 4 p.m. had diminished the urgency of a lot of the men's grievances.

He reached home at about 5 p.m. There came a knock on the door just as his wife put his evening meal on the table. It was one of the men from the mine, who was agitated as he burst into Croitoru's living-room. 'There's trouble in Bucharest again. Big trouble. These golani

have attacked the government, again. The government
buildings are all on fire. We must go to Bucharest immediately!' Croitoru agreed he would go back to his office and
make some phone calls to find out what was happening,
since he did not have a telephone in his house. He had
gone to Bucharest before, in February. He says, as the
Vulcan miners' leader, he could not refuse to go when the
men demanded it. He knew that this time, if they went, it
would be worse.

Croitoru is one of Miron Cozma's right-hand men in
the miners' union. Cozma is the leader of the miners in the
Jiu Valley, elected in March 1990. When Croitoru reached
his office, there was already a crowd there waiting for
news. He made a few phone calls and found that Cozma
was at the miners' welfare association in Lonea, another
of the string of small mining towns huddled round a pit in
the gloom of the valley.

Cozma came to the phone. 'What the hell is it, Nicolae?
I'm watching the football!' he demanded tetchily. 'They
say there's trouble in Bucharest; the government has been
deposed by the "*golani*",' Croitoru told him. 'You're
crazy! I've heard nothing. I would have heard if it was
serious. It can't be serious. I'm watching the Spain–
Uruguay . . .' Cozma said, but the insistence of Croitoru did
not allow him to finish. 'Miron, I'm telling you this is
serious. There has been a TV announcement,' he remembers telling Cozma. Cozma agreed to go to the union
headquarters in Petrosani and let Croitoru know what was
going on. 'You wait at Vulcan, and I'll phone you there . . .
This game's poor, anyway. It's worse than the Holland–
Egypt effort last night, and that was not up to much. Did
you see it?' Croitoru had to smile. 'No, I'm a serious man,'
he joked. He worshipped the ground Cozma walked on.

Claudiu Iordache was no longer the writer and philoso-
pher from Timisoara who became a revolutionary. He was
now engulfed in the hard-nosed world of politics, of trying

to make things happen, as Vice-President of the National Salvation Front. He had risen to national prominence, in part, because of his energy and ability, but also as a recognition, in some way, of what he had done in Timisoara. His position in the political pecking-order of the day allowed him to go to the cabinet room and become one of the select few of the political leaders of Romania who would grapple with the dilemmas of the day. He says he reached the cabinet room between 5 and 6 p.m.

> The situation in Bucharest had reached the doors of government. There was a crowd of about 400 menacing the headquarters and only a single line of soldiers defending it. There were about thirty people in the cabinet room when I went in, including Magureanu and Roman. It is not an exaggeration to say that there was an atmosphere of absolute despair ... I am convinced that if the mob threatening the HQ had tried to break through the cordon of soldiers, they would have succeeded, and lynched us. I'm telling you, lynch mob is not too strong a term to use. Things were in the balance.

Iordache says that after the appeal was made to the population to come to defend the government, phone calls were made to factories in the Bucharest area and then to surrounding towns like 'Ploiesti and Tirgoviste, in case the workers of Bucharest did not arrive'. The first detachments to reach the government headquarters were women textile workers. 'Their arrival was heralded by the noise of pro-Iliescu slogans being shouted. They stood in line with the soldiers. Their numbers doubled the line, as far as I can remember. You would have to have been there to believe it; the atmosphere was one of the government hanging by a thread,' he said.

Then Razvan Theodorescu, director-general of the Romanian television service, arrived. The stale smell of sweat and tobacco-smoke in the room was temporarily lightened since Theodorescu, an imposing, bulky, six-foot figure with his head shaved, has a penchant for expensive aftershave. But he too was in a sweat. He spoke directly to Iliescu and those around him, dispensing with the customary formal greetings normally required. One observer said that Theodorescu was in a panic. He told the President that there was now a mob at the TV centre and implored him to come on the television and address the nation on the crisis. There was argument about this. Pascu and Secares told Iliescu that this would 'raise the stakes too high', threatening to take the whole situation out of control. Roman agreed. A compromise was reached – the issuing of a second declaration to the people.

Iliescu says, 'On the one side we addressed ourselves to the people to come and support the government and to the troops of the army to support the government institutions and free the besieged buildings.' He is adamant that there was never a direct mention of the miners in any of these communiqués. A reliable source says the actual terms used were 'all conscious forces should gather round the buildings of government and the television to curb the attempts of extremist groups to use force, and to defend the democracy that was so difficult to attain.' It was decided at this time that the paratroopers at Boteni should be contacted directly since they had been the backbone of the revolution. If Iliescu had gone back to the TV centre with Theodorescu, he would have almost walked into the storming of the building.

Sorin Dumitrescu is head of TV programming of Romanian television. He went to work on 13th June about 6 p.m. At that time there were crowds of workers, mainly women, at the entrance to the TV centre, which, incidentally, is opposite the old residence of the British Ambassador which was shot to pieces in the fighting after 22nd December. One of the women said to him as he went into work, 'Don't worry! Now we'll knock the shit out of these bastards if they turn up here.' It was not a prophecy she and her compatriots fulfilled. When the enemy turned up, they were about a thousand strong. The 'defence guard' vanished, leaving the soldiers between the demonstrators and their objective. The demonstrators chanted, 'The army is with us!' and Munteanu's 'Fara violenta'. Dumitrescu says:

> By about 7 p.m. there were about 500 to 1,000 of them at the gate. I was watching from the first floor of the building. I could not believe my eyes. One of the army officers walked forward from the ranks of soldiers, and spoke to the demonstrators. Then he went back to the ranks and took an automatic rifle from one of the men. He removed the magazine and held it upside down to show that there were no bullets in it. I was absolutely dumbstruck. Maybe he was doing this with good intentions, but the moment he did it, the mob poured through the gates and into the grounds of the TV centre . . .
>
> I saw Cornel Pumnea, the sports commentator, among the demonstrators, discussing with them, and then suddenly they attacked him. He ran for it, but they caught him and beat him over a car . . . From the first floor I could see that on the other side of the TV centre, opposite the gate, there was a massive group of soldiers with full riot gear on, but they did not intervene as the mob tried to get into the building.

Alexandru Stark is a documentary film-maker with Romanian television. Later that night he was clubbed on the head by the invaders, but he recollects that around this time he was viewing events from Razvan Theodorescu's office on the eleventh floor. 'Until about 7 p.m. there were soldiers all around the television centre. Sometime after that, I can't say exactly when, each soldier turned and left

... marched away ... I turned to Theodorescu and said, "The game's up".'

Cornel Pumnea watched the demonstrators enter the grounds of the TV centre. 'They came, shouting, "The army is with us!" and, "Without violence", but a lot of them had iron bars and clubs and immediately they started to try and force an entry into the building.' He says he went down to ground level when he saw a police militia-man being beaten there. He reached the front door and tried to reason with the leading group. He said to them, 'We have hardly repaired the television network, and now you want to wreck it again.' One of their number shouted, 'The television has lied to the people!' A wisecrack sealed Pumnea's fate. He quipped, 'Who, me? Have I told you false football scores?'

A man next to him tried to stab him with an umbrella, a comment perhaps on the class composition of a section of the mob, since rolled umbrellas are seldom *de rigueur* in slums anywhere, even in Bucharest. Pumnea, a perform-ance gymnast, gave as good as he got to the first three assailants, then decided to run for it. He reached the car park, but was cornered there and beaten badly – suffering facial cuts, cracked ribs and extensive body bruising. But Pumnea is a tough nut. 'You can't see a devil dead!' he says. He got up and went back into the TV centre by a rear entrance, to seek revenge. He says he got it by making his way to the broadcasting studio as the demonstrators were pouring through the building, and declaring, in his dishev-elled, bloody, battered state, to the viewers of the nation: 'I have just come from a peaceful demonstration ... Look at the proof of that! "Fara violenta," they chanted at the gates, but I am witness to how peaceful these people who have come here are!'

By this time, two of the demonstrators were threatening Dumitrescu at the door of the main studio. They yelled, 'Come out, you bastards, or we will cut you to pieces!' Dumitrescu had managed to get a studio adjacent to the main one put on live broadcast. The TV transmission was cut to it, ironically interrupting a programme made by Alexandru Stark called 'Parliamentary Life', and Paul Solok, one of the announcers, said, 'The TV is under siege.' The plug was pulled after that, and screens across Romania went blank. The man who gave the order to stop broadcasting was the assistant director-general of the television service, Emanuel Valeriu.

That was around 8.30 p.m., and the advance guard of the rioters reached Valeriu's office on the eleventh floor shortly after. Those who followed wrought havoc in the building, destroying thousands of pounds' worth of equipment and priceless archive films, including the filmed history of the revolution. The rioters began to lay waste systematically to Valeriu's office as, next door, another group attacked Theodorescu's. In Valeriu's they tore out the telephone lines from the wall, upturned his desk and smashed anything they could get their hands on, including photos of his daughter and her family; Valeriu is a grandfather. They told him they were going to kill him by throwing him out of the window.

'The European Commission of Human Rights, when they came here after the June events, said that I provoked "race hatred" by calling these people "gypsies". But they were gypsies, as far as I was concerned. They were not students. If they were gypsies, what was I supposed to call them?' he told us in a heated fashion, still agitated when he talks of these happenings. When his life was threatened, the diminutive white-haired Valeriu went to the window and climbed up on the wood panelling beside it. He opened the window, and yelled, 'OK! Which of you is man enough to push? You want to kill me? Go ahead!' As they hesitated, men in the light blue berets from the Boteni Paratroop Regiment arrived. The demonstrators were caught in a pincer movement between them working their way down the building from the roof and soldiers coming up from the lower floors.

When news of the storming of the TV centre reached the cabinet room, it provoked the first talk of the day of a coup attempt against the government. Iordache says: 'When the TV programme was interrupted, there was open discussion about the nature of the rebellion against the government. Reference was made to Antonescu and the Iron Guard rebellion, and it was in this context that there was talk of the movement being of a fascist or legionnaire character. It was not defined as fascist or legionnaire specifically.' He says that, in the related discussions, Roman suggested that Iliescu should go to a secure military garrison to ensure his own safety. Iordache opposed, and argued that since Roman was the acting head of government, it was more appropriate for him to take such action. 'You cannot imagine how fragile the power seemed to be. I would not have given a penny for their chances,' Iordache said. In these discussions it was decided to send out two reconnaissance parties to ascertain the real situation because of all the contradictory information. Eight volunteers went from the thirty or so in the room – four in a Dacia car and four in an army jeep. Iordache went in the car.

Miron Cozma says that the interruption of the television broadcast put an end to all reason, and the consternation of the miners then became uncontrollable rage. 'After that, there was no stopping them ... An army division would not have stopped them,' he said. As the evening wore on, the union offices in the centre of Petrosani had become more and more crowded with miners, some of them straight off shift, demanding that the union leaders take them to Bucharest. When Cozma reached his office from Lonea, its two rooms were full and beginning to overflow. Then in the corridors in the building were miners all shouting: 'If they cannot keep order in Bucharest, then we will do it!' Before long, men were queuing down the two flights of stairs from the office to the street.

Some were there because they had heard Iliescu's appeal, but when pictures were shown of the mayhem at the TV centre and then the TV was cut off, all discussion was over. They were going. 'In any case, there was no reason for them to be called. They would have gone anyway,' Cozma says. When he went to the Petrosani railway station late in the evening, more than two thousand miners were there, ready to do battle. That night the station-master at Petrosani told Valerica Matei, the full-time secretary of the miners' union, that enraged miners told him that if he did not organise trains to Bucharest, they would kill him.

After order was restored at the TV centre, the second World Cup match of the day (Argentina versus USSR) was shown, and then Iliescu made the appearance on television that had been called for earlier. That was about 11.45 p.m. According to Petre Roman, the President's message, which had been recorded earlier, spoke of 'the danger to democratic institutions ... and specified the occupation of the TV centre and the chain of violence which showed that we were facing a rebellion of a fascist character'. The advance guard of the miners who terrorised the streets of Bucharest the next day did not hear it. The trains to Bucharest had left Petrosani before that. Miron Cozma, their leader, was not on any of them. He says he watched them pull out of the station, thinking, 'There is going to be a disaster.'

At 10.20 p.m. the Ministry of the Interior building was still burning. Iordache was with the three men he had gone on reconnaissance with, watching a group of youths stuffing a mattress through a ground-floor window, when a man of about forty or forty-five approached him. He was with a group of ten or so, all dressed similarly in suits. The man asked Iordache where he was from. He replied, 'Timisoara ... I have the right to watch what is going on.' They thought they had been rumbled, but the man moved off.

There were about fifty or sixty activists in the group attacking the Ministry, with the same number of on-lookers. Two armoured cars appeared at the rear of the attackers. 'I expected the crowd to scatter, but they didn't. Nothing happened. The armoured cars stopped, then drove away,' Iordache says.

It was near midnight when he got to the TV centre; it was still besieged by about a thousand demonstrators, but the main building and grounds were again under proper control. At 1 a.m. the soldiers from inside the grounds attacked the demonstrators ferociously. Many were badly beaten as they tried to flee. As the troops moved in, three cars parked to the left of the main building moved off simultaneously into the night. The ringleaders of this Armageddon at the TV centre were not going to be appre-hended in this last major law and order sweep of the day.

The streets of Bucharest were quiet as Roman and Iliescu prepared to sleep in the cabinet room. The day ended in the same swirl of rumour and contradiction that had characterised its every hour: Nica Leon, one of the leaders of the '*golani*', had been sighted leading an attack on the Ministry of the Interior; Petrina, the Peasants' Party Secretary, had been distributing Molotovs at the TV centre; Mihai Lupoi, the disaffected ex-Minister of Tourism, had plotted with CADA army officers to para-lyse the army's response; guns had been found in the Insti-tute of Architecture and crates of Molotov cocktails in the basement of the Peasants' Party headquarters; Ion Puiu, a Peasants' Party leader, had led the attack on the police at University Square.

Who knew what to believe? Both men were exhausted as the younger went to the ante-room off the cabinet room and lay on the floor under a single blanket. They knew the miners were coming. Roman remembers, 'I felt very uneasy, but the fears I had were as nothing compared to how it all turned out ... It was worse than my worst nightmare ... Oh yes, worse ... We thought we could convince them to behave responsibly, but what happened was really awful ... It was terrible.'

Iliescu slept only fitfully. When he woke about 4 a.m. he went to a bookcase in the cabinet room to find something to flick through as sleep eluded him. There were books by Victor Babes, the famous Romanian immunologist, Ministry of Technology and Science hardbacks and collected volumes of *Who's Who in Science in Europe*. He returned to his blanket on the floor. The first miners' train from Petrosani was less than an hour away, thundering with the hordes of Nemesis to the capital.

CHAPTER 19

14th June and the Aftermath

They came in an arrowhead, their hob-nailed boots thundering down the Nicolae Balcescu Boulevard in the heart of Bucharest.

One man in a grey suit walked out from the pavement, where the long bread queue afforded a weak, anonymous safety, into the middle of the street and tried to stop the arrow. He had no chance. The first miner swung his wooden club – the width of a man's fist – and the grey suit was down, a second miner kicked him in the head repeatedly, a third brought down a rubber cosh.

In an instant grey suit had disappeared, hidden by the boots and sticks pumping up and down like a demented threshing-machine.

It is a peculiarly nasty experience – far more frightening than the random menace of gunfire – to see a man beaten almost to death in front of your eyes and know that to intervene would be suicide. It must have been like this in the 1930s, when the Brownshirts stomped around Berlin.

One man was brave enough to try. He was an ox of

a fellow – at 6 foot 6 inches and weighing not much less than 20 stone, he towered above the dirty-faced runts in their pit helmets and boots. This second man showed a card to the new cluster of miners, but they were not in a talking mood. A wooden stave smashed down on his head and the ox, wounded, ran to the safety of a building, pursued.

More miners arrived, jumping down from a lorry, and charged the bread queue. Everyone, youths, old dears with bags of shopping, children, ran for it squealing like pigs in a slaughterhouse. A man in front of me lost a shoe, but kept on, half running, half hopping, desperate to flee. Later the ox turned up at the emergency hospital, to get his head bandaged. He turned out to be Gheorghe Daraban, former captain of the national rugby team, and a major in the police. Daraban is something of a national hero, but this had not helped him. His jersey, a gift from a touring British police rugby team, was dappled with blood. He said with a bruised grin, 'I was afraid I was going to lose my teeth.'

The first man, in the grey suit, was, by some miracle, still alive but so unwell that we were not allowed to see him. He too was a police officer. His name was Constantin Avram.

These words were penned by the *Observer* correspondent John Sweeney, and published on 17th June 1990. They picture some of the aspects of the miners' revenge. So does William McPherson, in his *Granta* article, already mentioned:

At the edge of the square the miners were beating a man in the face with sticks, then they kicked him. They kicked him twice in the face, then in the stomach, and then they clubbed him in the stomach. He was doubled over, bleeding, trying to protect himself. He was led to one of the waiting cars in the middle of the square. It took a long time, because they were beating him. I wondered if this was what it had been like in Nazi Germany when the Brownshirts were loose. A woman appeared to be on her way to work, but she was knocked to the ground, beaten, forced into a waiting car. Another man was being kicked in the face. The violence intensified, spread like an infection. Miners were shaking their fists at people on the balconies of the hotel, shouting, 'Photos are forbidden!' …

I returned to the hotel lobby. It was 7.20. The miners had chased a man into the hotel's revolving door and were beating him with clubs, chains, hoses. He was slumped there, his face bleeding, which he was trying to protect with his hands. He was picked up and dragged to a waiting car. I stood in the doorway for a minute, venturing out for a step or two. I wanted to make a list of the weapons I saw. Here is my list: thick chains, miners' drills … pipes, wooden clubs, tree limbs, rubber hoses with nozzles attached, chains in rubber hoses. I left before finishing the list, but in a few moments I went out again … I saw a miner carrying one of the distinctive yellow plastic 'Ratiu for President' bags. Ion Ratiu was the Peasants' Party's candidate. I assumed – correctly as it happened – that they had invaded the party's headquarters nearby.

The miners had reached Bucharest at about 5 a.m. By 9.30, they would stand accused of destruction, desolation, murder and mayhem. By then the offices of the two chief opposition parties, the Peasants' Party, on the Boulevard Republicü, and those of the Liberals, on the Nicolae Balcescu Boulevard, had been wrecked, several university departments had met the same fate and the miners began the policy – that they would pursue for the next two days – of becoming policemen, checking identity cards and arresting those they regarded as 'criminals'. The invasion of the offices of the opposition press followed. About three thousand miners from the Jiu Valley came first, but by the end of the day there would be five or six times that number, from mining areas all over the country, roaming the streets of the capital.

Vasile Secares woke Ioan Pascu that morning, by telephone, with the news that Marian Munteanu had been murdered. 'I cannot tell you how I felt. I felt sick in my stomach immediately,' Pascu said. Later in the day he was in University Square trying to control the wanton vengeance. He remembers: 'I have to say it was terrible. I never want to see such things again in all my life. They were merciless with anyone showing opposition. It was completely out of control. I personally intervened to stop them beating two people to death near University Square in the morning.'

Dr Emil Constantinescu is the Vice-Rector of Bucharest University, a man of strong opinions, who speaks them forcibly. We met in the common room of the Student League some months after these events, below a crude picture-graphic on the wall which showed the communist hammer and sickle transformed into a Nazi swastika in three easy steps. He says:

At dawn on 14th June and on 15th June the university was occupied and devastated by groups of miners and persons in plain clothes armed with crowbars, clubs and axes ... They were in a blind rage ... I cannot explain to you in words that are adequate ... Students were savagely beaten and severely wounded, at random, it seemed, teachers attacked, molested and insulted ... including one of the former rectors. It was a reign of terror.

Yes, a reign of terror. Classrooms, offices, laboratories, were destroyed. So was valuable technical apparatus obtained with great difficulties, and collections of high scientific value. This vandalism ... these irresponsible actions are unprecedented in the history of education in Romania.

'Who were the guilty parties? Who were responsible?' we asked.

Well, we would name the Romanian television and certain newspapers. They incited the miners to this. There was a permanent campaign of deliberate disinformation and extremely serious acts of instigating the population against the students and intellectuals in general. The students were blamed in the press and television for things which they did not do, and allegiance to fascist or legionnaire ideas which they are totally averse to. The papers and television were responsible for propagating these accusations, and so, to my mind, can be held responsible for what happened, in large measure.

A key question that emerges from Constantinescu's commentary is: who were the 'persons in plain clothes' he refers to? This has been disputed ever since. It is clear that the miners were led to various locations in the capital, but there is no unanimity about who these leaders were. The first detachments of miners were met by leaders of the National Salvation Front at the Gara du Nord station in Bucharest, who asked them to act in a reasonable manner, but they were literally swept aside as the miners' hordes passed, chanting 'Golani! Golani!' The miners had decided that their motto would be, 'If you cannot keep order, then we will', and damn the consequences. A high price would be paid – in broken bones and pulped flesh – the result of the brutality of the arbitrary justice that was to follow, and the shattering of the reputation of the government across the globe.

About 8.30 a.m., a crowd of some 3,000 or 4,000 miners gathered before the government headquarters in Piata Victoriei and demanded that Iliescu come out and speak. Instead, they were addressed by Cazimir Ionescu, one of the leaders of the Front in parliament. He told them, 'Iliescu is not here at the moment. I am Cazimir Ionescu, and I am speaking on his behalf. I have to thank you very much. But please don't go into town. We have arranged for food to be available for you at the National Exhibition Hall, and later today the football match between Romania and the Cameroon will be on TV screens there also.' The crowd continued to chant 'Ili-es-cu! Ili-es-cu!' Ionescu added, 'Please, friends, please be disciplined. Don't go into town, because that will harm your reputation and also our reputation.'

These appeals seemed to have some effect, because after Ionescu had spoken, the demonstration broke up and headed in the direction of the Exhibition Hall, up Kisseleff Avenue. However, not all the miners heeded the call to remain in order, for a section of this demonstration seemingly went to attack the offices of the opposition newspaper *Romantia Libera* in Free Press Square, formerly Piata Scinteii, next to the Exhibition Hall.

There are once again conflicting stories as to what happened next. The editorial offices of the paper had already been smashed by workers from the Bucharest area the night before, a long time before the miners arrived. Then the miners came, led by the notorious ex-Securitate man, Camaresescu. Petru Clej, who works as a journalist at *Romania Libera*, says that, contrary to popular conception, the miners did not gain access to the offices and then smash them to pieces. On the contrary, the sole journalist on the premises – the rest had evacuated – duped the miners into believing that everything was closed up because of the damage. The paper did not appear in print again until the following Tuesday, but that was a result of the printers' industrial action in protest against the anti-government line it had been taking, not because everything had been smashed to smithereens, as first reports suggested.

Marian Munteanu was not dead, either, although by this time he had been severely beaten. According to John Sweeney in the *Observer*, he sustained a broken left leg, a broken hand and a bad head wound. He was one of the 277 reported casualties dealt with in the emergency clinics of Bucharest's hospitals after the onslaught. There was only one death officially recorded – a man who died of a heart attack in the vicinity of University Square. Five died in the riots the day before.

It should be borne in mind that such division and days of riot, although shocking to those weaned on the mother's milk of parliamentary democracy, are not a new thing in Romania's history. Much comment was made at the time that the coming of the miners was a reflection of the politics of the Ceausescu era. A crucial difference, whether the journalists of the west liked it or not, is that, unlike in the Ceausescu era, the miners came to Bucharest largely of their own volition. In fact in February, in a similar mobilisation without the associated mass terror, they made that point by chanting, 'Noi sintem uniti! Nu sintem platiti!' (We are united! We are not paid!) at Piata Victoriei.

Comparisons were many with the Ceausescu era, but few made the point that both the historical parties in Romania in the 1920s and 1930s had street mobilisations which served to intimidate the opposition. In the entire period between the First and Second World Wars, there were only five years when the country was not governed under martial law; in 1932 the universities were closed to reduce unrest due to violent clashes within the students' ranks between supporters of the rising fascist Iron Guard and their opponents.

And just like some of the street battles of the past, Bucharest in June 1990 had its vanquished, who took a beating, and its victors, whose supporters celebrated. By the middle of the morning, Bucharest saw parades of workers who came from their factories to march with the miners and crowds of bystanders who cheered. The shouts went up: 'Hail to the miners!' 'Bravo, miners!' from ordinary people who were thoroughly disenchanted by the abuse of the democratic process that the continued protests of the *'golani'* represented, as they saw it, and now indignant by what many interpreted as an attempt to destabilise society to create conditions for the government to fall. The miners were cheered to the echo on the streets of Bucharest that day for saving democracy.

Emanuel Valeriu, the assistant director-general of the television service, reflected this, when he said later, 'Please, you with all your experience of democracy tell me which is the greater right – those of University Square to destabilise the country or those who came to re-establish order in favour of an elected government, which is the more democratic?' This logic might not have been accepted in the American Embassy in Kisseleff Avenue, nevertheless it was the logic of the 'silent majority' in Bucharest in those days.

All these mitigating elements of history and opinion were of no succour to Iliescu and Roman in the early hours of 14th June, however. Like Pascu, for hours they lived in dread that Marian Munteanu had been murdered; even when it was clear that this was not the case, their 'worst nightmare' was confirmed, hour by hour, as the rampage went on. The miners had come twice before since the revolution, but it had never been like this. At an early morning meeting in the cabinet room the plan was hatched to get the miners off the streets by creating special facilities for the viewing of the Romania-Cameroon World Cup match.

Thereafter, government officials worked flat out to make the Exhibition Centre, the Sports Palace and a military academy ready for viewing the football. This was one plan for the day that was successful. Pascu says that later in the day, Iliescu, in a rueful aside, told him ironically, 'Ioan, things are bad, but it could have been worse.

Romania might not have been playing tonight. Then what?' The adviser replied, 'Well, Mr President, it was the Romans who started "panem et circenses" – bread and circuses!' They both smiled, probably for the only time that day.

At around 10 a.m. Roman and Iliescu met Vasile Ionell, who had been acting commander-in-chief of the army in Stanculescu's absence, General Mihai Chitac, the Minister of the Interior, and others. Roman and Iliescu had both agreed to approach the meeting calmly, but the sight of those whom they considered had let them down so badly meant that the normally even-tempered duo displayed raw feelings uncharacteristically. They started first with Chitac.

They demanded to know principally why he had gone into hiding for three hours during the previous day as the growing crowd of workers outside in Piata Victoriei could be heard chanting for Iliescu for the second time that day. They both say he offered no explanation other than saying he had been out of contact because he was being pursued by the mob. 'You are telling us you went into hiding to save your skin from the mob?' Iliescu demanded. 'What about us? ... At one time the leader of the Guard came here yesterday and told us, "It looks as though we are alone." A single line of soldiers stood between us and the mob, and did we go into hiding?' he added angrily. Roman requested an adjournment.

He says that up to this point they had not decided what to do with General Chitac, although it had been widely rumoured that he would not get a place in the new government after the election. In fact this reality is said, in some quarters, to have been a factor in Chitac's insistence that the square be cleared; an attempt by him to capture lost glory. Roman said to Iliescu in the ante-room off the cabinet room, 'He's got to go now. We cannot afford to wait any longer. I have the man to replace him – Doru Ursu.' Iliescu nodded taciturnly.

'We do not consider your conduct or explanations satisfactory; you can go,' Roman told Chitac. It seems that he left without saying goodbye. Ionell was next in the firing-line. Iliescu demanded to know why it had taken so long for the army to do anything concrete on the streets. Roman added, his normal decorum vanishing, 'we are astonished at the performance, frankly, Mr General, and we have spent some time wondering if there are political explanations as to why the army did not counter the mob in a more satisfactory fashion?' Iliescu added subsequently, 'Just how far does the influence of the gentlemen of CADA stretch? Does it go to the top of the army? You have allowed the events of last year to influence your judgment?' Then, further, 'Yesterday had the outline of a coup.'

The General replied quietly and in measured words. There had been great confusion, which the absence of Stanculescu had not helped. The army had no experience still in street fighting, and it was only when the paratroopers arrived on the scene that they were capable of resolute action. When the counter came that this was not all that convincing, the General added, 'Well, order was restored after that, was it not?'

Iliescu's speech later that morning to the miners and workers assembled in Piata Victoriei carried the hallmarks of this discussion, and its frayed nerves. He said:

The events of yesterday had the colour of the attempts at destabilising the government that we have had to suffer on 12th January, 28th January and 18th February. But this time they were better organised. They had Iron Guardist-type detachments in their midst and were inspired by right-wing forces in the country and abroad ... who operated to a preconceived scenario whose aim was to establish rightist power in Romania ...

The people had declared at the ballot-box, but that

was not good enough ... and despite the open evidence of the violent character of these events, we have now some politicians and journalists who are blaming the government and the forces of law and order ... Well, let me say this: if there are criticisms to be made against the forces of law, they are to do with their slowness of response to the developing crisis ... These hooligans were allowed to do what they liked until late in the night precisely because the police and army tolerated their excesses for far too long.

Not surprisingly, the crowd roared in approval.

He finished by saying that the ringleaders had not been caught but that there would be an exhaustive investigation of those arrested to throw light on that, and he angrily condemned those in the army who were propagating the myth of a so-called 'passive army'. 'It is dangerous and could bring division between the army and the people, even though we have to thank those soldiers who restored order late in the day yesterday.'

At 7 a.m. that morning Ion Ratiu, who had been the Peasants' Party candidate in the presidential election, received word by telephone that the miners had come and were destroying the printing press owned by the Peasants' Party, which was stored in the basement of the National Theatre. One hour later Ratiu got word that the miners had been 'overheard saying they were coming to destroy my house and take me prisoner'. When he heard this, he decided to get out of town. He took his wife to the residence of the British Ambassador, who helped to arrange a flight to Chile for her.

Ratiu then headed for the quiet of Cimpulung, some 150 miles north-west of Bucharest. 'I remember sitting on the grass, looking at the mountains and thinking what a pity this country is so beautiful and we are making such a mess of it ... The people who are the aggressors are not happy; we are not happy ... People are unhappy because of the bloody system, but the country is so beautiful.'

Ratiu says he phoned the British Ambassador about 3 p.m. that afternoon. The Ambassador lives next door to him, so he was able to confirm that the miners had come and sacked his house. 'Then I phoned Roman. I told him that my house had been sacked, but he told me, "Not at all. I have given instructions that your house should be taken care of." Believe it or not, I believed him, and I told him I would see him in parliament the following day.'

About 11 p.m. Ratiu arrived back in Bucharest from Cimpulung. He says, 'I found the house completely smashed and all my clothes strewn all over the place; and, would you believe it, about fifteen minutes after my return the miners came climbing over the walls ...' He is aged seventy-three, and he fled. He went to the kitchen at the rear of his house and scaled the roof there, with the idea of jumping across the gap to the roof of the house next door. His aide, Ion Rodean, tried it, and broke his leg in the fall. Ratiu was concerned. He says:

Everyone had tried to run away and had been caught. I decided not to go any further. Then I saw this one come towards me with a bludgeon ... I thought, 'Well, this is it', because I knew that several people had been killed by this time. I was aware of my life passing before me ... When somebody yelled, 'Don't hit him!' I think it may have saved my life because these brutal people are difficult to stop once they have drawn blood ... It has been proved.

They frog-marched me through the yard and into the street ... There were two people there in army uniform near to this lorry with benches on it ... I said to them that they should stop them as I had immunity as a Member of Parliament, and they just looked at me blankly as though I were crazy ... This Senator Dan Josif ... he was one of the minions of the government

then ... he still is ... he was close to Roman then and
he still is now ... Why was he there? ... The whole
thing was organised by the government. I mean Roman
knew I was coming back ... Well, Josif spoke when
they were pulling me this way and that ... They were
calling me a criminal and such. Now I was very
properly dressed, as I usually am, and I said to them,
'Look at me. Do I look like a criminal?' That seemed to
defuse them a bit.

Ratiu was taken 'under arrest', held for a period of
time, and released. Six days later he was at the inaugura-
tion of parliament.

I was sitting next to Roman ... when Iliescu named him
as Prime Minister. I shook his hand and was the first to
congratulate him. When Iliescu finished, everybody
stood up, but I remained seated. I told Roman that he
should tell Iliescu that I sat down because he had
repeated this lie that there had been an attempted
putsch ... Because this was not a putsch ... This was
organised by him to bring the miners in ...

The world's press adopted Mr Ratiu's anthem in the aftermath of those June days. The message was spelled out in
printer's ink loud and clear: 'Ceausescu is back!' The three
days of rioting were treated as arbitrarily as the miners had
selected their scapegoats. The headlines from a selection
of the liberal press in Britain, typical of the rest of the
European coverage, tell their own story:

'Securitate-style thugs storm occupied square' – 14th
June.
'"Free Romania no longer exists" as opposition is
crushed' – 15th June.
'Iliescu imposes rule of iron' – 15th June.
'Miners terrorise Bucharest' – 15th June.
'Old ways die hard in Bucharest' – 16th June.

'Romania's divisions were exacerbated by Iliescu poll victory' – 16th June.

'Romania slides backwards towards tyranny' – 17th June.

'Jackboot returns to streets of Romania' – 17th June.

'Return of the Fear Machine' – 17th June.

'Romania on verge of civil war' – 18th June.

'Defiant students revive vigil in Bucharest square' – 18th June.

The *Independent*'s editorial of 18th June said it all: 'In Romania, the government of the National Salvation Front has behaved in a fashion virtually indistinguishable from that of the Ceausescu regime it overthrew.' Scarcely any headlines and stories broke with these themes, although *The Times* of 22nd June was an exception: 'Mobs of both persuasions menace Romanian liberty' – 22nd June.

The reaction of the world community was swift and also punitive. On 15th June Bruce Millan, the European Community Commissioner, announced that a proposed European trade deal with Romania was suspended. He said, 'I can give an absolute assurance that we will not proceed with the ratification procedure in the kind of circumstances that face us in Romania at the moment.' Three days later the suspension of the trade deal was officially ratified at a meeting of European foreign ministers. Only the foreign ministers of France and Italy urged that time to deliberate on an 'over-hasty exclusion of Romania from the EC's aid package' was justified.

In a press statement, the foreign ministers said: 'The twelve believe that major acts of violence ... constitute a major obstacle on the road to democratic change.' The following day Romania was removed from the aid programme launched by the group of twenty-four developed nations for all Eastern Europe at the insistence of the EC Commissioner for Foreign Affairs, Frans Andriessen.

In Copenhagen on 15th June, the United States

delegate to the Conference on Security and Co-operation (CSCE) invoked the CSCE mechanism allowing, under the CSCE Helsinki Accords of 1975, a delegation to be sent to Romania because of 'the violent repression of demonstrations in Romania'. The European reaction had been swifter and more immediately punitive than after the killings of Tiananmen Square.

On 14th June the American Ambassador to Bucharest was recalled to Washington, and the White House spokesman, Marlin Fitzwater, said:

> The United States condemns in the strongest possible terms the rioting of the past two days, and the government-inspired vigilante violence that departs from the commonly accepted norms of democracy and the rule of law ... We are concerned that the deplorable events of the last two days are being used to justify the suppression of legitimate dissent in Romania ...

CHAPTER 20

Guilty or Not Guilty?

So the world's press and the world community had pronounced its verdict. Now for the trial, in which the reader must be the jury. The chief witnesses for the prosecution arraigned before the court are Ion Ratiu, the parliamentary leader of the Peasants' Party, Anton Uncu, the assistant editor of the opposition newspaper *Romania Libera*, the foreign journalists John Sweeney, of the British *Observer*, and William McPherson, the Pulitzer Prize-winner, and Radu Campeanu, the Liberal leader. The defence has called Ion Iliescu, the President of Romania, Petre Roman, its Prime Minister, George Galloway, the British Labour MP, and Gelu Voican, who played a leading role in the revolutionary days and is now a member of the Senate. The trial is, of course, a fictional reconstruction, but all submissions are taken from material spoken verbatim to the authors or from published written material, and the order of submission will not follow the strict rules of a trial. Where appropriate, the authors will provide necessary questions.

The central thesis of the prosecution is that the miners'

coming to Bucharest was planned by the government in advance to crush all opposition forces; thereby, the events of 13th June represent a predetermined provocation to allow this to take place. The Defence case rests saliently on the destabilisation of 13th June being a scenario to create conditions for a *coup d'état* which, in the absence of resolute action by the police and army, justified calling on the workers, even if the resultant action of the miners was judged excessive by all concerned.

Ion Ratiu speaks first for the Prosecution:

The idea that the miners' riot was a response to a threatened *coup d'état* is absolute bunkum. It was a Reichstag fire re-enacted. At least two weeks before, there was a vicious campaign against me in *Azi* and *Dimineata*, the FSN newspapers, that I was an Iron Guardist and ... had paid for the demonstration at University Square in hard currency ... Gelu Voican, the former Deputy Prime Minister, had a telephone conversation with Petrina, who was our General Secretary ... He told him, 'Why do you defend this man? ... Make him a scapegoat, and we will let you be ... We don't want him in the country. Make him a scapegoat, and you will be all right.'

What was the justification for bringing in the miners? The justification was that the students came and demonstrated and attacked the forces who cleared the square in the morning ... Not saying anything about how violently they cleared the square in the morning. When the counter-demonstration started about lunch-time, who set the buses on fire? Who set the Police Headquarters on fire? Who set the Ministry of the Interior on fire? It is ridiculous to say that where you have the forces of state at your disposal you cannot defend against 300 or 400 demonstrators.

I have got to be clear on one aspect of it. A few days later I saw General Stanculescu. He invited me to his army headquarters ... I said to him, 'Do you really believe that Iliescu thought he needed the miners?' So he smiled, and he said to me, 'Well, I had only arrived from abroad that evening, and I rang him up at five minutes past twelve and I told him that the situation was under control.'

So how could Iliescu let loose this mob of criminals? It was not that they were let loose to do as they pleased; they were directed by the Securitate. How did the miners know my address? ... How did miners from Petrosani know my address? Their whole argument is an insult to intelligence ... The whole thing was orchestrated, there is not a shadow of doubt about it ... and I don't believe that anything was done without the knowledge of Iliescu and Roman.

Anton Uncu, one of the assistant editors of *Romania Libera*, is next on the stand.

That 13th June could have been a pretext for the miners could be true; that 13th June was the cause of 14th and 15th June is false. When the miners arrived in Bucharest, the police were masters of the situation, so they did not come to restore a balance, they came to punish ... On what basis did the miners decide that people were guilty? This was decided for them by the press of the government who linked the students with the '*golani*', said that the leaders of the opposition were traitors and legionnaires and that journalists were the agents of foreign capitalists ... So you cannot say that the events of 13th June were the cause of 14th and 15th June.

The guilty men are Iliescu, Roman and Stanculescu ... To say that the paramilitary action of the 14th and 15th is absolved because of the riots of the 13th is wrong ... The 13th was either a popular uprising or a provocation, and the key to answering that is the action of the police and the army ... The rioters were allowed to pass like a knife through butter ... There is a recorded tape that has the voice of Chitac discussing with Diamandescu, saying clearly that the variant established with the President is that we set the buses on fire ... The army and police were involved in a scenario ... a provocation ... categorically. It is a unique performance. They have compromised the most radical anti-communist revolution in the eyes of the world.

Petre Roman, the Prime Minister, takes the stand as the first witness for the Defence. He is asked to speak of the early part of 13th June.

The moment when we heard of the burning of the first police truck will stay with me for a long time. It marked the beginning of something which we did not expect; the scale of it took us completely by surprise ... The chain of violence, the paths that it took ... The places that were attacked were of great concern to us as there was no mistaking the logic of the process, it was leading to the government's door. The attacks were on the ... key elements of the security of the government, and then the TV ... In other words, this was not some random protest that got out of hand; shops were not looted; banks were not robbed; they did not attack people in the street. For us, the only conclusion was that this was an attack on our democratic institutions ... against the political power invested in us by the elections.

It was really the critical moment for us when we realised that the army could not stop the violence ... We did not want them to shoot, and without that, the situation got further and further out of hand, and that, combined with the further attacks, forced our hand ...

At that moment we decided that the President should appeal to the population.

The Defence then asks Roman about the coming of the miners. 'Miron Cozma, the leader of the miners in Valea Jiului, is on record as saying that the miners were led astray ... Who led them astray?'

Roman answers, 'Yes, there were people involved in leading the miners astray, it's absolutely true ... Those who led the miners to the home of Ratiu were former members of the Securitate. Three of them are now in prison.'

Defence Counsel then asks, 'But many in the west ask that if former Securitate men were involved in this provocation, why has the government not done more?'

Roman says:

Well, there are forces in every society that are difficult to control ... You might say that there is a huge drug problem in Washington, so why has President Bush not put them all in jail? ... We are dealing with a sort of Mafia here ... the former elements of the Securitate and the former privileged communist bureaucracy ... their common interest being to conserve their privileges and some of their power ... And as far as I am concerned, their activities are still a problem.

The defence case rests. John Sweeney is called for the Prosecution. The Prosecutor asks: 'What questions did you ask about the Securitate in the article you wrote on the June events on 17th June 1990?'

Sweeney replies:

I wrote as follows: 'Most depressing of all is the re-emergence of the Securitate. In the days immediately after the revolution it was they who were afraid, running from our cameras, weakly replying, "I don't know" when asked if they worked in the Securitate building they had just emerged from ... It would be madness to doorstep the Securitate today. They swagger round the streets demanding papers but refusing to show their own. In the middle of the night they donned fancy dress, wearing clean, freshly pressed miners' jerkins and boots ...

'Who else but the Securitate showed Ratiu's house to the miners? Who bussed them in, organised their keep? Who pointed out the newspaper offices to wreck? The miners left as smoothly as they had come, packed into trains which left Bucharest on Friday evening, the good organisation of their departure suggesting that it had all perhaps been stage managed from above ... The fear machine is making a comeback.'

'How did your newspaper describe Mr Iliescu in its profile of him in the week following this article?'

Sweeney quotes: 'At best, Iliescu appears too hidebound to change; at worst he is the Securitate candidate ... looking less like the man to heal Romania's wounds than Bob Hoskins' out of depth gangster in the film *The Long Good Friday* ... When the moment came, Iliescu fitted smoothly into Ceausescu's shoes.'

'Thank you, Mr Sweeney.'

Iliescu comes to the stand to answer some of these accusations. 'What do you say to those who accuse you of being the shadow of Ceausescu?'

This government should be judged by what it has done on all counts. For people capable of serious analysis, the idea that the government is simply the old communists with new faces is without foundation. It may be convenient for sloganising, but look at the record. We have created an elected parliament and Senate, not there before; we have established a legislative framework for reform, not there before; now we are in the process of implementing the economic reform ... Of course our generation had to live with communism and we all carry that weight of the past. No one can get rid of such a thing ... We were bequeathed an economic and social catastrophe and particularly a crisis of morale, the depth of which only showed itself after the revolution. The state of general suspicion, the lack of willingness to work, and the existence of corruption are even more difficult problems, in the short term, than the economic ones.

'So what of the accusation that there was a pre-planned scenario which created 13th June as a provocation to allow the calling of the miners?'

Anyone who considers this seriously must see that it is a preposterous idea. The government had just won an overwhelming mandate at the polls and desperately needed western help to promote the economic reform ... In any case, has the opposition been destroyed? The idea of a coup appeared in the circumstances of 13th June ... Whether that was a mature judgment cannot be said even now, nor can it be said who programmed the scenario; but judging from their actions and the objectives attacked, the idea of a coup is easily sustainable.

'Did General Stanculescu phone you on the late evening of 13th June to tell you that everything was under control?'
'No, he was out of the country.' Iliescu leaves the stand. The last witness for the Prosecution is William

McPherson, a journalist who was an eye-witness in Bucharest on 13th and 14th June. He is asked to give details of his knowledge of the existence of a tape he has heard, which implicates the government in a provocation.

A tape has surfaced of a low-frequency police-band radio, recorded on 13th June. The government has denounced it as a provocation, but it sounds convincing. The background noise, the sense of urgency, the confusion, are all there, and it appears to confirm what many of us suspected: that the terrible violence and bloodshed that began that day, leading to the rampage of the miners on Thursday and Friday, were deliberately provoked. On the tape, officer 53 says to officer 52: 'Do you see any possibility of informing the President? We are starting to burn all the buses. This was the agreement.' The recording implicates a Mr Magureanu. Virgil Magureanu is the head of the new Romanian Intelligence Service whose purpose is 'to gather data and information on the activity of espionage and terrorist organisations against Romania, of extremists or of individuals who plan subversive actions to undermine the national economy, to destabilise the rule of law.' No one has been able to see the rule of law for some time in Romania; the rule of force and rumour and manipulation prevails.

On the tape, officer 52 says to officer 53: 'I don't know how we can resolve this. Magureanu retreated, and we don't know where he is. This was his business ... The Prime Minister's orders were to keep order until the workers arrived.' Two people who have listened to the tape insist that one of the voices is that of the Interior Minister, General Chitac, who has since been replaced. I did not recognise General Chitac's voice, so I cannot say.

'Thank you for your testimony, Mr McPherson.'

George Galloway is called to give evidence. He is a Scottish Labour MP who was in Bucharest at the time of the June events. Defence Counsel asks Galloway his opinion of the media coverage of these affairs.

Well, since extensive attention has been given to John Sweeney from the distinguished *Observer* newspaper, I feel I have to make one important point about his report which in a way illustrates a general problem. I met John Sweeney in the restaurant of the Hotel Bucharest on the evening of Friday 15th June. He asked me my opinion of the miners' violence. I told him I found it regrettable but suggested that before we rush into print condemning the Romanian government we should consider the serious situation they were faced with. I made the point that stern action would have been forthcoming in Britain if the BBC's Bush House was under occupation, Scotland Yard ablaze, the Home Office on fire and the House of Commons besieged. Unfortunately, whether as a result of editorial control or not, none of these points made it into the story. In fact, Mr Sweeney even offers an explanation which attempts to excuse the leaders of the 'golanis'' responsibility for the riots, when he says, and I quote, 'That afternoon, students, teenagers, and a job lot of hooligans outside the 'golanis'' control went looking for their friends to liberate them. The BBC will be showing riots from Sofia and calling it Bucharest next,' he joked, since it had already happened. I'm bound to say that I have often wondered what the reaction of the world's press would have been if after the Nicaraguan election Sandinista-led mobs had stormed the offices of state security in Managua.

'The defence rests.'
'Call Radu Campeanu, the leader of the National Liberal Party. Mr Campeanu, can you tell the court what

your impressions are of the matters we have discussed today?'

The appeal to the miners came on the day of the 13th, but according to our information it was arranged one or two days before that. Twelve thousand miners could not just decide simultaneously to go and buy a ticket to Bucharest. Their conduct in Bucharest was an insult to the twentieth century. The offices of the PNL (the National Liberal Party) in Bucharest were destroyed completely on the morning of the 14th – everything in sight.

I consider the *coup d'état* story a lie, a shameful lie. There are two possible hypotheses. Firstly, that Iliescu was forced to make these moves by those around him, to compromise him. Or that Iliescu panicked; he was afraid of the street, and he over-reacted to things and called the miners, but in either case he is utterly and totally compromised. Let us be clear – without doubt, former members of the Securitate were involved; it is almost incontestable.'

Campeanu was the final witness for the prosecution. The last witness for the defence is Gelu Voican. He, like Campeanu, is asked by the defence advocate to give his general impressions of all that has gone before. Voican strokes his white beard, and begins:

First, I have to say that the June events are part of a series of events, part of a chain of 12th January, 28th January, 18th February, 20th March and the events of June. All these days are linked by the causal chain of violent disturbances propagated, by oppositional elements, with the aim of destabilising Romania internally and compromising our reputation internationally. Specifically, the June disturbances developed because of the delayed reaction of the state authorities towards the inadmissable gangrene of University Square; it must be said loudly that the University Square protest was neither democratic nor political, but the most abusive occupation of a public place, using the most blatant anti-democratic pretensions. Those who took part in those riots were from the gutter, who were manipulated by agents of destabilisation.

In all of this, the police behaved lamentably ... ceding ground to these hooligans everywhere. And this, combined with the TV pictures, provoked an over-reaction from the people. The miners came and decided they would become the unaccountable judiciary of Romania. The information on the TV had given the impression that the government had been deposed. So they came in a frenzy, but not afraid of anything, because the nature of their work makes jail the lesser of two evils.

There were vicious excesses, but partly as a function of the law of high numbers. About 15,000 came to act as voluntary policemen. Now even if you had 15,000 angels in town you would have had a bit of raping and pillaging. The western press presented the two days as a perpetual atrocity ... but this was not so ... If it was two days of perpetual atrocity, where were the thousands of dead?

Even the extent of the violence used is, in some ways, admissible, because of the nature of what was going on. People who want to play rough games should not expect the kid-glove treatment when they get caught. Take, for example, Livriu Petrina, Secretary of the Peasants' Party. He certainly had Molotov cocktails in his car, and maybe guns too. In the basement of the Peasants' Party HQ there were cases of Molotovs found; that is why I called for Ratiu to be expelled from the country. It would have been a mistake, but I was furious. I was at the front of the firing line in a day when the forces of law and order were in total crisis. Let me tell you, in the early hours of the morning of the 14th I went out on a sweep with the paratroopers to arrest the last of these lowest orders who still wanted to throw lighted bottles.

'Were the Securitate involved in these days of disorder?'

In the disorder, yes ... Elements of the ex-Securitate, but the main leaders were elements of the former privileged communists who had been excluded from their privileges, along with people who have power complexes like Munteanu: one day a communist leader of the students and Securitate informer and the next an apostle of anti-communism; like the robber, the leader of the gang who becomes the terrible policeman overnight. Or Nicu Leon, another pocket dictator, who can be used for trouble because he wants a place in the sun. These types have joined forces with all the former privileged Ceaus-istes to sabotage the democratic process. They are prepared to risk a civil war. You should understand that is what we are talking about still, and that is what has been at stake since the revolution.

Two non-Romanians sum up the trial. For the Prosecution, Jessica Douglas-Home, drawing on her writings published in the *Daily Telegraph* on 21st July 1990, and for the Defence, Conor Cruise O'Brien, the redoubtable Irish columnist and former politician, speaking to the script of his article published in *The Times* on 22nd June 1990.

Jessica Douglas-Home:

On 13th June President Iliescu ... invited miners to restore order against 'Iron Guardist extremists'. Those who led the miners had a sleek, well-fed appearance which no one who lived on a Romanian miners' wages could easily acquire. They also sported shoes which were, until December, an infallible mark of the Securitate.

The 'Iron Guard extremists', by contrast, consisted of young students, many of them women, under the leadership of a Christian activist who preached the need for non-violence from a balcony in University Square, while warning his followers against 'agents provocateurs'. Putting two and two together, and observing not only the violence exercised against the protesters (as well as passers-by) but also the fact that it was the victims, and not the perpetrators, who were jailed, most western commentators have remained sceptical of Mr Iliescu's version of the events ...

President Iliescu claims no longer to be a communist, but a believer in a new kind of Romanian democracy suited to the 'Latin temperament'. However, this new kind of democracy bears a close kind of resemblance to the 'fascism' which it claims to be fighting. Not only does it rely on mob violence to assert its supremacy, it also encourages racial hatred. The 'miners' who entered Bucharest two weeks ago, in search of the fascist enemy, had an uncanny ability to discover this enemy in every gypsy face. No doubt, when the supply of gypsies runs out, the Hungarians will be put to similar use.

President Iliescu is a child of the 1930s, and his speech to the miners is reminiscent of the mass politics of those years ... In describing his opponents as 'legion-naires', he refers to the Legion of the Archangel Michael, a quasi-fascist movement which arose in Iase, where Mr Iliescu was for many years First Secretary of the Communist Party.

But his own techniques, in fact, bear a remarkable resemblance to those used by the Legion when it worked to bring General Ion Antonescu to power in

1940. The Romanian fascists practised the same kind of radical populism, setting students against teachers, soldiers against officers, and engineering an 'armed workers' corps'.

Mr Iliescu, like Hitler, is given to issuing warnings against the dark international forces which are gathering on the horizon ... His party intimidates its opponents, while his followers attack their homes and persons with impunity. The party newspapers, which enjoy a virtual monopoly of news, now carry daily libels against individuals who dare not defend themselves, and who in any case, possess – in the legal twilight which prevails in Romania – no possible remedy.

Democracy does not mean mass movements or mobilised enthusiasm; on the contrary, it means the careful fostering of dissent.

Conor Cruise O'Brien:

The outside world is right to condemn Mr Iliescu's use of the miners, and to discourage any repetition. But the outside world should not forget that the Iliescu government is the first democratically elected government of Romania, and that any replacement brought into power by non-democratic means would be likely to be worse.

It is also wrong to forget ... that there were two kinds of mob violence in Bucharest last week. The first was that of the students; the second – in response to the first – that of the miners. The second is that what people think of exclusively when they hear the words 'mob violence in Bucharest'. The existence of the first seems already forgotten ...

The great difference between the two sets of violence is that the first was directed against the elected government, while the second was initiated by the elected government in its own defence. Western governments are right to condemn government-sponsored mob violence. They are also right to convey the message that acceptance of a country as a democracy ... requires more than a freely elected government. It also requires the rule of law and freedom of expression, including freedom to oppose the government by peaceful means.

Those messages must be conveyed, and continue to be conveyed. That said, some patience is required. What: patience with the people who called in the miners? Yes, patience with exactly those people. We should never forget that the present Romanian government – unlike any of its predecessors – was freely chosen by the people. I know that even that is now being questioned, but although it has been charged that there were serious irregularities in the conduct of the elections, hardly anyone has claimed that the present government did not win an overall majority. The fact that an elected government behaves badly does not retrospectively invalidate its election.

We should also remember that the government was responding to a real threat to its survival. The student-led mob could not have taken over power itself, but was creating anarchy in the capital. If that had continued, military intervention would have been on the cards, which would probably have meant the end of Romania's experiment with democracy ...

William Waldegrave, the Foreign Office Minister ... proclaimed last week that the Romanian government is 'just as bad as Ceausescu'. A Romanian might retort that if Iliescu is no worse than Ceausescu, Iliescu rates a knighthood. Ceausescu's was taken from him, not because of his misdeeds, to which a blind eye was always turned, but because his regime was collapsing. So the moral outrage which the Foreign Office can credibly export to post-Ceausescu Romania is quite limited ...

Then there is the question of the students. The un-
favourable coverage given to the miners was altogether
justifiable. The favourable coverage given to the
students was not. The students were trying to wreck
Romania's first democratically elected government at
the moment of its taking office. Their pretext for doing
so was that the government contained communists.
The principle asserted by the students was that a
communist, if elected, should not be allowed to take his
seat. That principle, when accepted by the Reichstag in
1933, brought Adolf Hitler to power . . .

The real case against the students is not that they are
fascists; it is that they are asserting a privileged political
status for their own order, irrespective of the democratic process; and that they have backed that assertion
by violence.

Guilty or Not Guilty?

Miron Cozma and the Miners of the Jiu Valley

When I asked Miron Cozma how long he had worked in the coal mines of Romania, he held up his hands in front of his face. 'Long enough for this,' he said, indicating the stump on his hand where a thumb should be. Then he pointed to the bridge of his nose, where he has one of the blue-black scars that are the hallmarks of men, from all parts of the world, who have worked hewing coal. According to where you stand in the Byzantine political mythologies of today's Romania, Miron Cozma is cast either as the Prince of Democracy or the Demon of Darkness. He is the leader of the Jiu Valley men who stormed Bucharest in June 1990.

To get to Petrosani you travel north-west of Bucharest through Pitesti to Rimnicu Vilcea, just over a hundred miles away. Another sixty miles due east lies Tirgu Jiu, and sixty miles or so north from there, up the twisting narrow mountain roads of the Jiu Valley, lies Petrosani. If you go in October, you will pass through villages where nearly everybody is out in their Sunday best celebrating the nuptials of two of their young people; October is the month for weddings, when the wine is newly harvested and there is plenty to spare. Our car was stopped twice and bottles of rich red wine were handed in through the window as good-luck gifts to the first passers-by when the new bride and groom left the village church.

These are the lands that communism forgot because the mountain small-holdings were too small to collectivise, although the villages were still large enough to fall under the gaze of Ceausescu's planners, marked for destruction in his megalomaniac dreams of 'modernisation'. Thus today the villages exhibit a strange dichotomy of dilapidation, where repairs ceased due to the coming communist razing, and fresh red-brick new buildings, with the promise of private ownership offered by the government of the revolution. Most of the villages have electricity, but water is taken from the well. On the roadsides, old women with hard hands and lined faces wore head-scarves and clothes in the manner of their grandmothers, and sold red apples for 25 lei a pound (10 lei = 15 pence).

Tirgu Jiu is a bustling reminder of the twentieth century: its traffic lights and hotels came as a surprise after the horses and carts and gaggles of geese on the way. The world-renowned sculptures of Constantin Brancusi are in a special park in the centre of town. We walked under Brancusi's 'Gate of the Kiss', we sat at Brancusi's 'Table of Silence' and stared at the concrete hexagons of the 'Endless Column'. Our thoughts were not on sculpture but on the endless columns that went to Bucharest in June.

As we travelled up the Jiu Valley, as dusk fell, an unmistakable atmosphere of crepuscular foreboding encroached. The River Jiu rushes black and polluted in the valley bottom, whose sheer black basalt valley sides are covered in dark coniferous forest. It needed only a Transylvanian castle or two to conjure up Bram Stoker's *Dracula*. Even in daylight, the head of the valley has a pervasive gloom about it. The haystacks are grey-green and the haystack tops are black, testimony to the polluting soot of the near-by Paroseni power station, which has operated without filters for years and blackens everything. The landscape has the permanent look of a colour television set tuned near the black and white spectrum.

The Hotel Petrosani stands in the centre of town like a threat. As we walked through its doors, a blast of cold air hit our faces, evidence, finally, of the old Romanian Ceausescu joke of the mother telling her child to close the living-room window lest a passer-by catch cold. There was no heating for the five days we stayed in Petrosani, no hot water, and nights of misery at 36 US dollars a time; only Ceausescu's communism could have yielded a town that shivered for lack of heat on the top of a coalfield.

Valerica Matei, Secretary of the Miners' League, the miners' union founded in March 1990 after the strike for higher wages, and Nicolae Croitoru, leader of the miners from Vulcan, came to see us the next morning. Vulcan is one of a string of mining towns in the valley which has fifteen pits; the four biggest are at Vulcan, Petrila, Petrosani and Lupeni. About 200,000 people live in the Jiu Valley, 60,000 of them working in mining, of whom 54,000 are members of the Miners' League.

Matei has an Arthur Scargill hairstyle; to camouflage his thinning on top he spreads his hair above his left ear and sweeps the strands over the top. The immediate similarities were compounded by his opening words, which concerned his distrust of journalists. He said that, since June, six different television companies had come to Petrosani to make programmes, all steadfastly promising that a video recording of their work would be sent. 'Only the BBC kept their word,' he said.

He had been a member of the Communist Party for fourteen years, joining in 1975 when there was a prospect of going on a student delegation to China. 'I was a member of the Party, but never a communist ... Millions were like me,' he said. So what did the Ceausescu era mean to him? 'It meant cold, hunger, thin white-faced children, and accidents in the mine ... In the last twenty years 900 people ... 900 people,' he repeated, 'have died in the mines of the Jiu Valley. The situation is desperate. You'll see that if you go down a mine. We need technology, but technology requires dollars, and we have none.'

In his earliest years in the pit, Nicolae Croitoru took part in the strike in 1977, the first serious thunder against Ceausescu's rule, between 3rd and 7th August. The Prime Minister of the day was Ilie Verdet, and when he came to negotiate with the miners, they took him down a mine, at Lupeni, and held him hostage until Ceausescu himself came. 'He spoke here,' Croitoru said, 'up on the balcony at the mine, without microphones, without flowers and without red carpets. When the miners whistled and jeered when he spoke, he realised how serious it all was. He promised us everything, for all time, but after 1985 he took it all back.'

It was an important point, because it explains why the miners are held in reverence by many in Romania today as the first, and thereby the bravest, dissidents, and why Ceausescu sent hundreds of Securitate men to work in the mines thereafter. Matei and Croitoru told us that the miners were not the rich men, the privileged workers, that some people say. 'Many have come here without an idea of how difficult the work is ... and most of them leave when they find out ... When Mr Binder of the *New York Times* was here and we took him down a mine, he told us that it was the closest he had ever been to Hell in his life; and he had been to Vietnam,' Matei said, evincing a certain pride drawn from a well-worn ability to make a virtue out of a necessity.

Francisc Appel is the Director of Coal Preparation in the Jiu Valley, who had been appointed to the position after the revolution. As if that were not enough burden to heap on any shoulders, he is also mayor of Vulcan. His demeanour and countenance are a manifestation of the worries he now faces daily. On the way to Vulcan we passed through Aninoasa, a 'new town' which looks like a large building site, where the problem of alcoholism in the area was corroborated by the queues in the street at 9 a.m. to buy illicit tuica, a potent local plum brandy. In the major cities of Britain, the worst housing units in the peripheral working-class housing estates are termed 'DTLs' by the weary assistants who adminsiter their allocation. The acronym comes from the definition, 'Difficult To Let'. Vulcan looks like one gigantic DTL.

When Francisc Appel was asked what he had achieved in his two-month period as mayor, he remained silent for a yawning thirty seconds. Then he replied, rather disconsolately, 'I should never have taken the job, because of the scale of the problems. All I can probably do is lose, and then I'll get the tomatoes for not producing the solutions.' Then he listed: 'Four kilometres of new road, the building of a new cemetary, a statue in the local park to the Romanian soldiers who fell in the First World War, reorganising some of the commercial practice in the local shops, and discussing with the local clergy about how people's attitudes can be improved.' He added, 'You can ask people to make sacrifice and effort in some circumstances how can you ask it in circumstances which are as difficult as ours? . . . We suffer material deprivations and a mentality inherited from forty-five years of imposed social thinking.'

If Appel had a magic wand, he would 'get people to pull together seriously, without pretensions'. He is a member of the Ecology Party. He told us that in the Jiu Valley they got a good vote, but not good enough to secure any position in the elections for the Senate and parliament. The Senator for the Jiu Valley is a Liberal, and the four deputies to parliament are split evenly between the ruling National Salvation Front and the Liberals.

The offices of the Miners' League are in the centre of Petrosani, in a large two-storey building that houses the community halls of the town. We interviewed Miron

Cozma there a day later. Cozma is of medium height and has an edge to his opinion as hard as the anthracite he has worked. In the union offices, he is immediately recognisable as a man without peer here. He is the one everyone is waiting to see. After the usual courtesies, he offered a question and a warning for openers: 'There are two types of journalist – those who tell the truth, who write as things are, and those who write as they want things to be. Which category are you in?' He then added, 'I want you to send me a copy of what you write ... Those who don't, don't get a second interview.'

Immediately, we were interrupted by a telephone call. He barked commands into the phone, then resumed. 'Would he pose for a photograph?' 'Yes.' But as he did so, he was banging on the table answering questions from others in the room. The interpreter told him in translation, 'They say that if you don't stop banging the table the picture will look as though you are the man from the Valea Jiului who always bangs the table!' Cozma paused, and said, smiling, 'It's not far from the truth.' When he was asked about Bucharest, he pointed to the table, and said, 'We'll start here in Petrosani first.' He pointed out of his office window to the slabs of grim, grey, four-storey concrete flats nearby.

Do you know that these houses have no heating just now and have to use bottled gas for cooking because Ceausescu insisted that they would have no chimneys in case the miners stole coal for their fires? We need 32,000 gas bottles a month, and this month we have had 16,000 only ... Do you know that eighty-six miners died in the Jiu Valley mines in 1989, twenty-nine of them on 10th September in an explosion in the Vulcan mine? Before you write anything about the miners, tell your readers that these are the worst mines in all of Europe.

The newspapers don't know the situation, even our

own newpapers; a miner at the coalface in his first year gets 3,914 lei per month; a specialist miner gets 7,100 lei per month and the average wage is 5,000 lei [the average wage in Romania is 4,000 lei], and these wages are payable only if the production targets are reached. All this talk of the miners made rich by the government is not accurate. Look at the place ... People had reached the limits of endurance here ... The idea that the miners marched to Bucharest to support communism is laughable.

Later he repeated this point, illustrating it by referring to the results of the May elections, emphasising that the National Salvation Front (FSN) had made far from a clean sweep. This last point was made by a number of miners who spoke over the course of the days in Petrosani. They insisted they went to defend an elected government, not the FSN.

The issue that Cozma, and others, raised about the difficulties of life in the valley is also accurate. It is incontestable that life there is grim. Petrosani, Petrila, Lupeni and Vulcan nearby are urban Stalags. In October, there was no heating in most houses because the local system had almost collapsed. Food is purchased from near-empty shops. Petrosani supermarket had its window filled almost entirely with boxes of dried Vietnamese prawns. The bad new was that there were only prawns. The good news that there were plenty of them. If you ask the mothers of these parts what they would like, the reply is universal: Chocolate or sweets for the children.'

Once the difficulties of buying food are defeated, it then has to be cooked on stoves fuelled by gas in bottles that were chronically difficult to replace when empty. The only commodity that seemed to be available in abundance was the local tuica. These harsh realities are, however, used by those who argue the miners' case as an implicit plea in mitigation. The unspoken inference has two dimensions:

one that harsh lives are some sort of explanation for harsh justice; the other that the prospect of the rays of hope shining from a new government being illegally extinguished drove some of the miners to apoplectic despair – and the Bucharest rampage was the result.

So while accepting Cozma's emphasis on the hard edge of life here, it was argued that this was no mitigation for the bludgeoning of Bucharest. 'How did it feel to be known in the west as the leader of men who clubbed women and young students in the street?' He says:

> There has been disinformation about all this … We had a government elected by the whole people … then on the 13th there were riots which threatened the democratic institutions, and the police and army who should have defended these institutions didn't, so the miners went to do it … I don't deny there were serious excesses, but I can say with all my conviction that the miners were misled by people who infiltrated their ranks and deliberately compromised them.

At this, he produced a copy of *Romanul Liber* (*Free Romanian*), a monthly newspaper published in Britain, with Ion Ratiu as its Honorary President. Cozma pointed out inconsistencies in the photographs in its June 1990 issue that showed miners beating people in Bucharest. In one, where a man was being beaten, it was clear that those carrying clubs had civilian clothes below miners' jackets. In another, a man with the miners was wearing Adidas trainers. 'These men are not miners,' Cozma argued.

'So, who were they? Who led the demonstrators on the 13th? Who took them to the television?' … 'There was a *coup d'état* attempted, a scenario, and when the miners came, they were used to confuse all this,' he replied.

Cozma argued: 'If the miners had gone to Bucharest to

wreck the opposition party headquarters, why did they not start in the Jiu Valley, where the people voted for opposition parties, and their offices were not touched? ... If they went to persecute students, why did they not start here at the Academy of Mines, where there are 4,000 students?' He said that one of the Vice-Presidents of the Peasants' Party, Jantau, had testified to the parliamentary commission that their offices in Bucharest were wrecked before the miners arrived on the 14th. Some months later the Liberal Senator who represents the Jiu Valley, Petru Jurcan, made a similar statement in the Romanian press about the Liberal Party headquarters.

Cozma said also that the miners were not called, but went when they saw the events of the 13th on television. From the stack of papers he was carrying that day, he produced railway-ticket receipts for the miners from Lupeni who went to Bucharest. The jumble of receipts totalled 75,460 lei for 462 tickets. 'They all bought their own tickets,' he said. The only thing he might concede in all this was that the road to Hell was paved with good intentions. He argued in the railway station that they should not go to Bucharest, from the practical point of view that the information about what had happened was confused, but 'They were listening to no one then.'

'So, what about Ratiu and his house?' 'Well, Mr Ratiu probably told you that a miner nearly killed him, but did he tell you that it was a miner who saved him? ... That it was a miner, a man from the Jiu Valley, who stopped him being beaten with a club? Did Mr Ratiu tell you also that five of the men who wrecked his house stole 100,000 dollars from him, and we caught one of them here in Petrosani and turned him in to the police, and he got 80,000 dollars back as a result of this?' In reply to Ratiu's other charges, he said, 'We have had piles of letters from all over the country thanking the miners for saving democracy.'

'So, what happens if the same sort of thing happens

again? Will the miners go to Bucharest again?' 'Yes, but this time all the leaders will go with them and there will be proper organisation and we will not be led astray by anyone of ill will to the country ... Bucharest is the beating heart of the country and there are those of ill intention who want to break that beating heart. The miners want a country with a beating heart.' It will come as no surprise that his farewell handshake was as firm and resolute as his defence of his men.

After the interview we spoke with the Vice-President of the League, Ilie Torsan. He that the wife of the leader of the Liberal Party had written on behalf of her charity organisation to say that they had forgiven the miners, adding that the Christian organisation was prepared to build a church in the valley for them. 'And will they accept?' 'Yes,' he said, 'but we would prefer them to build us a children's hospital. We have plenty of churches.'

They waited to go into the cage with faces like men on death row. Underground, under heaving pine timbers, in narrow seams, men stripped to the waist toiled with picks and shovels. Sweat droplets cut paths down the coal-dust on their backs, like snail trails glistening in the night. As slurries of coal fragments fell from the roof, the pages of Zola's *Germinal*, the epic story of the miners of France in the late 1860s, came to mind.

There is a chronic rage in these men. Their most frequent question was, 'How would you like to work down here every day?' When Bucharest was brought up among different groups, there were not always uniform answers, but always uniform anger. One miner remonstrated, 'Are we to work here in the ground so that they can sleep warm in their beds all day and come out to destroy the government at night?'

—— CHAPTER 21 ——

The Last and the First Chapter

The weeks and months that followed the June events were hard ones for Romania. The country was quarantined in Europe and the west. At the time of approaching economic reform, this ostracism meant that much-needed technical and financial aid was denied. The new government of Petre Roman was a government of technocrats: young men eager to change things, their élan seriously debilitated by the international boycott. The first administration that Roman inaugurated in Romania after the revolution had only three men who survived to become members of his government after the May election: Iliescu, Stanculescu and Roman himself.

In September, Adrian Severin, the Deputy Prime Minister in charge of the economic reform put it this way:

> We have paid and are paying an enormous price for the miners' advanture ... I must say that it is astonishing to me the way the west has turned its back on Romania ... How can genuine democracy evolve in Romania if the economic reform fails? ... The great paradox is that western governments helped with huge investments in

the Ceausescu era, which was part of an undeniably communist approach, while our appeals now for help to build a market economy fall on deaf ears ... We are asking for expertise to carry out the reform of communism, and the reply we get is that there can be no help for Romania because it is not reforming the old system. It is absurd.

That was in September. By the end of the year, the ice of ostracism had begun to melt. On 1st November 1990 Romania implemented the first stage of an ambitious price reform to begin the process of transforming the economy. This action, along with its resolute boycott of Iraqi oil, and its support for American policy in the Gulf conflict during its membership of the UN Security Council, demonstrated that the 'old communist' smear seemed, to say the least, questionable.

In the middle of November, in relation to these issues, Roman said:

Well, we have reached a very critical point of the reform of our economy ... We have to learn some hard truths now ... All the people of Romania have to face up to the realities of life in the free market now ... We have to recognise that the current structures of the economy are the product of more than forty years of communism ... No one has returned from Hell before ... but we are going to do it.

We have consulted experts across the world and we know what we are doing ... Of course things are going to be difficult, but I think we will see the winter through reasonably well.

Life in Romania is always interesting ... Not so long ago our opposition told us that we would never reform the Romanian economy, that the government wanted to talk about reform, but would never change the old system ... you know the arguments ... we are all still

really communists. Well, who can say that now, when
we are taking concrete steps to introduce the market
economy?...

He added that the reform had to be carried out at a pace
that took the people with the government and argued that,
of all the countries of Eastern Europe, Romania had made
the greatest progress in economic reform, if change was
measured against time. 'I believe we have actually covered
the ground towards privatisation of the economy in a
much more clear and decisive manner than the other countries of the Eastern bloc ... Now we face our greatest challenge: price liberalisation ... It will mean a great shock
for the country, but we have decided to do it because until
we do it a false impression can be given abroad of our
intentions.'

'Back from Hell' are the words for it. Whether Romania
traverses that route from state ownership to private
ownership successfully is the most important issue deter-
mining its short- and long-term future. If politics is
concentrated economics, Romania's political perspectives
will reflect how successful the government is in achieving
the goal of creating a capitalist Romania. The perils ahead
have to be acknowledged, for Romania lies in the shadow
of the economic disaster that is threatening all Eastern
Europe.

The breathtaking sweep of the 1989 revolutions in
Eastern Europe allowed the words of Marx's *Communist
Manifesto* to be re-written. A spectre was haunting Eastern
Europe – the spectre of Capitalism. But in 1990 the results
that followed indicated just how difficult it has been to
make substance of the spectre.

The joyous days of anti-communist coalitions, which
characterised most of the new governments of Eastern
Europe in 1989, have given way to societies racked by an
economic crisis which scars their politics with contradictions and deep divisions. It may be a consolation that the

early months of 1991 suggested that all of Eastern Europe was being Romanianised.

For the governments of Eastern Europe, economic reform is the 'poisoned chalice'. They see no alternative to economic reform, but they will have to deal with the enormous social and political crises that are consequent upon it.

Eastern Europe is bankrupt, as the figures in Appendix 2 show. The UN Economic Commission estimates that industrial production in Eastern Europe in 1990 dropped by 20 per cent on the calamitous achievements of 1989. On top, the 20 billion dollar bill for the boycott of Iraqi oil will have to be paid in 1991, as well as the price of the Soviet Union's wanting dollars for its oil exports from 1st January 1991. Economic disaster beckons.

In this context, the talk of 'Swedish' models and the relevance of the 'Japanese experience' is frankly hopelessly optimistic. What are the political implications of 'Argentina' being the more appropriate model? The London-based Centre for Policy Research estimated in a report published at the start of November 1990 that Eastern Europe could double its gross domestic product in the next decade. But, given the moribund state of these post-Stalinist economies – private enterprise still accounts for only 10 per cent of production in Hungary, for example – that would require investment inflow of 100 billion dollars per year. Those dollars are simply not forthcoming. If 1989 marked the end of un-socialist socialism, then 1990 was the year of capitalism without capital.

This may all seem catastrophic when Romania's first year after the revolution is looked at in this context. However, the caveat which might be offered is that Romania is certainly facing up to change in a way that its southern European neighbours, Yugoslavia and Bulgaria, are currently incapable of. And now, in circumstances that have some of its northern cousins looking over their shoulders, before they pay interest on the billions which they owe and which Romania doesn't, it is not fanciful to see the country re-emerge as the most powerful and influential in southern Europe in the next decade.

None the less it is not only the Romanian government and its people that will be put to the test in the coming years. Can capitalism provide substance to its promise to change things irrevocably for the better?

The cruel joke that did the rounds in Moscow in the early part of 1990 may have more to it than cynicism about the economic catastrophe that communism has bequeathed to the future of Eastern Europe: 'You can make fish soup out of an aquarium, but can you make an aquarium out of fish soup?'

So what is the spectre now haunting Eastern Europe? What will happen if the promised economic miracle does not materialise?

There may be a return to the politics of the 1930s. Then the region was plagued with xenophobic nationalism, territorial disputes, ethnic rivalries and Bonapartist dictators like Pilsudski in Poland, Antonescu in Romania and Horthy in Hungary, who marched in the streets before the coming of the Third Reich. Such perspectives may seem unduly pessimistic after the glories and the promise of the revolutions of 1989. But it does not require a great leap in imagination, in looking at present-day Romania, to see the real possibility of these spectres taking on flesh if the economic reform fails and the whole of life becomes a desperate struggle for bread.

John Pilger once said that journalism is history's first draft. His words have an applicable conciseness to the efforst we have made to chart our ship of record through these difficult and dangerous waters. We have also tried to obey the maxim of Herodotus, the world's earliest recognisable historian, who explain that if you wished to find out why the Greeks fought the Persians, you had to record both sides of the story. We have, however, done so without pretending that complete objectivity is either attainable or desirable.

So in our last paragraphs we first go to a Romanian historian to help us with our epilogue, for to contemplate the future, you have to look at the past. The historian is Dinu C. Giurescu, now a distinguished Professor of History at the University of Bucharest. His father was the renowned Romanian historian, Constantin Giurescu, who wrote the legendary *Forests in the History of the Romanian People*. For those who dwell in the nether world of Romanian politics lubricated by spite and venom, this introduction is no doubt enough to damn Giurescu for one reason or another. But the politicians and the journalists, have had their say.

Listen to what Giurescu says of Petre Roman: 'It was a good time for me when I heard that he was Prime Minister.' The reason was personal. Giurescu left Romania for a life in America in 1988. He was forced out after his six-year campaign between 1979 and 1985 against Ceausescu's destruction of Romania's architectural heritage. By the end of it he was banned from travelling, his family house had been destroyed and he could only teach history of the seventeenth and eighteenth centuries. In 1987, when his home was demolished, he had to disperse his belongings to relatives and friends. On that fateful day, only Petre Roman turned up to help him.

And Iliescu?

When I left for America, there was only one name on people's lips – Ion Iliescu – but a lot of people don't want to admit that now. In fact, now, they shout 'Jos Iliescu!' with more vigour than they ever shouted 'Jos Ceausescu!'

It's mostly intellectuals who do it, and it is a reflection of our past. In all Eastern Europe the intellectuals had a guilt complex and did something. Solidarity, the samizdat circles in Hungary, Charter 77 in Czechoslovakia ... Here they did nothing, partly because of the Securitate, but only partly, and now the louder they shout 'Jos communismul!' the better to wash away their sins ... I doubt if anyone else had been elected you would have got things much different, because everyone is a prisoner of history.

And what of his reply on the 'coup or revolution?'; question.

It was a popular uprising which succeeded because the army joined the revolution. In parallel, you had the normal endeavours of politicians and military people to change things, but it was the revolution that broke the dictatorship. The widespread psychology of a coup is based on a lack of knowledge.

And June?

June was terrible for the image of the government. To call on the miners and let them do what they did was a huge blunder, but none the less the government had been elected on a huge mandate and promised the market economy, civil rights and pluralism, and so I would give them time, with a constructive critical attitude. Those who say that nothing has changed are not facing the truth. Take the Securitate. Each country needs an intelligence service but it should not be the watchdog of every citizen that the former Securitate was before. Now if it no longer operates in that old way then why can't some of its old employees be used? Maybe some long for the old times but I think that now they are crippled because the people know it is all finished ... the people are afraid no longer ... They speak out, they are active and shouldn't Iliescu get some credit for that?

*

Giurescu says that all of communism was based on a lie.

> People said publicly that they supported the Party, and
> they didn't. That was for forty-five years. And for the
> last decade of that at least, there was a universal hate
> figure: Ceausescu. He was to blame for everything. It
> will take time before people get used to telling the truth
> again and not casting blame on the head of one man for
> all the problems of society ... You have to face it that
> people will not change in twenty-four hours ...
>
> Consider the June events ... Maybe there was a
> plot and the army did not intervene deliberately.
> Maybe, however, everyone was scared stiff of genocide
> indictments on the morrow, if they did the wrong thing
> today ... Maybe there was a calamity because Stancu-
> lescu was in a forest in East Germany and he had all the
> key codes of command.
>
> Romania needs some kind of co-existence; that will
> sometimes be very difficult, with muddy compromises,
> even with fingers pointed in accusation ... I have
> stopped reading newspapers that only criticise every-
> thing.

Harrison Salisbury, the veteran American foreign correspondent, went to the Eastern bloc for the first time in the
early 1950s. In 1957, leaving Poland after the 1956 insurrection, he wrote:

> In autumn 1957 I had not yet experienced the Japanese
> film *Rashomon*, the dramatisation of the classic enigma
> of truth, the inescapable, ordained contradictions, life
> distorted to infinity in its own mirror.
>
> I knew in Warsaw as I walked through the October
> events that I was walking in a hall of facets ... Thirty
> years later I cannot be certain what was real and what
> was imagined ... which has caused me to return to *Rash-
> omon* ... to study this metaphor of life and remind

myself that there is no truth. There are many truths, some valid for one, some for another. Things are not what they seem ... It is a lesson we must learn and relearn because always we keep searching for certainty, and certainty does not exist.

If you have journeyed through this reconstruction of the downfall of the Ceausescus and the early days of the Romanian revolution, you will understand now the significance of these words.

Romania – 20th May Election Results
Presidential, Parliamentary and Senate Elections

1. PRESIDENTIAL ELECTION

Total electorate	17,200,722	
Total votes cast	14,826,616 (86.2%)	
Votes cast: Valid votes	14,378,693	
Spoiled	447,923 (3%)	

Presidential election result

Name	Votes	percentage
Ion Iliescu	12,232,498	85.07
Radu Campeanu	1,529,188	10.64
Ion Rativ	617,007	4.29

2. PARLIAMENTARY ELECTION
(on proportional list system)

Name of party	Votes	Percentage of poll	No. of MPs
National Salvation Front	9,089,659	66.31	263
Union of Romanian/ Hungarians	991,601	7.23	29
National Liberals	879,290	6.41	29
Ecology Party	398,864	2.67	12
National Peasants and Christian Party	351,357	2.56	12
Romanian Social Democrats	73,014	1.05	5

3. SENATE ELECTIONS

Name of party	Votes	Percentage of poll	No. of Senators
National Salvation Front	9,353,006	67.02	91
Union of Romanian/ Hungarians	1,004,353	7.06	12
National Liberals	985,094	7.02	10
National Peasants and Christian Party	348,687	2.50	1
Ecology Party	341,478	2.45	1

—— APPENDIX 2 ——

Eastern Europe: the Economic Facts

Country	Population (millions)	Labour force (millions)	Per capita income (EEC=100)	National debt (billions of dollars)	Per capita national debt (dollars)
Poland	38	19	40	43	1131
Yugoslavia	24	10	45	18	750
Romania	23	11	35	1	43
GDR	16	9	75	21	1312
Czechoslovakia	16	8	70	7	437
Hungary	11	5	55	20	1818
Bulgaria	9	4	45	10	1111
Argentina	33			45	1363

(Source: Deutsche Bank, *Eastern Europe Special Report*, 1989)

SOURCES

All sources used in this book come from newspaper reports of these events, drawn chiefly from the *Independent*, the *Independent on Sunday*, the *Guardian*, *The Times*, the *Sunday Times*, the *Financial Times*, the *Observer*, the *Daily Telegraph*, the *Glasgow Herald*, the *Scotsman*, *Scotland on Sunday*, *Granta*, the *New York Times*, the *Washington Post*, the *St Louis Post-Dispatch* and the collected contemporary archives at *Rompres* in Bucharest.

Many verbatim accounts come from lengthy personal interviews undertaken by the authors with all protagonists in Romania, and journalistic colleagues and friends in Great Britain.

Selected bibliography includes:

Ascherson, Neil *The Polish August* 1981
Bradbury, Malcolm, *Rates of Exchange* 1982
Fischer, Mary Ellen, *Nicolae Ceausescu: A Study in Political Leadership*
Garton-Ash, Timothy, *We, the People* 1990
Kopacsi, Sandor, *In the Name Of the Working Class* 1989
Manning, Olivia, *The Balkan Trilogy* 1987
Pacepa, Ion *Red Horizons* 1989
Rosen, Moses *Dangers, Tests and Miracles* 1990
Salisbury, Harrison E. *Disturber of the Peace* 1989
Selbourne, David, *Death of a Dark Hero* 1990
Simpson, John, *Despatches from the Barricades* 1990
Teaffe, Peter, *The Masses Arise: the Great French Revolution* 1989
Tokes, Laszlo, *With God, for the People* 1990

———— INDEX ————

Academy of Mines, 280
Adevarul, 210
ADN, East Germany news
    agency, 117–18
Africa, 51, 58
agriculture, 14
Aids virus, 26, 57, 58–64
Alexandra, Tsarina, 100
Almond, Mark, 197
America, *see* USA
Andriessen, Frans, 255
Andropov, Yuri, 29
Angel Appeal, 62
Aninoasa, 277
anti-semitism, 67, 69, 71, 74,
    78, 81, 82; *see also* Jews of
    Romania
'anti-Sovietism', 14–15
Antonescu, Marshal Ion, 7, 67,
    70, 71, 72, 142, 238, 269,
    287
Appel, Francis, 276–7
Arabs, 20, 82–5, 211
Arafat, Yasser, 83–7, 177
architectural genocide, 90–94,
    102, 184, 186, 188, 273,
    288–9
Architecture Department, 137
Association of 17th December,
    120–21
Auerbach, Rabbi Leibish, 66
Australia, 62

Avram, Constantin, 243
Azi, 258

Baiu, Colonel Ion, 182, 200
Balan, Radu, 130
Balcescu, Nicolae, 124
Balthazar, Bogdan, 209
Baneasa airport, 172
Banes, Victor, 241
Begin, Menahem, 82, 84
Belgrade, 123
Berlin, 91, 100, 140, 229, 242;
    Wall, 100, 104, 208
Bessarabia, 142
Binder, Mr, 275
Birledeanu, 160, 163
Birsan, Livia, 42
birthrate legislation, 54–7
Black Sea, 14, 59, 73
Blandiana, Ana, 164
Bobu, Secretary to the General
    Committee, 145, 168, 170
Boeru, Captain Ion, 194–5,
    196–9
Borcea, Alina, 60, 61, 63
Borcea, Sabin, 60, 63
Borza, Maria, 176, 179
Boteni, 194, 196, 197, 234
Brancusi, Constantin, 273
Brasov, 99, 122, 123, 167, 169
Brecht, Bertolt, 36

Brezhnev, Leonid, 18, 23, 24, 29, 84
British Foreign Office, 90
British Royal College of Chemistry, 33
Brown Shirts, *see* National Socialists
Brucan, Silviu, 33, 160, 161, 163, 165, 178, 212, 216, 218
Bucharest, 4, 5, 7, 9–11, 14, 18, 24–5, 30, 38, 40, 42, 44, 51, 55, 61, 72, 78, 90–94, 114, 118, 134, 137–8, 140–65, 167, 169, 172, 175, 181–2, 188, 191–2, 200, 202, 208, 210, 212, 220–22, 225, 227, 231–3, 236, 238–40, 242, 244, 246–9, 252–4, 256, 258–9, 262, 264, 266, 269, 272–3, 277–8, 279–82; *see also* Central Committee building *and* Central Military Hospital
Bucharest Guild of Leather and Footwear Workers, 9, 30
Bucovina, 70
Budapest, 100, 123, 140
Bulgaria, 24, 286
Bush, President George, 261
Butariu, Viorica, 133

CADA (committee of army officers), 229, 240, 251
Cairo, 84
Calderon, Jean-Louis, 119
Calinescu, Armand, 70
Camaresescu, 247
Camp David agreements, 84
Campeanu, Pavel, 31
Campeanu, Radu, 215, 217, 223–4, 257, 265–6
capitalism, 186, 286–8
Caramitru, Ion, 160
Carlyle, Thomas, *The French Revolution*, 99
Carol II, King of Romania, 5–7, 67, 70, 142, 185
Carruthers, Garrey, 218
Carter, President Jimmy, 84
Ceausescu, Alexandra (mother), 5, 7–8
Ceausescu, Andruta (father), 5, 7–8
Ceausescu, Elena (wife), 29, 80, 99, 123, 132, 134; execution, 3–4, 196–9; meets Nicolae, 9, 10–11, 30–31; marriage to Nicolae, 11; education of, 30–32; 'Miss Working Class 1939', 30–31; Ph.D. in industrial chemistry, 32–3, 37; lifestyle of, 34–6; love of clothes, 35, 36; in politics, 36–8, 89–90; children of, 39, 41, 45, 47–9, 50–51, 52; visit to Asia, 88–9; emergency meeting of Romanian Communist Party, 114–16; and Central Committee, 145–7; escape in helicopter, 147–8, 151–2, 168–70; fall of, 156; arrest of, 159, 171; order for execution, 162; trial of, 178–9, 181, 183–95; sentence of death, 194–5; burial, 201–3
Ceausescu, Ilie (brother), 158–9
Ceausescu, Nicolae, 141, 173, 211, 213, 215, 231, 262,

277, 290, 291; execution of, 3–4, 196–9; birth and childhood, 4–5; early arrests and imprisonment, 7–10, 30, 40; meets Elena, 9, 10–11, 30–31; marriage to Elena, 11; leader of Communist Youth Union, 11–12; Marxism of, 12; new Romanian Workers' Party, 12–13; receives Order of the Bath, 14, 80, 90; leadership, 15, 16–22, 24–6, 28–9, 32, 76, 82; speeches, 18, 25–6, 28, 86, 128–9, 132–4; visit of Marshal Tito, 19; visit of Zhou Enlai, 19–20; visit of Brezhnev, 20; visit to Prague, 23–4; stand over Czechoslovakia, 23–5, 53, 84; personality cult, 28, 88, 97, 135; character of, 31, 35; lifestyle of, 34–6; children of, 39, 41, 44–5, 47–9, 52; 'state of morality', 53–64; birthrate legislation, 54; regime, 80, 97, 99, 101–5, 112–13, 142, 163, 208, 231, 248, 255, 271, 275, 285; emigration policy, 83; relations with Arabs and Jews, 84–7; visit to Asia, 88–9; architectural genocide, 90–94, 102, 273, 288–9; emergency meeting of Romanian Communist Party, 114–16; offers resignation as General Secretary, 116; telephone conference, 116–17; visit to

Iran, 117, 123, 128, 150, 186; broadcasts to nation, 128–9; addresses demonstrators, 132–4; gives orders to General Milea, Minister of Defence, 138–9; orders General Milea to be shot, 143–4; and Central Committee, 144–6; last message to people of Bucharest, 147; escape in helicopter, 147–8, 151–2, 167–70; fall of, 149, 156; arrest of, 159, 171; order for execution, 162; trial of, 178–9, 181, 183–95; sentence of death, 194–5; burial, 201–3; collected works, *On the Way of Building Up the Multilaterally-Developed Socialist Society*, 143, 147, 157

Ceausescu, Nicolae (brother), 8, 11
Ceausescu, Nicolina (sister), 8
Ceausescu, Nicu (son), 39–40, 41–6, 166–9, 172, 176
Ceausescu, Valentin (son), 39, 41, 42, 44, 45, 46–9
Ceausescu, Zoia (daughter), 39 50–52, 176
Ceausescu family, 10, 29, 40, 101
Central Chemical Institute, 32
Central Committee building, Bucharest, 129, 132, 139, 141–5, 147–9, 152, 158–61, 163–4, 167–8, 172–4, 177, 183, 210
Central Military Hospital, Bucharest, 144

Centre for Policy Research, 286–7
Cernauti, 67
Champion, Marc, 222
Charles, Prince of Wales, 90, 94
Chemenici, Colonel, 162, 179
Chernenko, Konstantin, 29
children and the Aids virus, 57–64
Chile, 252
China, 88–9, 275
Chiranescu, Ion, 199
Chitac, General Mihai, 149, 222, 228, 229, 250–51, 260, 264
'Christian National Peasants' Party', *see* National Peasants' and Christian Party
Cimpulung, 252–3
Ciobanu, Lina, 116
Ciortoioman, Henrietta, 56
City Hospital, Edinburgh, 62
Civic Forum, 208
civil rights, 289–90
Clej, Petru, 247
Cleveland, 78, 81
Cluj, 104
Cluk, 134
Codreanu, Corneliu Zelea, 6
Coman, Ion, 117
Comaneci, Nadia, 42, 45–6
Comecon system, 12, 14
communism, 12, 24, 28, 33, 65, 73, 155–6, 209, 212–15, 272, 274–5, 284–5, 290–1
Communist Parties, *see* Czechoslovak *and* Romanian Communist Parties
Communist Party Academy, *see*

Stefan Gheorghiu Party Academy
Communist Youth Union, 11–12
Conference on Security and Co-operation (CSCE), Helsinki Accords of 1975, 256
Constanta, 59, 60, 73, 74, 175, 223; hospital, 59–64
Constantinescu, Dr Emil, 212, 245–5
contraception laws, 54
Copenhagen, 255
Cornea, Doina, 164, 218
Cozma, Miron, 232, 238–9, 261, 272–82
Cracow, 66
Craiova, 7
'crivat', 141
Croitoru, Nicolae, 156–7, 231–2, 275
Cults, Department of, 102
Cultural Revolution, China, 88
Curticeanu, 116, 145, 146
Czechoslovak Communist Party, 21, 24
Czechoslovakia, 14, 20, 23–7, 53, 72, 74, 81, 84, 140, 208, 288–90

Daily Telegraph, 268
Dancea, General, 151
Daraban, Gheorghe, 243
Dascalescu, Constantin, 116, 128, 129, 145, 152, 154
Debreczemi, Istvan, 106
Deca, Nicolae, 171
Defence, Ministry of, 158, 161, 177–9, 182, 200–201, 211
Deletant, Dennis, 197
Demetrescu, Cerasela, 202, 203

democracy, 269, 270–72
Democratic Party of Labour, 154
demonstrations/riots, 98, 107–12, 113–21, 125, 131, 134–7, 140, 143, 154, 159, 207, 214–16, 220–28, 235–40, 242–9, 256
Deng Xiaoping, 18
Detroit, 78, 81
Diamandescu, 260
Diana, Princess of Wales, 94
Dimineata, 258
Dinca, 116, 145
Dinescu, Mircea, 99, 150, 159, 164
'Doctors' Plot' in Moscow, 74
Doftana Prison, 9
Dorohoi, Moldavia, 69
Douglas-Home, Sir Alec, 65
Douglas-Home, Charles, 65–6
Douglas-Home, Jessica, 65–6, 81, 268–70
Dubceck, Alexander, 23–4
Dumitrescu, Sorin, 234–5, 236
Dumitrescu, Vasile, 9, 30–31, 38
Dunca, Gheorghe, 228
Dynamo Bucharest, 46–7

Eastern bloc, 13, 20, 24, 25, 29, 33, 36, 43, 73, 74, 82, 285–6, 290–1; *see also* Europe, Eastern
Ecology Party, 217, 277
economy, the, 12, 37–8, 184, 214; collapse of, 57–8; in Eastern Europe, 294–5; reform, 283–6
Eftimescu, General, 145
Egypt, 20
Ehrenberg letter, 73

elections, 159, 215–16, 217–19, 220–21, 278–9, 283–4; results, 292–4
Elizabeth II, Queen of England, 4, 80, 147
Elle, 35
Ethiopian Ambassador, 137–8
Europe, Eastern, 4, 11, 13, 29, 37, 66, 74, 76, 77, 100, 124, 155, 197, 208, 255, 285–9, 294–5
European Commission of Human Rights, 237
European Community Commission, 255
European Cup, 182

Falik, David, 67, 70
fascism, 6, 8, 10, 56, 67, 78, 79, 142, 248, 269–70, 272
Ferdinand and Maria, King and Queen of Romania, 67
fertility decrees, 54–7
Finance, Ministry of, 37–8
Financial Times, 117
Fitzwater, Marlin, 256
Florescu, Major Mugurel, 182
food shortages, 35–6, 58, 188, 278–9
Foreign Affairs, Ministry of, 228
Fortuna, Lorin, 98, 107–8, 119, 122–3, 125–8, 129–30, 132
Fortuna family, 108
Frankfurter, Rabbi Naftule, 66
French Revolution, 99, 197
'Front of the Unity of the People', 149, 160
Fry, Stephen, 94

Galicia, 66

Galloway, George, MP, 49, 257, 265
Gapon, Father, 100, 110
genocide, 42, 117–19, 123, 175, 184, 186, 190, 193, 194, 199, 290–1
Germany, 6, 7, 244; East, 24, 208, 290–1
Gheorghiu-Dej, Gheorghe, 7, 10, 12–14, 16–17, 19, 21, 153
Giurescu, Constandin, *Forests in the History of the Romanian People*, 288
Giurescu, Dinu C., 90, 92, 289–91
golanis, 221–3, 225, 231–2, 240, 246, 249, 259, 265
Gorbachev, Mikhail, 23, 100
Gorbachev, Raisa, 29
Grand National Assembly, 124, 185, 186, 187, 189, 191, 193
Granta, 231, 243–4
Guardian, 62
Guild of Leather and Footwear Workers, Bucharest, 9, 30
Guse, General, 160
Gusi, Nicolai, 50

Hacham-Basha of Moldavia, 66
Haifa, 74
Halpern, Congressman, 79
Harrison, Olivia, 62
Health, Ministry of, 58, 61
Helen, Princess of Romania, 6
Hilton, Isobel, 218
Hitler, Adolf, 7, 11, 67, 68, 70, 79, 91, 270, 272
Homage, 39
Horthy, Nicholas, 288

Hoskins, Bob, 262
Hospitals, 59–64, 131, 144
House of the People, Bucharest, 91–2
Hungarian Reformed Church, 100–101, 104, 105–6
Hungarian TV, 103–4
Hungary, 7, 14, 24, 70, 74, 80, 103, 147, 286, 287, 288, 289

Iasi, 71–2
Iliescu, Ion, 88–9, 150–52, 159–65, 176, 178–9, 200, 207, 210, 212–15, 217–18, 221–5, 229–30, 234, 238–9, 241, 246–7, 250–52, 254, 257, 259, 262–3, 268–71, 284, 288–90
IMGB factory, 224
Imperial College, London, 47
Independent, 124, 137, 173, 218, 222, 230, 255
Independent on Sunday, 62
industrialisation, 21
Institute of Architecture, 224, 240
Institute of Construction Design, 97
Institute of Mathematics, 50
International Monetary Fund, 38
International Women's Day, 38
Interior, Ministry of, 227, 228, 229, 239–40, 258
Ionel, Vasile, 229, 250–51
Ionescu, Cazimir, 163, 178, 247
Ionescu, Paraschiva, 215
Iordache, Alice, 108–11
Iordache, Antoneta, 108–11

Iordache, Claudiu, 97–9, 108–11, 118–19, 121–2, 124, 126–7, 129–30, 132, 151, 175, 213, 232–3, 238
Iran, 117, 123, 128, 186
Iron Guard, 6–7, 10, 67, 70, 78–9, 142, 238, 248, 250–51, 258, 269
Ispas, Mihai, 161, 180
Israel, 20, 65, 73–5, 76, 77, 80–82, 90
Isserles, Rabbi Moshe, 66

Jacob, Paula, 40–43, 46, 47
Jantau, Vice President of Peasants' Party, 280
Jebeleanu, Eugen, 8
Jeory, Liam, 224
Jerusalem, 84
Jews of Romania, 6, 20, 47, 51, 54, 65–84; *see also* anti-semitism
Jilava Prison, 10, 40, 41, 46
Jimbolia, 123
Jiu Valley, 156–8, 215, 231–2, 245, 272–9, 281
Josif, Senator Dan, 154, 253
Jurcan, Petru, 281

Kennedy, Robert, 79
Khrushchev, Nikita, 14, 15, 29
Kim Il Sung, 88–9
Klutznick, Philip, 79
Korea, North, 88–9, 91
Korean War, 89

Laszlo Tokes, 101
League of the Archangel Michael, *see* Iron Guard
League of Students, 212, 230, 245
Lebanon, 20

Leia, Sorin, 119
Leipzig, 100, 208
Lenin, Vladimir, 17, 28
Leon, Nica, 240, 268
Liberal Party, 215, 216, 217, 223, 257, 265, 266, 277, 281, 282
Lod, 77
Loew, Great Rabbi, 66
Lonea, 232, 238
Long Good Friday, The, 262
Louis-Philippe, King of France, 124
Lucescu, Constantin, 182
Lupeni, 158, 274, 275, 279, 281
Lupescu, Magda, 6, 7
Lupoi, Mihai, 159, 161, 240

McPherson, William, 231, 243–4, 257, 263–4
Magureanu, Virgil, 182, 210–11, 229, 233, 264
Malutan, Lieutenant-Colonel Vasile, 168–71
Manescu, Corneliu, 164, 168, 170
Manolache, 154
Manole, Adrian, 223
Mao, Madame, 89
Mao Tse Tung, 28
Mares, Lieutenant-Colonel, 196
Marian, Ivan, 170–71
Mariuta, Mariana, 121
market economy, 289
Marx, Karl, *Communist Manifesto*, 286
Marxism-Leninism, 8–9, 12, 29, 31, 45, 47, 68, 155–6
Matei, Valerica, 157–8, 239, 274–5

Matenciuc, Sergeant-Major
  Trifan, 182, 201
Matusa, Dr Rodica, 60–63
Maurer, Ion, 75–6
Mazilu, Dumitru, 159–60,
  165, 178
medical services, 57–8
Meir, Golda, 77, 78, 82
Michael, King of Romania,
  6–7, 67, 70, 81, 82, 98
Michigan, 78
Miercurea Ciuc (concentration
  camp), 70
Mikoyan, 17
Milea, General Vasile, 112,
  114–16, 138–9, 143–5,
  190
Militaru, General, 160, 163,
  178, 212, 216
Military hospital, Bucharest,
  144
Millan, Bruce, 255
miners, 210, 215, 220, 224,
  231–2, 234, 238, 241–9,
  254, 257–64, 266–71,
  272–83, 290
Miners' League, 274, 278, 281–2
Mineu, 103, 105
Moinesti, 66
Mok, Dr Jacqueline, 62–4
Moldavia, 26, 32, 66, 69
Mongolia, 88
Moraru, General, 160
Moscow, 12, 13, 14, 18, 20,
  21, 288
'Most Favoured Nation' status,
  79–81
Mot, Petru, 107–9
Municipal Hospital,
  Constanta, 59–64
Municipal Hospital, Timisoara,
  131, 144

Munteanu, Marian, 212,
  230–31, 245, 248–9, 268
Muresan, Ana, 116
Muresan, Mircea, 129

Nasser, President Gamal, 20
National Cancer Institute, 63
National Council for Science
  and Technology, 37
National Council of Scientific
  Research, 32
National Liberal Party, *see*
  Liberal Party
National Peasants' and
  Christian Party, 123, 141,
  175, 212, 217, 220, 224,
  240, 244, 252, 257, 267,
  281
National Salvation Front
  (FSN), 160, 174, 176, 179,
  217, 218, 220, 223, 227,
  233, 246, 255, 277, 278;
  Council of, 164, 165,
  177–9, 185, 187, 189, 192,
  207, 209
National Socialists (Brown
  Shirts), 67, 242, 244
nationalism, 12, 26
nazism, 6, 7, 67, 68, 71, 79,
  244, 245
Neagoe, General, 168, 171
Neagra, 176
New York, 77, 78
New York Times, 275
New Zealand, 62; TV, 224
Nicholas II, Tsar of Russia, 100
Nicolaescu, Sergiu, 154, 159,
  199
Nistor, Colonel Ion, 182
Nixon, President Richard, 25,
  88
Nobel Peace Prize, 84

Noda Biyehuda of Prague, 66
North Korea, 88–9, 91
Nuclear Physics Institute, 47

Oancea, General Viorel, 151
O'Brien, Conor Cruise, 268, 270–72
Observer, 62, 133, 243, 248, 257, 265
Olteanu, Constantin, 38
Oltenia, 30, 38
Opruta, General Lieutenant, 168
Oradea, 101, 102, 134
Orban, Traian, 119
orphanages and children's homes, 57
Otopeni air force base, 170
Owen, Dr David, 80

Pacepa, Ion, 51, 85; *Red Horizons*, 45, 85
Pacoste, Cornel, 128
Palestinians, Romania and the, 72, 82–7, 211
Pancea, Lieutenant-Major, 201
Panorama, Hungarian TV, 103–4
Papp, Bishop Laszlo, 101, 103, 104
Paris, 91, 123, 142
'Park of Joy', 9, 15, 27, 30
Paroseni power station, 274
Pascu, Ioan, 226, 228–9, 234, 245, 249–50
Patriotic Guard, 157–8
Pauker, Ana, 12–13, 74
Pauker, Marcel, 13
Peasants' Party, *see* National Peasants' and Christian Party
Pentagon, Washington, 91

People's Socialist Republic, 133
Petreanu, Victoria, 93–4
Petrescu, Anca, 91
Petrescu, Barbu, 38
Petrescu, Lenuta, *see* Ceausescu, Elena
Petrescu family, 29
Petresti, 38
Petrila, 274, 278
Petrina, Livriu, 176, 240, 258, 267
Petrisor, Nicolae, 171
petroleum deposits, 14
Petrosani, 157–8, 232, 238–9, 241, 259, 272–4, 278–9
Philadelphia, 77
Pilger, John, 287
Pilsudski, Joseph, 288
Pircalabescu, Colonel, 152
Pitesti, 5, 170, 272
PLO, 82–3
Ploesti, 190, 233
pluralism, 289
Poiana Brasov, 65
Poland, 24, 80, 140, 147, 208, 288, 291
Police Headquarters, Bucharest, 227, 229, 258
Pop, Iftene, 141–2, 175–6, 212–13
Popa, Colonel Gica, 182, 184–93, 197, 203
Popovici, Vasile, 218
population, 54
Postelnicu, Tudor, 112, 114–16, 145–6
Prague, 66, 100, 140
'Prague Spring', 21, 23, 197
Pravda, 73
Preda, Ion, 42, 167
Prina, Isabela, 129, 175
Provisional Council of National

Unity (PCNU), 207–8, 215–16
Pumnea, Cornel, 134–6, 235–6
puritanism, 53

Radio Free Europe, 141, 157
Rafferty, Sister Chris, 63
Rashomon, 290
'Rational Nourishment Commission', 36
Ratiu, Ion, 123–4, 209, 216–17, 224, 244, 252–4, 257–8, 261–2, 267, 279–81
Red Army (Soviet), 7, 10, 14, 72, 133
'Renasterea', 175–6
Revista Economica, 38
Revolution, *see* Romanian Revolution, *also* French Revolution *and* Russian Revolution
Rimnicu Vilcea, 272
riots, *see* demonstrations/riots
Ripan, Raluca, 33
Rodean, Ion, 253
Roman, Mioara, 134
Roman, Petre, 134, 136–8, 143, 147–50, 152, 158–61, 163–5, 176–9, 199–200, 207, 224, 229–30, 233–4, 238–41, 250–51, 253–4, 257, 259–61, 283–6, 288–9
Romania Libera, 210, 247, 257, 259
Romanian Child Aids Appeal, 62
Romanian Communist Party, 5, 10–12, 14–15, 18–19, 21, 30, 33–4, 39, 53, 65, 68–9,

72–3, 82, 86, 113, 115, 128, 130, 133, 141, 150, 153–4, 156–7, 163, 166–7, 187, 209, 214–15, 227, 230, 269, 274; Central Committee, 4, 17, 26, 37, 144–5, 146, 150, 174, 215, 217; Ninth Congress, 17–18; Tenth Congress, 25; Department of Propaganda, 31; elects Ceausescu for further five-year term one month before his execution, 196–7
Romanian Democratic Front, 126
Romanian Intelligence Service, 85, 211, 227–9, 264
Romanian National Day, 37
Romanian Orthodox Church, 78, 92, 99, 203
Romanian Revolution, 33, 45, 57, 59, 86, 93, 94, 122–30, 134–9, 140–65, 173, 175, 212–13, 216, 284, 290, 292
Romanian TV, 123
Romanian Workers' Party, 12, 13, 16
Romanul Liber (Free Romania), 280
Rosen, Chief Rabbi Dr Moses, 65–70, 72–81, 85
Roth, Julius, 124
Rugina, Dr Claudia, 63
Russian Revolution, 100

Sadat, Anwar, 82, 84–5
Safran, Chief Rabbi, 72–3
St Louis Post-Dispatch, 218
St Petersburg, 100
Salisbury, Harrison, 290–91
sans-culottes, 99, 119, 155

Scinteia (Spark), 11, 16, 19, 20, 37, 38

Scornicesti, 4, 7

Scruton, Roger, 66

Secares, Vasile, 226, 228, 234, 245

Securitate, 61, 99, 101–3, 106–9, 112–15, 118, 123, 125, 132, 138, 145–6, 154, 157–8, 160, 166–8, 170, 173, 175, 178, 181, 190, 193, 210–12, 214, 228, 247, 254, 259, 261–2, 266, 268–9, 275, 290; Training School, 11

Sever, Camil, 167

Severin, Adrian, 283–4

Shazar, President Salman, 77

Sheridan, Michael, 173–4, 176

Siberia, 141

Sibiu, 42, 43, 44, 134, 140, 166, 169, 172

Sinaia, 84

Sirbi, Nicolae, 90

Sirbu, Adrian, 229–30

Six Day War, 77, 82

Slatina, 5

Social Democratic Party, 215

socialism, 24, 91, 133, 287

Socialist Party, 12

Socialist Party of Labour, 153–4

Sofrone, Romeo, 107, 111, 114

Solidarity, 99, 147, 208, 289

Solok, Paul, 237

Sorin, Dr, 63

Soviet Union, *see* USSR

Spectator, 65, 81, 82

Stalin, Josef, 5, 7, 12, 13–14, 17, 26, 28, 29, 68, 74, 81, 88, 128, 208

Stalingrad, 72

Stanculescu, General Victor, 131–2, 144–5, 146, 158–9, 162, 163, 178–9, 181–3, 197, 200–202, 217, 229, 250–51, 258–9, 263, 284, 291

Stanislawow, Galicia, 66

Stark, Alexander, 235–6, 237

'state of morality', 53–64

Steaua Bucharest, 46–7, 182, 200; incident at stadium concerning Ceausescu bodies, 200–201

Steele, Sir David, 147

Stefan Gheorghiu Party Academy, 154, 155–6, 210–11

Stelica, helicopter co-pilot, 168, 170

Stevens, Siaka, 89

Student League, 212, 230, 245

students, 111, 259, 265, 269, 271, 272

Suez crisis, 74

Sweeney, John, 243, 248, 257, 261–2, 265

Syria, 20

'Systemisation' programme, 102

Tanasa, Sergeant Jan, 182

Tarnovski, V., 8

Technology and Science, Ministry of, 241

Teodorescu, Nicolae, 182, 184, 191–2, 194, 201

Thatcher, Mrs Margaret, 221–2

Theatre Almanac, 97

Theodorescu, Razvan, 222, 233–6

Times, The, 117, 123, 124, 197, 255, 268
Timisoara, 97–111, 113–21, 122–30, 134–5, 137, 140, 150–51, 158, 166, 175, 184, 186, 190, 192–3, 195, 208, 212–14, 232–3, 239; hospital, 131, 134
Timisoara County Communist Party, 113, 130
Timisoara Society, 213, 218; Declaration of the, 213–14, 216, 217
Tirgoviste, 144, 162, 171, 179, 181–3, 196, 233
Tirgu Jiu, 272–3
Tirgu Mures, 216
Tito, Marshal, 19
Titu, 170
Tokes, Edit, 105
Tokes, Father Laszlo, 100–110, 123
Torsan, Ilie, 281
Totu, Nicolae, 67, 70
Transcendental Meditation sect, 138
Transnistria, Ukraine, 70–71
Transylvania, 7, 26, 70, 72, 101, 103, 142
Treaty of Friendship, Co-operation and Mutual Assistance with the Czech Government, 23
Treveleanu, Cornelia, 55–6
Trifa, Bishop Valentin, 78–9, 81
TV centre, Bucharest, 148–52, 155–6, 161–3, 165, 172, 174–7, 179, 199, 221–2, 227, 234–6, 238–40

Uitea, Constantin, 153

Ujvarossy, Ernö, 104
Uncu, Anton, 257, 259
United Nations, 72, 79, 81; Economic Commission, 287
University of Bucharest, 90, 212, 245, 289
University of Cluj, 33
University of Iasi, 32
University of London, 197
Ursu, Doru, 93, 94, 250
Ursu, Madame, 94
USA, 18, 58, 63, 78, 79, 83–4, 90, 92, 218, 255–6, 289
USSR, 14, 15, 19, 20, 24, 29, 33, 43, 53, 71–3, 76, 83–4, 287

Valea Juiful, 261
Valeriu, Emanuel, 237, 249
'Velvet Revolution', 140
Verdet, Ilie, 152, 153–4, 275
Vienna, 77
'Vienna Diktat', 7, 70
Vietnam, North, 88, 275
Virgiliu, Professor Ancar, 56–7, 58
Vissarion, Aexa, 153–4
Vlad, General Iulian, 115, 146, 154
Vladescu, Daniela, 167, 169, 172
Vogue, 35
Voican, Gelu, 138, 152, 159–63, 165, 177–80, 182, 184–6, 189, 197–200, 202–3, 215, 257–8, 266–8
Voican, Sanda, 203
Voinea, Major Dan, 182, 197
Voinea, General Gheorghe, 145–50, 152, 158, 217
Vulcan mine, 156, 231–2, 274, 277, 279

Waldegrave, William, 226, 271
Wallachia, 26
Warsaw, 140
Warsaw Pact, 14, 20, 23, 24, 229
Washington, 80, 256, 261
Who's Who in Science in Europe, 241
'Workers' and Peasants' bloc', 6
World Cup, 231–2, 239, 247, 249
World War I, 248, 276
World War II, 19, 71–2, 142, 248

Xenopol, A.D., 18

Yash pogrom, 71, 78, 81
Yiddish Theatre, 71
Yom Kippur, 75
Young Communist League, 120
Yugoslavia, 19, 286

Zeca, Colonel, 151
Zhou Enlai, 17, 19–20
Zionism, 73–6, 81–3
Zola, Emile, _Germinal_, 282